Wrestling With
Elephants

The Authorised Biography Of Don Black

Printed in the UK by MPG Books, Bodmin

Distributed in the US by Publishers Group West

Published by Sanctuary Publishing Limited, Sanctuary House, 45–53 Sinclair Road, London W14 0NS, United Kingdom

www.sanctuarypublishing.com

Copyright: James Inverne, 2003

Photographs: Courtesy of Don Black unless otherwise stated.

Cover photograph: © Getty Images.
Posters from the London stage productions of *Aspects Of Love* (TM© 1989), *Sunset Boulevard* (TM© 1992) *Tell Me On A Sunday* (© 2003) and *Bombay Dreams* (TM© 2002) are each reproduced with the kind permission of The Really Useful Group Limited. With thanks also to Dewynters Plc.
Additional images courtesy of Moviestore Collection.

Lyrics reproduced with the kind permission of The Really Useful Group Limited, EMI United Partnership Limited/International Music Publications Limited, Jobete Music (UK) Limited, Ardmore & Beechwood Limited, Universal Music Publishing Limited, Essex Music Group, Sony Music Publishing (UK), Sony/ATV Music Publishing (UK) and Warner Chappell Music Limited//International Music Publications Limited.

ISBN: 1-86074-468-0

Wrestling With
Elephants

The Authorised Biography Of Don Black

James Inverne

Foreword by John Barry

Sanctuary

Acknowledgements

Have you ever noticed how book acknowledgements often begin with the phrase, 'I could not have written this book without the help of the following people'? I'd like to be more specific than that.

The following people I could have written the book without, but it would have been much harder:

Thank you to John Ashby, Michael Ball, John Barry, Elmer Bernstein, Barbara Broccoli, Christopher Hampton, Kenny Clayton, Andrew Lloyd Webber, Lulu, Denise Van Outen, Elaine Paige, Tim Rice, Marti Webb, Bob West and Michael Winner for sharing your time and memories.

To Jan Eade, Tris Penna and Paul Tucker at the Really Useful Group, and to Michael Brunton at *Time* magazine.

To Don's family, especially Grant, Clive, Nita, Michael and Adele.

To Jodie and Daniel Cohen, and also to Marcel and Shirley Cohen, for your encouragement.

To Dalia Cohen for cheering me up whenever things looked bleak.

A special thankyou to Kareen Cartier for support and for patiently listening to endless chapters, frequently interrupted by me saying, 'Hang on, that's not right – wait a minute,' and tapping away on my computer. It's not the easiest way to digest a book.

The following people I certainly could not have written the book without:

Thanks to everyone at Sanctuary Publishing, especially Iain MacGregor, for your patience and understanding and for being a pleasure to work with.

And thanks most of all to Don Black for asking me to write what turned out to be a fascinating adventure story, and to Shirley, the power behind the throne.

For my mother, Sue, a wonderful woman who is deeply missed, and for my father, Richard, one of the finest men I know

James Inverne

For Shirley, my secret weapon

Don Black

Contents

Foreword

Composing music is a lot easier than writing lyrics. Music is instinctive. I always hate it when people ask me to explain my music, and avoid talking about it like the plague. Because it comes from deep inside me, there is no easy explanation. Lyrics need that feeling from deep inside, but they also require the germ of insight that Don Black brings to them.

Don is very diplomatic, he gets on well with people. But he is also a very astute observer of life and people. And it is his gift to be able to put his finger on what he sees, in his songs. That's a vital skill for a lyricist. He's also very theatrical, which I love because I'm a theatrical composer. I love reacting to a given script. Don immediately catches on to that sense of drama.

Beginning in the 1960s, from *Thunderball* and *Born Free*, Don has been my best lyricist and my best friend. Our writing partnership has grown into a deep mutual respect that will last forever. I love him for the trust and loyalty that he has always shown towards me.

And, as for the work, we've done good things together. Some of the best work in both of our careers.

John Barry

Introduction

I had known for some time that various publishers were trying to get Don Black to agree to an authorised biography. He kept mentioning it over lunch. I also knew when he finally agreed to go with Sanctuary Publishing. It still took me by surprise when, one evening in August 2002, I received a phone call from Don, which was typically to the point.

'Hi, James. I'll be brief. We lyricists are good at that. Do you want to write this biography?'

Don's was one of the last great untold showbiz sagas of his era, although he has outlasted many of his famous contemporaries and is still as busy as ever. I admired Don's work, had struck up a friendship with him after interviewing him for a *Time* article – had even partaken of the Black bagels at a family lunch – and knew that I would enjoy writing the book.

There were various uncanny coincidences which became apparent as the book developed. It transpired that Don and Shirley had spent their honeymoon at my family's kosher hotel in Bournemouth (the Cumberland). A friend of mine turned out to be a long-lost relative of the Blacks. But the one coincidence I recall with a tinge of sadness is that I found out my mother was a long-standing Don Black fan.

Sadness because, while I was writing, my mother (still young, at the age of 49) was declining from a lethal cancer. She died in January 2003, after which I returned to work. Work helped to ease the sadness somewhat, and the fact that I was writing a book I *know* that she would have enjoyed turned it into something of a cathartic experience. Don epitomises much of what she – and, for that matter, most people – value in life: kindness, humour and ease of character. 'He seems such a *nice* man,' she would always say.

My mother was far from alone in that opinion. A fellow critic calls Don 'the nicest man in show business'. He, of course, would put it another way. Don would explain that he's simply a down-to-earth guy working in a profession populated by an awful lot of people who seem to have their heads in the clouds.

It was fun spending a book's worth of time in the company of Don Black. I hope you find the same.

James Inverne, London, April 2003

Overture

'Wrestling with elephants', says the writer Christopher Hampton, 'seems to me a wonderfully accurate description of the process of putting on a musical. Everything is so big. It's a much more industrial process than anything else in the theatre. Go into the rehearsal room on the first day of full rehearsals, and everything is going on around you. It's like being on the set of a movie.'

Hampton, collaborator with Don Black on two musicals, suggested the title of this book perhaps without realising how many appropriate resonances it has. As well as grappling with the beasts that lurk in the rehearsal rooms of a big musical, Don has also had to face those that are the outsize personalities he has worked alongside over the years. The Hollywood producers, full of empty promises; the inspired composers, driven by their gifts; the troubled stars, losing contact with the real world – these are elephants too.

And Don wrestles with yet more elephants every day. It is the job of a lyricist to harness the stampeding images in his head, and to parade them in the confines of his verses. Sometimes he must turn them into characters: a faded silent film star, a girl searching for love abroad, a boy dreamer, a man struggling to escape the squalor of a Bombay slum for the excitement of Bollywood.

Don Black's most fabulous elephants, with the richest plumes, are to be found in his songs.

2002. It's a cold winter's night, so the 200 or so dinner guests walk briskly into the plush London hotel to divest themselves of coats and scarves and let a little wine warm them. A member of the public would easily recognise some – certainly Andrew Lloyd Webber, sexy-TV-presenter-turned-glamorous-musicals-diva Denise Van Outen, director and restaurant critic Michael Winner, television queen Cilla Black. What they might not realise is that, concealed among the faces is a large slice of their musical heritage. There is enough songwriting talent in that dining room to cater for several radio stations – among them, Tony Hatch ('Downtown'), Geoff Stephens ('The Crying Game'), Les Reed ('It's Not Unusual'), Mike Batt ('Bright Eyes'), David Arnold (resident James Bond composer), Barry Mason ('Delilah'), Bill Martin ('Congratulations') and Marcel Stellman ('Tulips From Amsterdam').

Taking his place at the top table, a few heads down from the Lloyd Webbers, is Hollywood legend Elmer Bernstein, the man who scored countless movie classics – *The Magnificent Seven*, *The Great Escape*, *The Ten Commandments*. He's come over from the States especially for this evening, a Royal Variety Club of Great Britain tribute dinner.

And who is the titan who could have assembled such a gathering? Some superstar? A former Beatle, perhaps? Nope. A mild, engaging Jewish boy from the East End of London called Don Black. As the boy became a man, he had discovered a talent for words and a feeling for people that saw him develop into one of the foremost lyricists of his generation. He has, he calculates, worked with over 100 top-rank composers. The names sound like a roll call of a musical hall of fame – including Andrew Lloyd Webber, John Barry, Elmer Bernstein, Quincy Jones, Michel Legrand, Jule Styne, Charles Aznavour and Henry Mancini. His hit songs have been recorded by the likes of Michael Jackson, Barbra Streisand, Tom Jones, Lulu, Elaine Paige, Michael Crawford, Michael Ball, José Carreras, Bernadette Peters and kd lang. He was the first British songwriter ever (alongside John Barry) to win an Oscar, for the song 'Born Free'. He has won a Golden Globe, two Tony Awards, Ivor Novello Awards, as well as plenty other, more obscure, prizes. His songs have been No.1s in music charts around the world; they have sometimes even become part of popular culture (as in the case of 'To Sir With Love', sung at American graduation ceremonies, and 'Born Free', which became a song of freedom for black South Africans during apartheid). In 1999, the Queen told him he could put the letters 'OBE' (Order of the British Empire) after his name.

It is all pretty impressive. However – and, cliché or not, this is true – he has always remained what he always was: a cheerful, warm, modest London boy making a living at what he enjoys most. And loving every minute of it.

Michael Winner puts it amusingly in his after-dinner speech. 'I'm Don's next-door neighbour,' he smirks. 'I live in a 30-room mansion. Don lives in a maisonette. And he insists on parking his eight-year-old blue Golf outside my house. It's like living next door to a hamisha version of the Osbournes!'

Perhaps it is this very ordinariness that makes Don Black, as well as a marvellous artist, such a great witness to the maelstrom of trends and scenes in which he has stood for years, calm and solid, alongside his wife Shirley. He was part of the Jewish East End, and worked alongside John Barry, The Beatles and many of the iconic figures of 1960s London. He helped create the enduring image of 007 – in *Thunderball*, *Diamonds Are Forever* and others – equipping James Bond with classic lyrics to go with his Martini and Walther PPK. He has experienced both the craziness of Hollywood and the very different lunacies of the pop music industry. As a manager, he has dealt with the demands of artists from Matt Monro to Elton John. He has also been a mainstay of the British musicals revolution – with the smash hit musical *Billy* in 1974, through his famous collaborations with Andrew Lloyd Webber, *Tell Me On A Sunday*, *Aspects Of Love* and *Sunset Boulevard*. He was there. He's seen it. He helped to do it. And, as you would expect from a lyricist, he has some darn good stories to tell...

1 The Boy From Hackney

Betsy Kersh and Morris Blackstone were a well-matched couple. Jewish, they had both moved to England from Russia when they were children (and when Morris Blackstone was known as Morris Koperzuch). The life for Jews in Russia was not good, and was to get worse in later years. Oppression, in the form of limited rights and violent pogroms, was rife. England was seen as a promised land, a place where a better life could be won. But by God you had to work for it.

Morris was a handsome man, with deep, determined eyes. He arrived in England aged 14, and lived in Hartlepool with his brother Solomon. He hated it there, and by pretending to be two years older managed to enlist in the British army and move out. A man of few words, there was something of the loner about him. Which was fine, because Betsy was sociable enough for both of them. Small and dark-haired, she was the soul of gregariousness.

They married in January 1924 at Alexander Hall in Sunderland, and it was in that town that Betsy gave birth to their first child, Myer, two years later. Soon after, they moved to the East End of London, where Jewish immigrants grouped together to find work. Morris went first, leaving his wife and child in Sunderland until he earned enough money to rent some rooms and send for them, and eventually they were able to move to a cramped third-floor council flat in Hackney. Their new home, 10 Tornay House, Shore Place, became an oasis of hospitality in the midst of the tough, industrial East End.

Over a period of 13 years, Morris and Betsy had five children to provide for: in order of age, they were Myer, Nita, Cyril, Adele and Donald. Don. Who came along on 21 June 1938.

East London was not an easy place to live in the early 1940s, when the war reduced swathes of it to rubble, and air-raid sirens regularly pierced the streets. The night sky would often be shot through with flares, while light-bulbs were hurriedly extinguished to avoid the sights of enemy bombers. But underground, in air-raid shelters, the determination of Jews who had already gone through much to reach England was fortified. As families and neighbours huddled together, keeping up their spirits with Vera Lynn songs, the will to succeed burned bright in the gloom.

Succeed many did. And those who found a way out, like the famous Jewish boxer Jack 'Kid' Berg, were celebrated. They became folk heroes, examples to follow. Why did so many enter show business? There are dozens of well-known examples, from Harold Pinter to Lionel Bart, and a similar phenomenon occurred among the poor Jewish districts of New York. Because films and theatre gave those living the humble life a vision of another world. Fred Astaire would dance on a glass piano, the music-hall comics would bring smiles to the faces of hundreds at a time. It was there. And, with talent, it was attainable.

Morris was a conscientious worker. He worked as an underpresser, a job title which his sons upgraded to tailor for the benefit of prospective girlfriends. Bringing up a large brood was expensive, and Morris worked long days, and when he didn't work he gambled. 'He loved playing cards, and betting on the dog races,' remembers Nita. 'It wasn't gambling for gambling's sake; it was all to get extra money to give to my mother.'

Betsy, who worked in a clothes shop by day, set the tone at home. She was full of joy, loved having visitors, and would go to great lengths to make them feel welcome. Guests would always arrive to find her in the kitchen baking yet another cake, and the flat became locally famous for the wonderful cooking smells that pervaded the neighbourhood. When visitors were present and the cakes were ready, she would bring them out with a delighted smile and sit down to talk. Only when the visitors had gone – and it was often late into the night – would she go back to the kitchen and begin the washing-up. And there she would stay, sometimes until the early hours, until it was done. Then bed, and ready for work early the next morning.

She adored her children. The boys shared one room, the girls another. And Betsy's indulgence was boundless. On a cold day, it was only with the greatest reluctance that she would wake them up to go to school or work. 'Oh, let them sleep,' she would smile at Morris. Her husband was far stricter.

'My father was very tough, a very hard man,' says Nita. 'I was never allowed to wear lipstick. He used to watch me come home at evenings from the window of the house to check that there wasn't a boy with me.'

The toughness never worked with Myer, who became rebellious. In his early teens he wanted a bicycle; it cost half a crown, which Morris saw as a waste, so he refused. Myer somehow scraped together the money and bought it anyway. 'When Dad came home and saw it there,' Myer remembers grimly, 'he put it over his knees and smashed it into pieces.' Morris loved his children, though. 'Beneath the harshness, he had a heart as big as a mountain,' says Myer. And the kids had a happy childhood.

'It was joyful,' says Don, and proceeds to paint the picture as though he's describing the opening of a show. 'The scene is my mother singing gypsy Yiddish songs all day long, and my sister having piano lessons and forever playing "Legend Of The Glass Mountain". We had a piano in the flat. There would be non-stop music and drama.'

Betsy encouraged evening talent competitions. Don and his brothers would do impressions of their favourite movie stars, Don's specialities being Maurice Chevalier, Peter Lorre and Sydney Greenstreet. Adele would play the piano and sing Doris Day songs. Betsy, Morris and Nita would judge. 'It was a non-stop laugh,' chuckles Don. 'My mother would yell out, "More Maurice Chevalier!"'

Don, the baby of the family, was a handsome, thoughtful-looking boy with a slightly toothy smile (though in his teen years, thin and bespectacled, there was something of the Buddy Holly about him). He was also the quietest, so quiet that Myer, 13 years older and by this time living in his own flat in the West End, would worry. He'd walk in the door to see his baby brother reading dictionaries. Then Don would thrust the book at him or Nita, and demand to be tested on how to spell the hardest words they could find. He never lost.

Betsy loved anything to do with show business. Every week there would be a family trip to the cinema, and they would all be re-acquainted with their heroes – James Cagney was the favourite. Then along came a movie that, for Don, changed everything: *The Jolson Story*. He was entranced. 'I saw that movie 32 times. I felt an incredible empathy with this Jewish kid who wanted to be something in show business. Of course he ends up on Broadway, and all of that seemed fantastic to me. Where was this place, Broadway? Far from the council flat in Hackney, that's for sure.' He still treasures *The Jolson Story* on video and watches it often.

It was many years later when Don, now a Broadway success himself, attended a Los Angeles party for Michael Jackson and found himself sitting next to Evelyn Keyes, the actress who had played Al Jolson's wife. 'This incredibly gnarled, little old woman came and sat down. I couldn't recognise the beauty she'd once been, but I had to tell her what the film meant to me. "Miss Keyes," I said, "I've got to talk to you. You changed my life. When I was a kid I saw *The Jolson Story* 32 times. I can't believe I'm sitting next to you!" She looked at me and smirked. "I saw it the other night. What a load of hogwash." I was so disappointed.'

It was Betsy's ambition to enter show business as well. However, where Don now dreamed of Broadway, her aim was closer to home. Her dearest wish was to be an usherette at the Hackney Empire music hall. Every so often, for a special treat, she would take Don on the number six bus to the Hackney Empire and she would gaze up at the lights and, in the thick north English accent she had acquired in Sunderland, say, 'Eee, Donald, look at those chandeliers!'

She thought the acts were just wonderful. And many of them were. There was the famous comedian Bernard Miles, the Jewish singer Leo Fuld, who would sing Yiddish melodies in a midnight-blue suit ('Eee, look at the style of him!' Betsy would gush). Ted and Barbara Andrews were regulars, with their little daughter Julie, who would trot on stage and sing 'Love Is Where You Find It'. She, of course, became rather more famous as a solo artist, with a nice line in warbling nuns and nannies!

The singer Steve Conway lived near the Blackstones in Hackney, and Betsy would marvel at him walking past her window in his camel coat. 'Look at the style of him,' she'd murmur. Later, Hackney had its other show-business success stories, too – Lionel Bart and Anthony Newley among them. But for now, it seemed unlikely that the quiet boy who read dictionaries would do anything special in that field. No, Myer was the one who was going to raise the roof.

Myer left home in his early 20s . He knew he was funny, and decided to have a go at becoming a comedian impressionist. He auditioned for the famous impresario Carol Levis, who was sufficiently satisfied to give Myer a three-year contract for £17 a week. To a poor boy from the East End this was a fortune and Myer, seeing the good life dangled in front of his eyes, seized it hungrily. 'I went crazy,' says Myer, 'and spent it everywhere, staying in five-star hotels, and so by the end of every week I would borrow more from Carol Levis. I was forever in debt.' Years later, in an eloquent demonstration of the dangerous unpredictability of show business, Myer answered a knock at his door. It was Carol Levis, asking for a handout.

Myer Blackstone changed his name to the more audience-friendly Michael Black and he did OK. Then one day everything changed. A friend phoned and asked whether he would like to earn a fiver and if he was free that Saturday night. The friend was putting on a show at an American Air Force base in South Ruislip and needed a compère. Michael, needing the money, readily agreed. He was a smash.

'I did impressions of stars the soldiers knew. Peter Lorre, Jimmy Cagney, Humphrey Bogart, James Mason. They fell about. I mean I tore them apart! At the end I got a standing ovation, and the commanding officer said, "That's one of the best god-damn acts I've ever seen. Will you come back next week? Whatever you're getting, I'll triple it." I thought fast. "Well, I'm only getting £20," I lied. He promised me 60 quid a night!'

So Michael began the vast circuit of air force and army bases, putting on shows and booking acts. A clever, outgoing operator, he was in his element. 'I was like Bilko,' he laughs. 'I was forever wheeling and dealing, I had the colonels running round and getting me whatever I needed. Soldiers used to grab whisky and cigarettes for me. And everywhere they loved my shows!' Demand became so great that he would have 20 or 30 shows every weekend in bases all around Europe.

And that was how Michael Black became one of the most important agents in the UK. He handled all the stars of the day – in fact, many of them became stars thanks to his help. 'I gave them all a break,' he says. 'Shirley Bassey, Des O'Connor, Dave Allen. I booked Lulu for seven quid a gig, and Tom Jones for 25 quid.'

He returned home infrequently, but when he did it would be a red-letter day. Betsy would cook for hours and welcome him like returning royalty. And Morris? He was always proud of what all his children achieved and, despite their differences, Michael was his first-born and held a special place in his heart.

In 1947, when Don was 9 years old, a calamity befell the family. Morris set off one day to the Southend dog track, and on the way became involved in a horrific car accident. Betsy was telephoned with the news that her husband was in hospital with a fractured skull. He remained unconscious for six tortuous weeks.

'That changed all our lives,' remembers Don. 'When he came back, he wasn't the same. He'd been a mountain of a man, physically strong as well as emotionally. He even kept chest expanders in the house and loved to show us how strong he was.'

After his return from hospital, Morris seemed diminished. The might was now replaced by frailty, the strength of will by floods of emotion. He would suddenly start crying at the slightest thing, or simply while watching television. Yet Betsy and the children supported each other, the family pulled through. And eventually he found a new kind of strength, channelling the emotion into determined cheerfulness. Years later, in 1973, when Morris got diabetes from smoking and was told that the doctors wanted to amputate both his legs, he brightly replied, 'Take 'em off!'

For now, though, the children pulled closer – to their parents and to each other – than ever before, and it was an emotional bond that never slipped.

At 15 years old, Don's first big break came. A big break? Well, a break's a break, and you take what you can get. He answered an ad for a job at the most famous variety theatre in the world – the London Palladium. He was polishing the brass and ushering people to their seats so it wasn't exactly a career-maker, but to Don it was great fun and he was able to boast that he was working at the London Palladium (while being deliberately hazy about the details). For his mother, it was an achievement beyond imagining. Never mind the Hackney Empire; her youngest son was an usher at the Palladium!

Lucky that she enjoyed it while it lasted, because it didn't last long: Don was fired after only three weeks. The reason? The same thing that made him take the job in the first place – he adored show business.

'When I was taken on,' explains Don, 'the great comedian Danny Thomas was topping the bill there. He was an American icon, who had played the part of Gus Kahn in one of my favourite films, *I'll See You In My Dreams*. He was a kind of American Eric Morecambe – everyone knew who he was. And in his act he did this mesmerising thing. He sang "I'll See You In My Dreams" as the closing number, and told the audience to take out a match or a lighter. On the line, "They will light their way tonight", everyone had to ignite their matches. And on that line the whole dark auditorium just lit up! It was an unbelievable effect, and I watched it in awe every night.' Unfortunately for Don, Thomas's act closed the show, and he was supposed to be standing at the exit to show people out of the theatre. The management heard about this kid who spent every night watching the performance when he should have been ushering people out, and he was duly shown the door himself.

Now back in Hackney, Don took to putting on variety shows for local Jewish youth clubs with his brother Cyril and some friends. One night they were entertaining at the Harmony club in nearby Clapton – not far from Hackney, but a definite step up the social ladder. Cyril had brought along one of his old flames to watch the show. She was an attractive girl, with short blonde hair framing a face full of warmth. 'Don,' said Cyril, introducing her to his brother. 'This is Shirley.' For the first and only time in his life, Don fell deeply in love.

For a lyricist who was to become best known for his romantic verses, Don describes Shirley in a down-to-earth way. 'I knew she was the girl for me when I went into her flat and saw that her mother had three matching plates!' he jokes. 'In the world I came from, that showed she was quite well-to-do.' Pressed, he opens up a little. 'She was a reader – that was the thing. I'm touched by words, and people's reactions to them. She talked about *Little Women*, which she loved. She was interesting; she didn't just want to go dancing the whole time.'

Shirley, for her part, found Don uplifting company. 'I thought Don was very funny. Most of the people I knew were quite serious. He and all of his family are much more fun-loving. Lighter. He always had a good, dry sense of humour, not in a joke-telling way, but he was very influenced by American comics with their throw-away remarks.'

Shirley's family, who lived in neighbouring Clapton, were indeed more well-to-do than the Blackstones, but it was not that much of a jump. 'My father was by profession a cabinetmaker, and later he became a taxi driver,' she says. 'We were very modest, we lived in a council flat.

But compared to Don we were upper class because we lived in a borough council flat, and Don was county council! So we were like snobs to them! But we were a poor family. The difference was that my father always worked and brought in money. Don's father was in a business that wasn't so good.'

With girls he liked, Don had always claimed that his father the presser was actually a tailor. He *really* liked Shirley, so… 'He told me his father owned a factory!' she laughs.

Shirley adored Don's family, but Betsy most of all. Through her entire life, with all the famous people she has met and befriended over the deacdes, she still says that Don's mother made the greatest impression. 'She was a very ordinary Russian Jewish housewife with this strong northern accent. But she changed my life and my attitude to life, because she had such a wonderful soul, such a spirit. She was always ready to laugh, and in the same breath she'd cry. With no education as such, she still seemed to have such a good foundation about what makes people work and how to accept everyone.

'She was so star-struck, when Michael would bring stars round she would love it, rush around making food. There was always so much food. However little money, there was always plenty to eat. "Eee, she's so clever," she'd say of me, in her little northern accent.

'I saw something in her that has stuck with me. She was a deeply good person, with no bad word to say of anybody. Her life was hard, but she saw the best in everyone and everything.'

And Shirley saw the best in Betsy's son.

It was two years before Don proposed. He remembers the delay as being entirely a question of money. 'I wasn't a great catch. What did I do? I was floundering, and had to get on my feet. Luckily her parents were prepared to wait. They liked me, and had faith that one day I would establish myself.'

His ejection from the Palladium may not have seemed the best omen, but he would be back. 'I had got the smell of it all in my nostrils. I don't know what I was trying to build up to, but I felt this irresistible connection to the world of show business.'

And pretty soon he would be introduced to the street where showbiz and sounds converged in a daily cacophony of chaos – Tin Pan Alley.

2 The Living Joke

Someone once described Tin Pan Alley, or Denmark Street as it is more properly known, as '200 yards of hokum'. It's a very small side-street off the Charing Cross Road in London's West End, and easy to miss. But in the 1950s every shop in that street was connected to the world of music publishing. It was the hub of the British music industry, and even the two cafés – Julie's and the Suffolk Dairy – would be crammed with musicians, songwriters, agents and publishers complaining, gossiping, hustling. Making connections to make sales.

Michael managed to get Don (now, like his brother, using the 'slicker' surname Black) a job at the *NME*, or the *New Musical Express* to give it the full title nobody used. It was run by the impresario Maurice Kinn, a quietly spoken, kind man who was besotted by show business. He also reeked of money and power. Kinn took a liking to the thin, bespectacled boy who was so eagerly trying to get his foot in the door. Don was taken on as an office boy, and a new world was revealed.

'It was unbelievable,' he grins. 'I loved the smell of the newspaper, I loved the deadlines, the urgency, the drama in the office. And there'd be Johnny Ray phoning Maurice Kinn from Las Vegas – I didn't even really know where Las Vegas was – and people like Billy Eckstine would come in to see him.' There wasn't a day when a gawping Don wouldn't bump into a Frankie Laine in the corridor, or pass a Dickie Valentine on the stairs. 'These were the superstars of the day,' he explains. 'To get a sense of them you have to compare them with Robbie Williams or Britney Spears today. The name "Dickie Valentine" means little now, but put it in context – this guy would appear at the London Palladium and there'd be a four-mile queue to get in!' On one unforgettable occasion, staff reporter Mike Butcher took an overexcited Don to sit in on his interview with the biggest star in the world, Nat 'King' Cole.

A 1953 Christmas issue of the *NME* features an amusing caricature of the magazine's staff on a long train, with Maurice Kinn sitting by himself in first class, and everyone else in other carriages. Well, almost everyone, for right at the back, pushing the train, is a puffing Don. The text, introducing the staff members, finishes, 'Last, but by no means least, comes our office-boy and tea-maker-in-chief, Donald Black, and it is typical of the tough jobs he does for us so willingly and cheerfully that he didn't even mind when we asked him to push the train...!'

The *NME* was, at last, steady work, and Don decided it was reliable enough for Shirley and he to marry. They vowed their lives to each other at Brenthouse Road synagogue on 7 December 1958. A good day to get hitched? It was the anniversary of the day the Japanese bombed Pearl Harbor. 'The day', Don grins, 'I landed on Shirley.'

There were, happily, no bombshells during the wedding and the Blackstone clan turned up en masse from Manchester, Darlington and Sunderland. When the new Mr and Mrs Black checked into the Westbury Hotel for their wedding night, however, they had a nasty surprise. 'Single beds!' exclaims Shirley. 'I wanted the perfect night, so we checked out again and went to the Strand Palace Hotel. All they had left was a tiny room right at the top, and it was so freezing we went to bed with more clothes on than we'd worn all day!' The rest of their honeymoon passed pleasantly enough in Bournemouth, at the popular Cumberland Hotel (which, as I mentioned earlier, my family owned and where I passed much of my childhood).

Back in London, the office boy almost lost his second job, early in his *NME* career, when he severely tested Maurice Kinn's affection for him. One morning Kinn came storming out of his office, furiously looking for his secretary, who was nowhere to be seen. He was waiting for a telephone call from New York and needed someone to take vital information down in shorthand. It so happened that Shirley, working as a solicitor's secretary and skilled in shorthand, had been giving Don lessons. He wasn't very far into them yet, but – hell! – he figured it was worth a try. 'Mr Kinn,' he smiled, 'I think I can help you out.'

Kinn was delighted. He called Don a godsend and invited him into his office. In came the call, a detailed list of forthcoming performance dates, and Don busily scribbled them all down. Frankie Laine here, Guy Mitchell there. After 20 minutes, Kinn hung up the phone, and let out a great sigh of relief. 'That was close,' he confided. 'Don, I can't thank you enough. Type this up and take a couple of days off.'

Don was thrilled, until he got back to his typewriter, when he found he couldn't read a word of what he had just written. Try as he might, the dots and squiggles were suddenly completely incomprehensible to him. In a panic, he phoned Shirley and asked her to translate. 'It doesn't work like that,' she told him, adding for good measure. 'Why on earth did you say you could do it?'

It was obvious that his job was on the line. He turned for help to the news editor, Peter Charlesworth (a notoriously bad speller, who later became Joan Collins' agent). Charlesworth heard him out with sympathy, but it was clear there was only one course of action. The young employee had to throw himself at his publisher's mercy. 'You've got to knock on his door, Don,' he advised sagely, 'and say these words. "Mr Kinn, I've overreached myself." It's all you can do, Don, it's all you can do.' He shook his head sadly.

It was a very nervous office boy who knocked on his boss's door some minutes later. 'Yes, Don, what can I do for you?' was the pleasant response. Then came the phrase which became famous around the *NME* offices for years to come: 'Mr Kinn, I've overreached myself.' Equally famous was the loud shout of 'WHAT?!!' that followed it. Says Don, 'He went absolutely barmy. And he cancelled the days off.' Nevertheless, although he was treading on thin ice for a little while, he was allowed to keep his job.

Don got to know the Alley's music publishers, and would hang around their offices. He became fascinated by the lonely songwriters – 'battered, street-wise, world-weary figures' – who would chase after the publishers with their latest efforts. They lived from fiver to fiver, which was all they expected for their efforts. These people, to Don, were professional dreamers. They got paid to capture their dreams in print. 'I used to walk around the park with them,' he says, 'and listen to them talk about what they did, and it seemed bloody marvellous! Better than my Dad schlepping that presser.'

At the time there was a dearth of decent lyricists. The call went out from Tin Pan Alley, and the hunt was on. There was decent money to be had for those who made it. Don became friendly with the lyricist Mike Hawker, who'd recently written the No.1 song 'Walking Back To

Happiness' for Helen Shapiro. He and Don were chatting one day, when Hawker casually pulled out a cheque that he'd received from the Performing Rights Society (PRS) for £1,200. To astonished Hackney eyes, this was a fortune, and more than enough to convince Don he should have a go. So he began writing the odd song or two. Some got recorded – 'April Fool' ended up as the B-side of an Al Saxon record, 'Crazy Over You' was picked up by Perry Ford and his group the Ivy League – and he would start getting cheques through from the PRS for £10 (equivalent to a week's wages at the *NME)*. Don sensed opportunity, if he could only work out how to have a big hit.

Of more pressing concern, however, was the job with the *NME*. After two years there, Don had tried almost every position going: office boy, the circulation department, the advertising department, writing. None of it suited him as a long-term prospect, and none of it paid enough. He was bored and he was broke. Then he was rescued by the man who'd got him the job in the first place – his brother Michael.

One night in 1954, Michael needed a compère for one of his shows. Don may have been the quiet kid of the family, he reasoned, but he was no slouch in the living-room shows they used to put on for their parents. So he took a chance. 'Do you want to do a show tonight, son?' Don gulped, and asked what he meant. 'I need a replacement. Just go out there and introduce Dave Allen.'

Truth to tell, Don had always fancied himself as a bit of a comedian. 'Great,' he said, and his stage career began.

Soon graduating from hosting his brother's shows, Don got himself an agent and a memorable name, and thus was born 'Don Black – A Living Joke'. He spent 1954 and 1955 touring clubs, music halls, charity functions and Jewish weddings. The posters used to dub him 'Britain's slowest-rising comedian'.

The act was, he fancied, a lively mix of jokes and impressions, with Groucho Marx and Marlon Brando his specialities. According to Shirley and his sister Nita, however, it was, frankly, terrible. 'He did all these mother-in-law jokes as though he was a middle-aged man,' chuckles Nita, 'and he looked about 12!'

Shirley agrees. 'The material was OK, but it really didn't suit him. They were jokes for someone older. His impressions were quite good, though.'

Michael is far less tactful, saying gravely, 'He was the worst comic in the world.' After one of Don's turns, an agent Michael knew bumped into him in the gents' toilets. 'That comic Don Black is the worst I've ever seen,' he groaned. Michael nodded in agreement. To his dismay, the agent continued, 'You know, Michael, he looks a bit like you, and he's got the same surname. You're not brothers, are you?'

'Brothers?' snorted Michael. 'If I had a brother who was that bad a comedian, I'd disown him!' Don was known as the shoe comedian, adds Michael – he walked off to the sound of his own footsteps.

Of course, the family never told Don how bad he was and boisterously supported him. They'd take up an entire row at Collins Music Hall. 'I'd come out and say, "I hope you're a good audience because I'm very critical,"' says Don, 'and if the family were in, amidst the polite laughter there'd be this huge collective "Wa-hey!" from where they were sitting.'

When the family weren't in, however, the reception could be a lot less welcoming. One of Don's regular spots was at the Panama strip club in Windmill Street, then (as now) the centre of Soho's sex industry. And it was hard work. The comics were required to do five shows a day to give the girls a break. If only the impatient audience had given the comics a break... 'It was a ridiculous place to do comedy. As I'd walk onto the stage, everybody in the audience would lift up their newspapers and start reading. Because they've come to see the tits, and who gives a shit about what I've got to say?'

He'd give them his best lines (such as they were). No reaction. One night the singer and songwriter Al Saxon, a friend from Denmark Street, came by to watch the act. Don was struggling as usual to get any sort of response from his newspaper-engrossed spectators, who were waiting for him to introduce 'The amazing Maria and her fans!' Spotting Saxon from the stage, Don gave up and started having a conversation. 'Hello, Al!' he cheerfully hollered across the footlights.

'Hello, Don. What are you doing?' came the bemused reply.

'I've got to introduce the next act, but I could meet you for coffee after.'

Saxon looked around. 'Is this the sort of audience you usually get, then?'

'Yup.'

'How long will you be?'

'About 20 minutes?'

'OK, great.'

Don turned back to the audience. No one had noticed a thing. He shrugged, and with a flamboyant gesture announced, 'The amazing Maria and her fans!'

Today Don looks back at the job and sighs ruefully. 'It didn't matter what I did. They just wanted to see the knockers.' One wonders how many unsuccessful comedians have that phrase carved on their gravestone.

The comedy circuit attracted some real eccentrics, and Don loved mixing with them. One of his favourites was the comic Dickie Dawson, made famous by the TV series *Hogan's Heroes* and also married to Diana Dors. Dawson made a great impression on young Don, who thought him impossibly glamorous, with his Canadian accent and his talk of friendships with Frank Sinatra and the Rat Pack. Until, that is, it transpired that he had creditors in every corner chasing him for certain unpaid debts. Dawson owed thousands of pounds. The reason he owed the money was even more unexpected, for his oft-boasted contacts with American megastars like Sinatra were completely one-sided. If he heard, say, that Sinatra – whom he had met perhaps once – was playing in Las Vegas, he would send an expensive present with a note, saying, 'Thinking of you, love Dickie'. Dawson even turned out not to be Canadian in the end – he was from Southampton. His best act was his life.

Don did stand-up for two years, but it was no kind of career for a young married man, and not just because he wasn't especially good. The music halls were dying around him and the work was drying up. The big music halls struggled on – Collins, the Metropolitan in Edgware Road – and he was playing these places, but he would look at his diary and see bookings three weeks apart. 'Variety was dying,' quips Don. 'I blame myself.'

Don was now a husband and had responsibilities. And there were a lot of bills. It wasn't just the money, though. Comedy was hard work. Constantly writing new material, going through the pre-performance nerves, scouring the country for bookings. But in some ways it was ideal training for a lyricist. He explains: 'I always had a thing about comedy. And it's very closely linked to lyric-writing. A great comedian never wastes a word. Analyse Ken Dodd or Bob Hope. You couldn't edit out a word that they say. It's compression. That is what lyric-writing is about as well. And in the pacing, the timing of comedy, there's an almost musical quality. I didn't realise that at the time, of course.'

It was time to leave comedy, and Don went back to the street he loved best – Tin Pan Alley. But this time the street was to be the start of a genuinely new direction. In professional terms, it was to be the start of everything. And it was to introduce him to one of the most important people in his life. Matt Monro.

3 Enter Matt Monro

Matt Monro's story is one of optimism, luck, blessings, curses and tragedies. It has never been fully told. But nobody knew him better than Don Black, and he is finally ready to tell Matt's secret.

The story begins as the tale of Terence Parsons, the name his parents gave him when he was born in Shoreditch, London, in 1930. It was a tough childhood: when he was 3 years old, his dad died and that was followed by his mother contracting a serious illness. He was moved into a foster home, where he lived for two years.

Terry left school at 14 and tried his hand at a variety of jobs – working in a tobacco company, as a milkman, brickie's assistant, builder, fireman on the railways, and even helping out in a custard factory. It was when he joined up, and the army sent him to Hong Kong, that he discovered the God-given talent that was to pull him out of manual work and place all of the world's riches within his grasp.

He was assigned to the tank division as an instructor and heard about a weekly talent show at the local Cheerio Services Club. Enticed by the prize – Hong Kong $10 and 200 cigarettes – he decided to give it a try. Although back in school he had been banned from singing with the choir because he was always so out of tune, he knew that his voice had improved a great deal – he had even been paid to give the odd show at the Tufnell Park Palais back home. So he entered as a singer.

He won. He won the next week too, and the week after that, and the following week. After seven wins in a row, he was barred from entering again because it didn't seem fair on the other contestants!

As well as the cash and the cigarettes, the talent show also gave the winner a half-hour spot on Hong Kong's Rediffusion radio station. Private Parsons was such a hit that they gave him his own show, called *Terry Parsons Sings*. The show was a success, and by the time he returned to London in 1953 he knew that singing was his future.

Well, that was the dream. The reality was that Terry was forced to finance his efforts at kick-starting his singing career with the rather less glamorous job of driving the number 27 bus from Tufnell Park to Holloway. He drove the bus during the days, and touted for singing engagements at night.

It was a slog, but it wasn't to last forever. Winifred Atwell, the hugely popular black pianist, heard this singing bus driver and was deeply impressed by his coppery, burnished voice – manly and warm, yet with a vulnerable mellowness to it that was greatly endearing. She took the grateful Terry under her wing, and persuaded her contacts at Decca Records to audition him. They were so impressed that they immediately put him under contract, not bothering with the usual practice of releasing one record and assessing the response.

The Decca execs knew one thing for certain: their new discovery could not be called Terry Parsons. Something more catchy, more romantic was called for. 'Matt Monro' was perfect, though its origins are rather bizarre – 'Matt' (White) was the name of the first national newspaper journalist to run an interview with him, and 'Monro' was the first name of Winifred Atwell's father. Together, they went with a swing.

Matt Monro turned up for his first recording session still looking very much like the old Terry Parsons, and was so nervous that (for comfort) he kept on his bus driver's jacket! The nickname which was to stay with him for his entire career – 'the singing bus driver' – never seemed more apt. The recording went well, the musicians breaking into applause after his first number, and Decca were confident that they had a new star to rival the best America could offer.

It didn't happen. Not yet, anyway. Although he left bus driving and recorded four singles and an album for Decca, they were failures. Good reviews, bad sales. That was the story of Matt Monro's early career. Decca dropped him.

He became one of the dream chasers, hanging around Tin Pan Alley desperately trying to get recording work from the music publishers there. And that was where Don came in.

Don had returned to Denmark Street and landed a job as a song-plugger for the publisher David Toff. His responsibility was to get the company's songs played on the airwaves, either as a record played by a DJ, or performed live with a band. So he would spend his time schmoozing BBC producers and DJs, and getting artists to record the new songs so that he could tout them around. It was ruthless and adrenalin-fuelled, and he loved it.

'That was a fantastic, competitive world,' says Don. 'Your whole life revolved around getting those songs played. You'd take a producer out to lunch and your eyes would be scouring the restaurant to see who else was there, and if you saw a rival talking to the producer of *Family Favourites* – one of the best shows to be on – you'd go crazy with jealousy! Because it was deliver or die.'

Matt Monro was, if not dying, then struggling. And Don was a lifeline. They met just as the Decca deal was collapsing: 'Matt used to come into my office. He used to go into any office where he thought there might be a prospect. He wasn't doing anything really, only getting the odd gig. He was drifting, and would come and see me to ask if I would record him for the demo of our latest song. He had this great voice, and anyway we struck up a friendship immediately.' At one point Matt was broke, and turned to his friend for help. Don, short of money himself, lent him £7, enough to get by until the next pay cheque. A grateful Monro never forgot that favour.

Matt's star was to rise again, but not in a way anyone could have envisaged. George Martin, a record producer with a big Beatles-fuelled future ahead of him, was making waves in the industry as a producer of comedy records. In 1959, he and one of his star turns, Peter Sellers, were working on an album called *Songs For Swingin' Sellers*. The comedian was known for his uncanny impersonations, and he was eager to try his hand at Frank Sinatra. But he was having trouble, and felt he needed a guide track from a real singer. Martin, who knew of Monro, asked him to supply an Ol' Blue Eyes-style rendition of the song 'You Keep Me Swingin''.

Matt was furious. He wanted to record himself, not be a warm-up guy for Peter Sellers. But then again, a job is a job, and money is money. He did it – rather well, in fact. So well that Sellers declared he couldn't possibly do any better and it was Matt's track that opened the album. *Songs For Swingin' Sellers* was released, was a hit, and the identity of the Sinatra impersonator was kept a secret. Soon everyone wanted to know who this gorgeous voice belonged to, with many believing it was Sinatra himself playing a joke!

The truth leaked out and it was as well for Matt that it did. Suddenly he was in demand. George Martin signed him up to Parlophone, he started singing big dates in London and New York, and followed all this up with one of the hit records of 1960, the melting 'Portrait Of My Love'. It reached No.3 in the British charts and made Matt Monro a household name. Before long, Sinatra declared that Matt was the best singer in Britain, one of the best in the world. Bing Crosby said the same.

The bus driver was, at last, a star. And he needed a manager. 'Someone had to do it,' shrugs Don, 'and we got on so well that he asked me. It was a very good job, not easy, but we became joined at the hip, him and me. Money-wise, there was a definite income. Matt was in demand.' It was a job that Don never relinquished. Even when he was so busy that he really had no time to look after Matt, he could never bring himself to tell him. As far as they were both concerned, they were in this crazy world together and that was that. Besides, it was Matt who kick-started Don's writing. He'd done a few bits and pieces, but never seriously, and he had more or less given up. Matt, meanwhile, had faith in his friend's potential.

For Matt, 1963 was yet another golden year. He'd been picked to sing the title song for the second James Bond movie. *Dr No* had been a smash, but *From Russia With Love* was to be the first with a song. Lionel Bart, author of the fabulous musical *Oliver!*, wrote it, an easy, sweeping romance with more than a touch of the sinister. It suited Monro perfectly.

Bart and Black had much in common. They were both Londoners, East Enders, Jewish, working-class boys. And Matt saw no reason why Don couldn't do what Lionel Bart was already making a lot of money at. With the name Matt Monro on the records, he reasoned, he could help establish his friend as a first-class lyricist, and he approached him with the line, 'If Lionel Bart can do it, why can't you?'

It wasn't quite as simple as that. Don knew that Matt wanted to be a singer in the Sinatra mould, so he set about delivering a Sammy Cahn-style lyric. The result was the song 'April Fool', with music by Al Saxon:

I'm a fool for April,
Yes I'm an April fool.
Not just for one day a year,
Every time she's near.

'I reasoned that there'd never been an April Fool song,' laughs Don. 'There had been songs for Christmas, Easter. And I thought that if Irving Berlin can have an Easter classic with "Easter Parade", there was no reason why this couldn't become an April Fool's Day classic!' There is still no April Fool's Day classic. Despite the song not doing well – as the B-side of a record, it never had a chance – Matt liked it and urged Don to continue.

In 1964, Matt was asked to sing the British entry for the Eurovision Song Contest in Copenhagen, 'I Love The Little Things'. He came second. But the song he really fancied was the Austrian entry by Udo Jürgens, called *Warum Nur Warum*. That it bombed in the contest didn't deter Matt – he felt the tune was a winner. All it needed was some decent English lyrics. His manager was with him. 'Over to you, Don.'

This time the new lyricist felt confident. 'Udo Jürgens was this very popular composer in Austria, their Sinatra. He'd sit at the piano and sing these wonderful, melodic, gypsy Jewish tunes that are right up my street.' Don delivered a beautiful, agonised lyric, with the title 'Walk Away':

Walk away, please go,
Before you throw your life away.
A life that I
Could share for just a day

We should have met,
Some years ago.
For your sake I say,
Walk away, just go.

Walk away and live,
A life that's full with no regret.
Don't look back at me,
Just try to forget.

Why build a dream,
That cannot come true?
So be strong, reach the stars now.
Walk away, walk on.

If I heard your voice,
I'd beg you to stay.
So don't say a word,
Just run, run away.

Goodbye my love.
My tears will fall now that you're gone.
I can't help but cry,
But I must go on.
I'm sad that I,
After searching so long,
Knew I loved you, but told you
Walk away, walk on.

It was a huge hit, and these were the verses that launched Don Black the lyricist. Over the years the offers were to pour in. Would Don write lyrics for Elmer Bernstein? Michel Legrand? Lalo Schifrin? He found himself straddling two careers – as Matt's manager, and as an in-demand songwriter.

However, the partnership benefited them both. If Matt had helped Don, Don could now help Matt by suggesting he be the vocalist on Don's songs. So over the years Don got Matt's voice onto hit songs he wrote with the likes of John Barry, Quincy Jones and Michel Legrand.

The future was inviting for Don and Matt. They were both hot, artists of the moment, and there were plenty more triumphs to follow. But a cloud was to keep hiding the sun for Matt – a cloud comprising alcohol vapours.

'To understand Matt,' says Don, 'you have to understand that he always stayed an ordinary guy. Through all the fame and success that was to come his way, he always remained, at heart, the singing bus driver. He was resolutely unimpressed by people's reputations, as I found out when I managed him. He'd be playing at, say, The Talk Of The Town nightclub in Leicester Square – this was the biggest date around, the epitome of chic. Lena Horne played there, Shirley Bassey, Johnny Mathis. And I'd go backstage to Matt and tell him excitedly, "Great audience tonight, Matt! Sammy Davis is out there and Tony Bennett's also in, and they want to come back and say hi after the show!" He'd just groan and say, "For God's sake, Donsie, I thought we were gonna have a game of cards." And he'd actually mean it! I'd be left stammering, "But it's Sammy Davis…" He'd sigh and say, "Alright, well, for goodness' sake, let's get 'em in, 'ave a quick drink and let's get out of here."'

No one thought more highly of Matt Monro than his 'Donsie'. But part of Don's job, which he's never talked about till now, was to hush up the problem that was to blight Matt's career and keep him from attaining the heights Don believes were his for the taking. Matt Monro was an alcoholic.

Don used to kid him, 'The only difference success has made to you, Matt, is that you've gone from pale ale to champagne!' He'd grin back good-humouredly and say, 'Have a bleedin' drink and don't be so uptight.' His non-drinking manager would never quite reconcile the cultured, stylish vocalist with this pub-loving guy who often seemed as though he'd still be happiest drinking with his mates from the bus depot. Strange, he would muse to himself, the gifts that people are given in life. One man can spend his whole life taking perfect care of himself, practise all the time and still not be able to get a note right, while someone like Matt could smoke 100 cigarettes a day, drink himself silly and *still* sing like an angel.

'Time and again before a show,' marvels Don, 'I'd watch him lurch into the theatres completely drunk, throwing up backstage. Then he'd splash water on his face, say, "Right, off we go!" and bound onto the stage to launch into a gorgeous rendition of "Around The World".'

Champagne wasn't actually Matt's favourite; he was a beer man, or a Scotch and water man. And once he started, he just kept on drinking. Not that it ever showed on stage – that was part of his talent. But from the first days of Matt's success Don felt that the alcoholism was damaging his career. Yes, he could pull it off in front of an audience, but it was harmful in more subtle ways.

'This is what would happen. He'd be at The Talk Of The Town. Sensational. The audience would go mad. Standing ovations. And everyone would come up to me and say, "He's the greatest singer ever to come out of this country." Meanwhile, Matt would be back in his dressing room, gulping down the booze.' Don would often bring back luminaries and important industry players to meet his star client. And there the problems would begin.

'Bernard Delfont, the owner of the club and a very powerful figure, would come back to congratulate him. And there would be Matt, in a fog of cigarette smoke and drinking away. He'd see Mr Delfont and shout in a lary way, "Allo Bernie, how are you son? Have a drink?" Mr Delfont would politely decline and Matt would keep nagging, "Oh go on, 'ave a drink, what difference does it make?" So by the time they left his dressing room these people, who were key to his career, would only remember the smoke and the booze, not the standing ovation of an hour before.'

It was the only subject they argued about. Don would scold Matt, reason with him, plead him. 'What's the bloody difference, as long as I go out there and sing all right?' the star would argue. 'Matt, it does make a difference, because the impression you give them after you stop singing will eventually get on their nerves.' Eventually, later on, it did catch up with him.

Despite his usually reliable ability to cover it up, there was one tell-tale sign that Matt was drunk on stage. He would talk too much, suddenly convinced that he was the funniest man in the world. It is a memory shared by Matt's old musical director Kenny Clayton: 'When he'd had a few too many, he would go on and on. I'd often give him a musical nudge to stop him, by getting the band to play the intro to the next song while he was still talking!' It could almost ruin his act. And, according to Don, one night in particular he never quite recovered from. It was the most important night of his professional life.

Nat 'King' Cole had just died. Capitol Records had lost their major star, perhaps the biggest star in the world at the time. And they were hunting for a replacement. Matt was seen as the heir apparent.

Capitol signed Monro, brought him over to America and he started having hits there – 'My Kind Of Girl' reached the Top 20, 'Walk Away' made the charts. People were talking about him, and his admirers included Dean Martin, Tony Bennett, Sinatra, Crosby, Sammy Davis Jr – they all said how great he was.

Everything was going right, and the London boy was poised to take America, the world, by storm. All he had to do was claim the mantle, and Capitol arranged the night for him to do it.

They set up a fabulous engagement at the Westside Room at the Century Plaza Hotel in Los Angeles. This was going to be his night, the night Matt would formally take over from Nat.

Everyone who counted in the music business was there , all the record-company big boys. Jack Benny, Liberace, Bobby Darin – they were all eager to see the emergence of the world's new superstar. Don was on the top table, next to Jack Benny. And, if everyone else was excited, he was nervous – because he'd been backstage and seen the state the new superstar was in.

He'd been drinking, and Don had been trying to coax him to put the drinks away. 'Everyone's here tonight, Matt,' he cajoled. 'This is the night – you've got to go out there and do it!' But he knew that the singer, no doubt nervous himself, was plying himself with Dutch courage.

So it was a relief when Matt Monro was announced and the singer walked steadily to the front and launched into 'Around The World'. And it was great. The audience lapped it up, cheering and applauding, and Matt looked like he was enjoying himself. The stars in the audience were saying things like, 'What a voice!' and 'This guy's got nine lungs!' They raved about his phrasing. The next number was the same, and the next. Don began to relax. After the third number, though, came that sure sign that Matt was under the influence. He began to talk.

'Matt loved to do comedy,' grimaces Don. 'He always thought of himself as a great raconteur. And sometimes he could be pretty good. But when he drank, he went on and on. And that night… It was so embarrassing.'

He started by saying, 'I see we have Mr Benny here this evening!' and launched into a terrible Jack Benny impression. The room began to get quiet. Don, who was sitting next to the poor man, cringed. 'I was dying. He just went on and on, and I was desperately thinking, "Just sing, Matt, for God's sake sing!" But he was determined to show that he could do the whole "big star" bit, and the longer he rambled, the further his chances of superstardom flew away.'

Joke after bad joke followed, and the feeling of disappointment among the audience was palpable. When he did sing the evening lifted, and when he talked it sank. Matt's chance was gone. He was still a star, he still had a great career. But he was not, never became, a superstar on the level of Frankie or Nat. And, thinks Don, he should have been. Could have been. If it wasn't for the drink.

'Great stars', says Don, 'must have a mystique about them. A mystery. There has to be something unknowable, untouchable about them. You need to elevate yourself from the masses. When Matt drank he became so obviously one of the people. And the people don't worship someone they might meet in the pub.'

To an extent, of course, attitudes have changed, as Black readily acknowledges. Today it's even fashionable to admit to alcoholism or drug abuse. Stars are almost expected to check themselves into a trendy drying-out clinic as a grim prerequisite of celebrity. 'But then you didn't talk about it,' he says. 'His wife Micky asked me to try and get him to stop, and he did try but always failed.'

Once, when Matt was in hospital for a sinus operation, he called Don and urgently asked him for some drink. Shocked, Don told him there was no way he would be allowed booze in a hospital. When he turned up to visit him, however, Matt had a bottle of Scotch hidden in the bed.

The public knew nothing of this, and that was vital for Matt's career. There were times when the mask publicly slipped. At a Frank Sinatra concert at London's Royal Festival Hall, Matt was so drunk that he fell down and broke his wrist. 'We hushed up the reason for the fall,' reveals Don. 'It wasn't hard to do. Journalists liked Matt, he was one of them! He'd buy them all a drink. So they purposely didn't pry that much.'

The real problem was one of character. Matt's drinking was part of who he was. Even when he tried to kick the habit and checked himself into a rehab centre in Roehampton, he still spoke and acted like a drinker. When it was time to leave and Don went to pick him up, he insisted on going straight to the pub. 'Let's have a drink. My shout, son.' He was on the wagon, but still stood at the bar, smoking a cigarette and gulping a 'bitters' (bitter lemon) for all the world as though he was in the middle of a heavy drinking session. 'He loved the whole atmosphere of drinking,' says Don. 'It was the cigarette, the glass, the whole image. Even without the booze, he was a drinker.'

John Ashby, who in the mid-1970s handled the day-to-day details of Matt's work when Don moved to Hollywood (from where he still supervised his client and friend's career), tells a marvellously illustrative story of Matt at his best, and at his worst.

'In 1975, I booked Matt to tour the Far East and Australia. We had already been forced to postpone the tour once because he was on a bender. Although he did manage to stay dry at times, this was during one of his drinking periods. So Australia had been put back for six weeks, and now, come what may, we had to go. He was still pretty shaky, having just come out of hospital.

'On the plane Matt sat in first class, and I and the music director were in business class. I made him promise not to drink. "Don't worry, son." He assured me he'd be fine. But when we had to change planes in Bombay, I walked through first class to see that he'd been having a *very* good time! There were lots of empty glasses lined up in front of his seat. Again he assured me that he would be fine.

'We got to Singapore and the promoter met us. He saw Matt was not with us and, no doubt noting my worried expression, asked, "Is everything OK?"

'"Fine," I told him, "Matt has been as good as gold." At that point a porter rushed up to us, pointing behind him and frantically shouting, "He very drunk! He very drunk!" I smiled encouragingly at the now-panicking promoter, grabbed the reeling Matt and put him to bed.'

But the next night, says Ashby, Matt turned up completely sober at the Neptune Theatre and gave a magnificent performance to 3,000 fans. 'It was,' he says in awe, 'the best concert I've ever seen in my life, and I've seen a lot. He was electric. Every number, they stood and cheered. On his day Matt could be the greatest showman of them all.' The more they cheered, the more Matt, lifted by the reception, gave. He had been nervous before the tour because drink had stopped him singing for ten weeks. Now, not 24 hours after the episode in the airport, here was the same man giving a 24-carat show. Even the drink could not destroy his talent.

To Bob West, Matt's road manager between late 1964 and 1969, the greatest thing about Matt was his generosity of spirit. West accompanied the singer on his South African tour in 1967. Monro, he says, felt very strongly about racial equality – after all, his mentor Winifred Atwell was black – and he had stipulated in his contract that black people should be allowed in to watch his concerts.

When he reached his Cape Town hotel, the black *maitre d'* approached him and urgently told him that blacks were being warned away. 'But', he pleaded, 'we must hear you sing. "Born Free" is an anthem to us.' Matt was outraged, and went to see the mayor of Cape Town. He was told the only way he would be allowed to sing to the black population was to give another concert after his contracted evening show, in private.

Matt willingly agreed, and after one evening performance he went with his drummer, pianist and bass player to a small cinema on a street corner in the middle of one of Cape Town's black neighbourhoods. 'We had secretly rehearsed there in the afternoon,' says West, 'and when we got there that evening, Matt walked in through the auditorium. The entirely black audience cheered and surrounded him so he couldn't get to the stage. He sang "Born Free" right there on the floor, and the audience went crazy! Finally making his way to the stage, he sang "Born Free" another three times in a row before they would let him continue to another song. And they had hooked up speakers in the streets, where immense crowds gathered. When he sang "Born Free", we could hear the roar from outside. It was never reported.'

Why did Matt drink? West has his own opinion. 'He was an ordinary Cockney guy who liked singing. He was never seriously ambitious. He didn't chase the fame and would have sung for anyone. I'm absolutely convinced the drink was a response to the pressure of all this celebrity he found himself with.'

West remembers that Don would complain miserably to him about the singer's latest stumbles off the wagon. 'It would upset Don. He would ask me, "Why does he do this, Bob, he's going so well?" And I would reply, "Don, he just wants to sing. He's not as ambitious as you want him to be." Some people wanted Matt to be more than he wanted to be himself.'

'When people ask me why I don't drink,' says Don, 'I tell them about Matt, and what the booze did to this great talent and this wonderful, kind-hearted man. I hated the stuff.'

However, Black knew about Matt's drinking right from their days in Denmark Street, from the times a hard-up Matt would earn a sought-after £5, then head straight into the White Lion pub to spend it. He signed up for the ride anyway, and what a ride it proved to be.

4 Barry, Black And *Born Free*

The 1960s saw the creation of a movie phenomenon, and with it the rise of an icon. The phenomenon was James Bond, licensed to kill and make a killing at box offices around the world. The icon was 007's resident composer, John Barry. Or should that be the other way around?

There was something of the Bond style to Barry himself. He had moved down to London from Yorkshire, and was enjoying the bright lights, the glamour of the big city. Already a star thanks to his hit band, the John Barry Seven, Barry's music for the first three James Bond films, *Dr No*, *From Russia With Love* and especially *Goldfinger* (with its unforgettable title track), had established him internationally as one of the leading film composers of the day. And the music was so integral to the James Bond image that some of that mystery could not help but rub off on the way the public perceived him. They wanted him to be glamorous, and he did not disappoint.

'John Barry was the guy around town,' remembers Don. 'He was the womaniser, the hell-raiser of his time. A very handsome guy who used to drive this white Citroën Mazarati. He always looked the part, always had beautiful girls around him.'

As well as the Bond films Barry, five years Don's senior, had also won success with pop songs, TV themes for big shows of the day such as *The Persuaders* and *Juke Box Jury* and the soundtrack for the movie hit *Zulu*. He, like the rest of the music industry, would spend a lot of time around Denmark Street and every so often would bump into the young song-plugger-turned-agent-turned-lyricist. They liked each other, and would have lunch and swap gossip and trade news. 'We got on well,' says Barry, 'and that's very important to a composer–lyricist relationship. I liked his songs, and thought we might work well together.'

So one day the two men were having lunch, and John Barry dangled a commission in front of him. 'How do you fancy having a go at the new Bond song?' Don was ecstatic. Not only was this the chance to work with the major British film composer, but it was Bond! This, Don knew, was a rare chance. What, he asked, was the title? There was a pause. '*Thunderball*.' Don accepted, though he had no idea what the word meant As soon as he got home he ran to the dictionary to look up the word 'thunderball'. It wasn't there.

'I always get lumbered with bad titles,' he moans. 'Other people get *The Way We Were*. I get *True Grit* and *Thunderball*!'

He wasn't the only one who could make no sense of the word. 'It was gibberish, an awful title to work with. Good for a movie, terrible for a song,' sniffs Barry. 'I kept asking the producers, Cubby Broccoli and Harry Saltzman, if we could write something different, but they insisted. They'd had success before with this formula, and it was important from a marketing aspect to get the title of the film into the song. Well, that was fine for *From Russia With Love* and *Goldfinger*, where you could talk about the villain. But *Thunderball*?'

Meanwhile, Don was racking his brains for a solution. Eventually he decided to treat it like a code word: 'He strikes like Thunderball.' If nobody knew what it meant, it didn't matter. It was code, right? And he used the fact that the word was such an enigma to pack a powerful punch. And, says Black, this song was about the hero of the saga. Bond. Determined. All-conquering. And ruthless.

He always runs while others walk.
He acts while other men just talk.
He looks at this world and wants it all.
So he strikes like Thunderball.

He knows the meaning of success.
His needs are more so he gives less.
They call him the winner who takes all.
And he strikes like Thunderball.

Any woman he wants he'll get.
He will break any heart without regret.
His days of asking are all gone.
His fight goes on and on and on.

But he thinks that the fight is worth it all,
So he strikes like Thunderball.

Barry was delighted. 'I once called the Bond genre "million-dollar Mickey Mouse music", because the music must follow the action – right from the title song, it has to be almost cartoony. You can do anything, but subtlety isn't a virtue and it has to have a lot of style. Don got that right from the beginning.'

He had, undoubtedly, caught the Bond style. But what is that style? 'Provocative, enticing, seductive, wordly in a sophisticated way,' says Don. 'You want the whiff of the boudoir and the sip of the Martini.'

Barbara Broccoli, daughter of Cubby and current keeper of the Bond flame, is a great admirer of Don's Bond lyrics. 'Here's a film called *Thunderball*,' she says. 'The producers want the title in the song for marketing, but also to prepare the audience for what they're about to see. And you also want to set up all the Bond ingredients – the sex, the danger, the suspense. That's hard enough to do in a two-hour movie, let alone a three-minute song! But he does it. Those lyrics capture Ian Fleming's world. Bond's world.'

Having conquered the title, Barry and Black set themselves to address the next pressing decision. Who should sing it? Matt Monro had done *From Russia With Love*, and of course there would be no trouble getting him again. Shirley Bassey had scored big with *Goldfinger*. 'What it really needs', said Don, 'is a steely, manly voice.' Could any voice match the testosterone levels in those lyrics? One, undoubtedly, and he was an old friend of Don's. Tom Jones.

'We were worried about telling him the title.' recalls Barry, 'but he didn't ask any questions, he just sang it straight out. And the good thing was that, when someone like Tom Jones sings, you don't question what the words mean!'

Barry's music, just as full on as the lyrics, as broad and driving, is a hard push for any singer, even one as hardy as Tom Jones. In the recording studio, they rehearsed the number two or three times, and then Jones indicated that he was ready for the take. He seized on the song, pushing himself harder and harder, and then – when he reached the last, high note – he blacked out, tottering around in the booth. Jones managed to finish the note before he collapsed. The exhausted star was given a chair and a glass of water. And the recording was absolutely fantastic.

Don tells an enjoyable story about a subsequent encounter with Tom Jones. They were both, by coincidence, staying at the Hyatt House Hotel on Sunset Boulevard. Don was there with Matt, Tom Jones there for a concert. Spotting Don, Jones took him aside and asked for a favour. His American agent was Lloyd Greenfield, who also looked after Liberace. Greenfield was eager for Jones to go and be seen at a Liberace concert in nearby West Covina, and then to go backstage and meet the pianist.

'Tom, like Matt, is a very straightforward guy, very down-to-earth, and the last person you'd expect to want to hang around with Liberace, and he wasn't looking forward to it,' remembers Don. 'He wanted some company, and I agreed.' So off they went to West Covina. Liberace was playing to a packed auditorium, and they were seated near the front. Liberace made his habitual grand entrance, glittering in diamonds, to tumultuous applause. Then he held up his hand for silence, and spoke. 'There are two people here today and I'm so thrilled because they've come a long way and they're so wonderful. One of them is No.1 in the charts with "It's Not Unusual" – Tom Jones. The other is the brilliant lyricist Don Black.' A spotlight hit the surprised pair, and the applause was deafening.

Liberace began to play. 'It was all very flowery, florid stuff,' says Don. 'Tom's getting increasingly impatient because, after all, he's a ballsy rock 'n' roller. He leans over and whispers, "I can't take any more of this. There's a bar over there. Let's go and have a drink."' Don, as fed up as his companion, nodded vigorously and, while the audience's attention was on the stage, the two sneaked across to the bar and Tom started drinking Screwdrivers. When eventually they made their way back to the auditorium, they were horrified to hear Liberace saying, by way of concluding the evening, 'And I'd just like to thank my two special guests, Tom Jones and Don Black.' This time, as the throng applauded and turned to gaze, the spotlight hit two empty chairs. It was one of the most embarrassing moments of Don's life.

They went backstage as promised, with Don frantically whispering, 'What are we going to say?' Jones appeared completely unfazed, and when they met Liberace, who was drenched in sweat from his exertions and presumably none too pleased that they had been wasted on his VIPs, the singer simply remarked, 'You really worked hard out there!' None of them ever referred to the incident of the empty chairs.

'Thunderball', released in 1965, was a hit, reaching gold record status. And Don was now, as he puts it, 'hot'. But the good news was just beginning. For, in John Barry, he had found one of the three great writing partnerships that were to mark Don's career, and he teamed up with Barry again for his next film. It was to make his fortune and seal his reputation.

Barry was keen not to be pigeon-holed as the James Bond composer; so, aware of how dangerous that trap might be, he chose a completely different kind of film to follow *Thunderball*. Guns and glam girls (er, and seriously cheesed-off Zulus – 'fousands of 'em') had marked most of his movie work thus far (*Bond, Zulu, The Ipcress File*). At the time, then, the true-life story of lions captured and nurtured by an English couple in Kenya may have seemed an unlikely theme for his themes, but in the event Barry created an easy, flowing sound-world for the comfortable family film. The entire score flowed from the title song, for which Don wrote the lyrics, and which was (again) named after its movie – 'Born Free'.

Both Don and Barry thought that the warmth of Matt Monro's voice would be ideal. He came aboard. Don fancied writing for a lovely, mainstream film. But the experience proved to be fraught for all three men: 'At every turn of the coin there was another problem,' groans Barry. 'I was so delighted when it was over.'

For a start, the original director did not like John Barry and wanted him off the picture. Needless to say, if John went, Don went. And if Don went, Matt went. However, after many headaches, the producer Carl Foreman replaced the startled director instead.

From being the hero of the hour, however, Foreman became another obstacle to be bested. To start with, he wasn't at all sure he even wanted a title song. And he was not happy with what Black and Barry delivered. 'He didn't like John's tune,' says Don, 'and he thought my lyric was too much of a social comment. The movie was about lions, so he wanted lines to do with cages and bars and that kind of thing.'

Don fought his corner. 'Carl, we've got to get a universal thought on this. You have to keep an eye on the charts, and go for something that will have a meaning for everybody.' So 'Born Free' became a song not about lions, but about freedom. It drew from Don some of his most popular verses, and they eloquently hugged the contours of Barry's easy, deep-breathing music. Together they created a song that seems to embrace life, nature and the joy of liberty:

Born free,
As free as the wind blows,
As free as the grass grows,
Born free to follow your heart.

Live free,
And beauty surrounds you.
The world still astounds you,
Each time you look at a star.

Stay free,
Where no walls divide you.
You're free as a roaring tide,
So there's no need to hide.

Born free,
And life is worth living.
But only worth living,
'Cause you're born free.

Opening out the subject was a trick Don also employed to good effect years later, when asked to come up with a song about a boy and his pet rat. 'Ben' became a No.1 hit for Michael Jackson in 1972.

It wasn't just the music men who were having a hard time on *Born Free*. When John Barry consulted the lead actors, Virginia McKenna and Bill Travers, he discovered that the old adage about never working with children or animals was proving true. The lions were being most uncooperative, refusing to do what they were told. Progress was painfully slow and, in the end, the director became so fed up that he resorted to taping penknives to the ends of sticks and using them to jab the animals into place. So much for a film about the humane treatment of lions!

It remained touch and go whether Foreman would relent over the title song. 'That song was absolutely essential,' says Barry. 'Don's lyrics were right on the money. The movie needed them, to stop it all seeming terribly corny.' The lyrics made the film a metaphor for freedom. And in an ironic twist, the song has nw become an anthem for anti-abortionists across America.

Black and Barry felt they had done enough persuading and arguing to win the battle with Carl Foreman. But they were in for a nasty surprise.

There was to be a royal première in London and, although the writers could not make it, Matt Monro decided to attend. He went along, posed for the photographers, sat down and prepared to enjoy the song.

Some hours later, he made a hasty telephone call. 'Don, it's not there! They've cut the song!'

Foreman had re-edited the film without the song, and the movie opened with an orchestral version. Had Matt not decided at the last moment to go to that screening, they would never have found out in time and the music history books would have looked rather different. Don, Barry and Matt were livid, but it looked like they had lost. However, still they continued to argue, to harass. But Foreman wouldn't budge.

Luck intervened. At the same time, the popular American bandleader Roger Williams took a shine to the song. He recorded 'Born Free' and it shot up the US charts. It was a sign the producers couldn't ignore.

'Suddenly,' grins Don, 'the film bosses smelled success. They fell over themselves to quickly get the song back in the film while it was still eligible for the Oscars. The publishers, Screen Gems, the producers, everyone started screaming, "Get this song back in that film!"'

The producers were forced to go back to every individual print of *Born Free* and put the song back in. More than that, they put the full weight of an Oscar campaign behind it.

The song was sweeping America, and Don found that people kept coming up to him and assuring him that he was 'bound to get an Oscar nomination for this one'. Still a relative newcomer to the movie business, he was amazed at the aggressiveness of the marketing campaigns. 'I'd pick up *Variety* and see all the huge adverts – "*Born Free*, for your consideration", and that would be on a page opposite similar ads from our rivals, *Alfie* and *Georgy Girl*. It's a huge offensive, an Oscar. It's not "Cross your fingers and hope": it's advertising, marketing. Machiavellian tricks. So much goes into it. In a way that's the bad part of growing up. What you thought was a world of dreams and joy, you see is actually a hard marketplace.' The nomination was duly announced, and the momentum started to build.

What did all this mean to Don? Principally, that his song would be popular, that it might be sung in households, on buses and over the airwaves, and, yes, that here was a chance – perhaps – to finally make some real money. By this time he and Shirley had two children, both boys. There was Grant, born in 1961, and Clive, who came along in 1963. They were living in a small house in Mill Hill (a pleasant, but hardly splendid, borough in northwest London). He had a responsibility to his family, and a mortgage to pay, so he might make a few quid. But Don had no idea of the scale of what was about to hit him.

He was soon to find out. John Barry had found working on *Born Free* such a rotten experience that as soon as it was finished he sighed to himself, 'Thank God that's over', and wanted nothing more to do with it. Even when the nominations were announced, he remained in London, convinced that nothing good could come of this film. When the ceremony was happening, he didn't even bother watching the broadcast, and only got the news of how they'd done because a friend telephoned him.

For Don, however, the nomination was unbelievable. The boy who had so loved sitting in the East End movie-houses was now, for this moment, Hollywood royalty. Determined to enjoy it, he took Shirley across to America a few days before the ceremony. It was one of the best holidays they ever had. They stayed in Palm Springs, rented a Mustang, and saw the sights. Everywhere they went, people (noting the British accents) asked in a friendly way whether they were on holiday. Don couldn't resist: 'Actually,' he'd say, 'it's business. I'm here because I'm nominated for an Oscar.' The reactions were always explosive. The expression of polite interest would turn to one of disbelieving awe. 'An Oscar?' they would invariably shriek. 'Oh, my Gad!' It never failed to amuse Don, and hell, it was certainly a better reaction than he ever received from the newspaper-reading audiences at the Windmill Club. It was probably even better than 'Maria and her fans!' ever got.

10 April 1967. Oscar night. Hollywood turned out to the Santa Monica Civic Auditorium in force. Charlton Heston, Jimmy Stewart,

Richard Burton, Elizabeth Taylor, Walter Matthau, Steve McQueen. Michael Caine and Vivien Merchant, flushed with their nominations for *Alfie*; Paul Scofield, about to claim his own slice of Oscar history for *A Man For All Seasons*. This was the year of *Blow-Up*, of *Who's Afraid Of Virginia Woolf?* and *Georgy Girl*. It was also, of course, the year of *Born Free*.

Don and Shirley were driven to the famous red carpet in a shining stretch limousine. As they stepped out, all they could see wherever they turned were screaming fans, stretching to see all their celluloid gods. Don and Shirley had planned this, the dignified walk up the red carpet. Enjoying the fact that they had made it. They were among the chosen few. Don's composure lasted for just a few seconds. Until he glimpsed Jimmy Stewart. 'Look, Shirl!' he shouted, beside himself with excitement. 'Look who it is!' While the other nominees grandly strode into the hall, Don hopped about outside, pointing and laughing. 'I was just like one of the public, straining to get a glimpse of the stars!' he says. 'You can't believe you're there with them.'

Don took his seat in this auditorium full of poster people, twisting his head this way and that to take them all in. He was amazed to find himself sitting next to the legendary lyricist (most famously for Burt Bacharach), Hal David. On their other side sat fellow Brit Jim Dale, also stunned by his surroundings. 'Can you believe where we are?' asked Dale. Don slowly shook his head.

This was the major league, and Don was up against tough competition, really tough. Vying with *Born Free* were Jim Dale and Tom Springfield for *Georgy Girl*; Bacharach and David for *Alfie*; Elmer Bernstein and Mack David for 'My Wishing Doll', from the film *Hawaii*; and Johnny Mandel and Paul Francis Webster for 'A Time For Love', from *An American Dream*. The young Londoner felt overawed: 'These guys were my heroes. At the time I was a huge fan of Paul Francis Webster's. He'd written so much great stuff – "Calamity Jane", "Shadow Of Your Smile", "Love Is A Many-Splendoured Thing".'

The rest of the field were, as they say in America, no slouches either. Elmer Bernstein was already part of the Hollywood dream, having scored classics from *The Ten Commandments* to *The Great Escape* and *The Magnificent Seven*. Bacharach and David were already 'Bacharach and David'. Jim Dale – a favourite film star from the *Carry On* movies

– had turned to songwriting with his friend Tom (brother of Dusty Springfield) to create a beautifully memorable hit, which captured the vivaciousness of the 1960s (as did the film *Georgy Girl*).

Before the Best Song award came round, Don had the distinctly weird experience of appearing on stage to accept an Oscar for someone else. Ken Thorne, winner for his film scoring of Stephen Sondheim's musical *A Funny Thing Happened On The Way To The Forum*, couldn't be there, so Don accepted the award on his behalf. As he made his way back to his seat, he wondered nervously whether that might be the only time he went up that night, or whether he might be lucky enough to experience some highly pleasurable *déjà vu*!

Did he expect to win? Even against such names as Bernstein and Bacharach, could Barry and Black possibly be the Bs to lift the prize? Honestly, he didn't know. There was, however, one moment in the evening when he felt they might have edged it.

As is customary, every nominated song was performed on stage. For 'Born Free', the producers really pushed the boat out. The Roger Williams Orchestra, who had had such a smash with the song in the American charts, came on to perform it. And with them appeared a huge choir comprising singers from all different races. Black, white, Asian, it was a world choir in the best sense. 'It was so moving,' says Don. 'When all these people sang "Born Free", the lyrics took on their full meaning. It became a social comment about how we should all live together in harmony, and that was a powerful moment. The audience loved it, and at that point I thought we might have a chance.'

When the time came and his name was read out, Don was delighted to see that the Oscar was to be presented by another of his heroes – Dean Martin. He made his speech and, three brief minutes later, retook his seat, clutching the coveted gold statuette. From now on descriptions of him would often carry the two most prized words in show business – 'Oscar-winning'.

What he did not expect were the tellings-off he received about his speech. He had thanked everyone he could think of. Yet, when he came off, he kept being accosted by people, upset that they had not been mentioned. He was shocked. 'They kept coming up to me, saying, "Why'd ya thank that cocksucker when, if it wasn't for me, there wouldn't be any fuckin' Oscar?" I'd thanked Donnie Kirschner, a big music publisher. Someone said, "Kirschner had fuck all to do with it! You should have thanked so and so!"' He realised very quickly how important all those bland Oscar speeches are to so many behind-the-scenes careers. That is where a great many fortunes, and friends, are won and lost.

After the ceremony, Don joined the queue of celebrities waiting for their cars. Bruce Forsyth, then at the peak of his fame, had happened to be in Los Angeles and had come to watch the proceedings. They knew each other from Michael Black's shows, so Don and Shirley went to chat and wait with him. Ever the joker, Don couldn't resist finding a way to liven things up.

There was an announcer, patiently calling out the cars as they rolled up, and inviting the stars to meet them. 'Mr Jack Lemmon, your car is ready. Mr Edward G Robinson, your car is ready.' Now, Don and Bruce Forsyth knew of a singer from London called Alan Breeze, who used to sing with the Billy Cotton band. Compared to the Oscar crowd, he wasn't even on the scale, but he was a well-known local character. So Don went to have a word with the announcer. Within minutes they heard, 'Mr James Cagney, your car is ready. Mr Alan Breeze, *your* car is ready.' Forsyth doubled up. 'Alan Breeze?' he gulped, when he could catch a breath. 'His car's outside the Golden Egg cafe in Tottenham Court Road!' The Americans, who didn't have a clue who Alan Breeze was, were bemused to see the two men in hysterics at this mysterious private joke. It's an episode that tells you a lot about Don. If he was about as far away from home as it felt possible to get, he couldn't resist bringing a bit of home with him – even if only his sense of humour.

There was an enormous party afterwards, and the Oscar sat proudly on Don's table. Everyone kept coming over to congratulate him – Marilyn and Alan Bergman, James Mason, Richard Burton. Charlton Heston patted him on the back, for Pete's sake! 'This is the thing about America,' he enthuses. 'They love a winner. If you're a success, folks you don't know come over and hug you. In England, they don't have that overriding sense that winners should be congratulated.'

The best moment of the night, though, came when Don and Shirley returned to their hotel, the Hyatt House (the same hotel where he had been staying when Tom Jones talked him into going to that embarrassing Liberace concert). They walked in the front doors, and saw that the entire staff of the hotel had lined up and were applauding him. Astonished and deeply touched, he walked past them, murmuring thanks. 'That', he says simply, 'was one of the big moments of my life.'

When he phoned home early the next day, his sister Nita told him something else that he has never forgotten. 'Your name is on the front page of the London *Evening Standard*,' she gabbled joyfully, 'and it's on placards all around the city. "East End boy wins Oscar". You're front-page news!'

Don thought back to the days when his mother used to take him to the Hackney Empire, to when he used to polish the brass at the Palladium, to all the shows in the living room at his parents' home. And now he was on placards around London, the first British songwriter to win an Oscar. 'The placards meant a lot to him,' remembers Shirley. 'He felt like he'd won respect.'

He had made it. Still only 28 years old. He was just getting started.

5 Hand In Hand With Brian Epstein – The Trials Of An Agent

Tragically, Don's 1967 Oscar triumph came too late for his mother. In 1966, after a lifetime of caring for her family, and having seen them all embarked on successful roads, Betsy passed away. She was 63. Don remembers the night.

'That was a tragedy. I spoke to her the night before she died, and she had seemed perfectly well. She used to phone up and laugh. She would have these laughing attacks. On that night, she asked whether I had seen Bruce Forsyth on television, and she was laughing her head off. I held the phone out for Shirley to listen and said, "Can you hear that?" She was laughing and laughing. The next morning my brother-in-law, Nita's husband Woolfy, phoned. "I've just had your father on the phone. He can't wake Mummy up. It sounds bad, Don." She had died in her sleep of a heart attack. She would have felt no pain, and the neighbours all said the same thing: "She died like a queen."'

After the Oscar, 'Born Free' was the song everyone wanted to record. To date it has been recorded by over 600 artists. Johnny Mathis, Frank Sinatra, Andy Williams, Mantovani, Liberace – they all recorded 'Born Free'! Don was staggered by the sheer size of the reaction. Offers poured in for him to write for film after film. And all this time he was still working as an agent, which was itself a hugely eventful career.

By now his work with Matt Monro had made him a respected manager in his own right, and he had been invited to join the powerful NEMS agency, at 35 Curzon Street in London's Soho. NEMS, which stands for 'North End Road Music Stores', was Brian Epstein's family business. It began by selling pianos and radio sets, then expanded to incorporate records and artist management. Epstein built it up and eventually made its fortune, and made himself a figure of pop music legend, by taking on The Beatles.

Don had brought Matt into an agency run by the popular bandleader Vic Lewis, but soon after, the Lewis business was bought out by Epstein, and Lewis and Black joined NEMS. It worked out well for everyone, at least for a while. For Vic Lewis, it was a coup joining Brian Epstein and being able to boast that the company he helped to run managed The Beatles. Epstein, for his part, now had access to Lewis's already-impressive roster of artists, which included big British singers of the day like Matt and Donovan. Also important to Epstein was the reciprocal deal that Lewis had sealed with the GAC agency in America, by which Lewis would take care of their American artists when they were in England, and vice versa. So Lewis and Don found themselves charged with the wellbeing of great figures like Tony Bennett, Nat 'King' Cole, Mel Torme, Johnny Mathis, Henry Mancini, the Supremes. It was a very showy list, and Epstein wanted in on the action.

Being part of a big company was good for Don. Lewis had a lot of artists to keep happy, so Don – in addition to handling Matt – would help out. In return, when Don was too busy with his songwriting to cover Matt, his NEMS colleagues would fill in.

Brian Epstein was very pleased to be able to impress new clients with the calibre of his staff by pointing to Don's room and saying, 'You know, the fellow in the next office has got an Oscar!' And one evening, Don realised just how important the Fab Four's guru had become.

Epstein was in a meeting late that night, and everyone else had gone home apart from Don. The phone rang. It was the Lucille Ball Show calling from California, and they wanted to speak to Brian Epstein urgently. 'I'm sorry,' explained Don, 'I'm the only other one here and Mr Epstein is busy.' They said that they had been trying to reach him for days. Lucille Ball was coming to London to film an episode of her ratings-topping show. She had this grand idea that she would walk down Piccadilly and simply walk past The Beatles in the street, doing a comic double-take as they walked by. That was all – a few seconds. And for this, they told Don, they would pay $100,000. That would be fairly impressive now. In those days, it was a staggering amount of money.

They had to know quickly. So Don knocked on Epstein's door. 'Sorry to bother you,' he apologised, and quietly, excitedly, took him aside to explain. Feeling sure that even Brian Epstein must be impressed by $100,000 for a few seconds' worth of filming, he scribbled the incredible sum on a piece of paper and handed it to him. He was wrong. 'Oh no, no, no,' tutted Epstein. 'We're not interested.'

At the time, the incident impressed upon Don just how big Epstein had become. That is one perspective. Others whispered that he might have a flair for handling artists, but Brian Epstein was no businessman. The fact that he turned down such a formidable sum was not, after all, merely an indication that he didn't need the money. It also showed that he was not really interested in business dealings.

Epstein's biographer Ray Coleman, who says that 'Epstein admired Black's combining of creative talent and business dealing', tells the story of Don and the Lucille Ball offer in a different way. He cites Vic Lewis, to whom Don swiftly and incredulously told the story: 'I said I wouldn't mind being interrupted for a hundred grand. But that was typical of Brian. There were many instances of his aloofness or detachment from any kind of immediate material gain with The Beatles.' Coleman argues that the very compassion and care for personalities that made Epstein such a great man-manager for his star group prevented him from seizing the best business deals.

In a way, though, Don's take was spot on. People who need it would seize on an offer like that. Maybe he could have made more, but Epstein was huge. NEMS had some pretty big names on its books, but Epstein had The Beatles. Don and most of his colleagues handled stars, whereas Epstein had the superstars.

Had he wanted to be a full-time agent, Don was presented with golden chances. In fact, he had the opportunity to take on another genuine superstar in the making.

Elton John was on the NEMS client list, and one morning he and Bernie Taupin came to see him in his office. They were full of complaints about the agent who was now handling them, Dick James (one of Brian Epstein's trusted confidants, who had been instrumental in The Beatles' rise). They weren't happy, they told Don. 'He doesn't understand us,' sighed Elton. Then came the big question. Would Don take over their management?

It was tempting. Don could feel that Elton John had a big future if he was properly guided, and he knew he could do the job. However, he also knew that if he added to the burden of managing Matt, he would have to give up the writing. He turned them down.

But he was still able to help, and claims some credit for getting Elton John on the path to fame. Fast-forward a few years, to 1972. Don was No.1 in the American charts with the song 'To Sir With Love', an important hit for the pop star Lulu. He had gone out to Los Angeles for the song's American launch, which had gone swimmingly. While he was there, he spent a lot of time with the man who ran the American office of the Dick James publishing company, Lenny Hodes ('A lovely yiddisher man, looked like the actor Keenan Wynn'). One of the reasons they enjoyed each other's company so much was a private game they often used to play. It was a game two Jewish boys were born for – who could drink the most chicken soup? Hodes used to pride himself on his capacity, but he had reckoned without the rigorous training course that had been his opponent's childhood, for if there was one thing Betsy Blackstone had known how to cook, it was chicken soup. Her son could gulp down three or four bowls of the stuff, while Lenny Hodes was trailing and gasping for a break! It was a fine way to cement a friendship.

However, one day over lunch at their favourite coffee shop, Hodes looked troubled. Don asked what was wrong. 'It's this kid,' groaned Lenny, in utter misery. 'Do you know him? Reg Dwight, changed his name to Elton John. Dick James has told me I've *got* to place him with a record company. My job's on the line. I've been everywhere and no one wants him.' He hardly touched his chicken soup.

At that moment, Russ Regan walked into the coffee shop. He worked at Uni Records, one of the hot record companies of the day and was, as far as Lenny Hodes was concerned, make or break. Uni was undoubtedly a label Dick James would approve of (besides, he'd already tried almost everybody else), and Regan was the man who signed their record deals. He started to badger him about Elton John. 'Russ, you'd love him. He's going to be huge! Trust me, Russ.'

Regan listened impassively, then turned to Don. 'What do you think of him?' Don had a lot of faith in Elton John, who at the time had just released his first single, 'Skyline Pigeon'. He liked it, thought it sounded a bit like an English José Feliciano. 'He's fantastic,' he told Regan. 'A great performer, a writer, the real thing.'

Regan nodded. 'That's good enough for me. I'll take him.' And Elton John was offered his first big recording contract.

There was another time when Don helped Elton. The singer had his first major LA concert coming up at the Troubadour Club. This was the show that sealed his reputation in America. Don called Quincy Jones, Elmer Bernstein, Henry Mancini – all these big stars he knew – and he urged them to come to the concert, which they did.

He never regretted not taking on Elton John. Management was a lot of trouble, and he had his hands full with Matt. All artists can be temperamental, Elton as much as any of them, and Don got a taste of that side of him, too. Some years later, when Elton was a big name, he was due to appear in an important televised concert in Paris. Dick James couldn't be there, and asked Don to go in his place. So Don agreed to go and supervise.

Off they went to France and all seemed fine. Rehearsals began and Elton was singing like an angel. Suddenly he threw a tantrum. 'I'm not going on tonight!' he stormed. 'It doesn't feel right! My throat's not right!' He didn't like the atmosphere, he didn't like the sound. There were a hundred reasons.

Don could not believe his eyes. 'It was so childish.' This was an extremely important show, and Elton had shut himself away in his dressing room. The producer begged Don to do something. Elton, though, was adamant.

There was a phone on the wall outside the dressing room and Don hurriedly dialled Dick James's number. 'I'm here in Paris with Elton,' he reported, trying to keep his voice calm, 'and he won't go on.' There was a pause, then, 'Well, tell him it's very, very important that he does go on. He must go on!' Don spoke to Elton through the open dressing-room door, phone still in hand. 'Elton, Dick says you and he can talk about this tomorrow, but tonight you must go on.' Elton looked up sourly and, without skipping a beat, replied, 'Tell Dick to go and fuck himself.' Don did skip a beat, then relayed the message. 'Dick,' he said into the receiver, 'he says "Go fuck yourself."'

They tried everything, even prevailing on Petula Clark (also on the bill) to go and talk to Elton. 'You're a fellow pro,' Don pleaded. 'Please talk to him, he'll listen to you.' She did, and he didn't. The show, as far as Don remembers, went ahead without Elton John.

Don had never met Brian Epstein before joining NEMS. But the two men liked and respected each other. They didn't socialize. Don always remained a family man who never thrived on the rock 'n' roll social scene of which Epstein was a staple member. But Don was there on the most famous day of the legend of Brian Epstein – 27 August 1967. The day they found him dead.

Disturbed by reports that Epstein had not left his house for two days, his secretary Joanne, general manager Alistair Taylor and a doctor broke down the door of his flat in Belgravia. They found him slumped on his side in bed. It was thought that he had taken an accidental overdose of pills (which he tended to gorge on to get through the days).

Don had just returned from a restful holiday in Malta when he took a panicky telephone call from Vic Lewis's driver and minder Don Murfitt. 'Brian Epstein's just died,' he gabbled. 'I can't get hold of Vic. You're the only one I've managed to get on the phone.'

He asked Don to go to Brian's flat, and to hurry. Don rushed over. He found Geoffrey Ellis ('Brian's right-hand man and probably a bit more than that'). Ellis, beside himself with grief, managed to explain that the body had just been taken away. The doctor had said that it was probably an overdose. Maybe accidental.

Don was, of course, shocked, but remained mindful of the situation. The press would quickly get wind of what had happened and hotfoot it to the flat. They probably had minutes before they were besieged by reporters. Don and Ellis took to the phones.

The first person Don called was Dick James. James had always been extremely close to Brian, and Don knew this wouldn't be easy. But the reaction he got wasn't what he expected. 'Dick,' he said gently, 'you'll never believe what's happened, but you might want to sit down. Brian's just died.' There was a pause, then calmly, quietly, came the reply, 'It doesn't surprise me.' Epstein had been known to threaten suicide in the past, and if his flirtations with death in fantasy had, accidentally or not, become fact, he had always danced close to the fire.

As he put the phone down to Dick James, Geoffrey Ellis phoned Brian's brother, Clive Epstein. Don could hear the screams echoing down the line. The brothers' father had died only weeks before, and this new blow was more than Clive could bear. He was inconsolable,

One by one, they told everyone who needed to know right away, including The Beatles. As Don left the flat, the press were beginning to gather outside. 'It was', he grimaces, 'a terrible morning.'

6 Blowing The Bloody Doors Off

By 1969 the name Don Black had appeared on song sheets next to some very notable names indeed, including John Barry, for 'Thunderball' and 'Born Free'. Between those two hits, there had been a collaboration with one of Don's heroes, Charles Aznavour. His mother, Betsy, adored Aznavour, so when the music publisher David Platz mentioned to Don that he handled the Aznavour catalogue, and that he thought the two might work well together, it was a special moment. And, appropriately, the song they were to write was called 'For Mama'.

Aznavour had already written French lyrics for the song, and wanted an English version. It was a minor-key, gloriously schmaltzy ballad about a dying mother's last wish for her children. Pretty sad stuff.

Don did the job, and went to meet the dapper Frenchman in his home just outside Paris (though born in Poland, Aznavour had adopted France as his country). Aznavour was courteous and charming, and insisted that Don's lyrics were not sad enough.

Don was taken aback. He thought they were as sad as he could possibly have made them. For goodness sake, they included lines like, 'She said my son I beg of you/I have a wish that must come true/The last thing you can do for Mama'. Then it continued to describe the mother's melancholy instructions for her son to look after the other children and take her place. Hardly cheerful. In fact, Don had been worried it was *too* sad!

Aznavour tutted. 'In French,' he explained, 'the mother is dead, and the singer is holding her cold, dead hand.' Don was wide-eyed. 'Erm, you just can't do that in English, Charles,' he ventured. Aznavour raised an elegant eyebrow. 'Why not?' Don explained that 'Sad is sad, but this is macabre. It doesn't suit your beautiful melody.' Aznavour continued to insist, but Don fought his corner. 'Charles, you cannot have someone singing in English, "I'm sitting here holding my mother's cold, dead

hand." There are certain words you just cannot sing in this language.'
Aznavour demanded an example. 'Divorce,' replied Don. 'You can't
sing the word "divorce" in a ballad in English.' Aznavour looked amazed
– 'We sing about divorce all the time in France!'

Don won his case and the song did well, particularly in America,
where it was a chart hit for Connie Francis and Jerry Vale. And his
mother, of course, loved it. More top-notch collaborations swiftly
followed, with Michel Legrand (the theme song for a film called *Pretty
Polly*), Francis Lai ('One Day Soon', for the movie *I'll Never Forget
What's 'Is Name*) and Maurice Jarre (the title song for *Isadora*) .

There were some less than top-notch projects, too. Does anybody
remember the schlocky horror flicks *The Vengeance Of Fu Manchu*
(with Christopher Lee as the Oriental criminal who deserved awards
for his moustache alone) or *House Of A Thousand Dolls* (an everyday
story about a white slavery ring run by magician Vincent Price)?

Oh, and there was *Boom!*, an adaptation of Tennessee Williams'
play *The Milk Train Doesn't Stop Here Any More*. Richard Burton and
Elizabeth Taylor were looking for a hit, and thought this tale of a dying
rich woman and the young man who comes to ease her passing might
be the one. The great Italian director Joseph Losey seemed an extra
guarantee of success, as did Noël Coward as Taylor's homosexual friend.
It died. America's *TV Guide* magazine has called *Boom!* 'one of the
biggest bombs in Hollywood history'.

The problem for Don was that the success of his film songs was tied
to the popularity of their movies (the flip side of that is, of course, that
when the films do well they perpetuate the songs). On the other hand,
he was at last getting well paid and, as Michael Caine once said of his
involvement with dubious pictures like *Swarm* and *Jaws – The Revenge*,
'I have a very high standard of living. It takes a low standard of picture
to support it.'

Having said that, Don was in huge demand, and in 1967 alone wrote
for eight movies. By the law of averages, he reasoned, one of these at
least had to come good!

In the event it was an old friend of his who handed him his next smash.
He had known the singer Lulu from his song-plugging days. She was on
the way up. A string of hit singles ('Shout', 'Here Comes The Night',
'Try To Understand') had led to her being voted Britain's Most Promising

Newcomer by the prestigious *Melody Maker* magazine in 1965. In 1966, though, she was ready to step up to real stardom. She broke away from her backing group The Luvvers, and started putting herself forward for film work.

Columbia Pictures were looking for a bright young unknown to cast in their new Sidney Poitier movie *To Sir With Love*, and Lulu fitted the bill. She was cast as Babs Pegg, one of the riotous students whom new teacher Poitier inspires to mend their ways. A song was needed, and Lulu recommended Don.

She was already a Don Black fan, and talks about 'plucking up the courage' to ask him to supply her with a lyric. 'His talent goes very deep,' she says. 'He could have been great at so many things.' Lulu is convinced that in the right circumstances Don could have been a great comedian. 'He and his brother Michael have got such a hysterically dry sense of humour. They would reduce me to tears of laughter. One line of Don's I still use myself, though I don't have Don's poker face. When the phone would ring, he'd say, "Hold it. This could change everything."'

To Sir With Love was an almost unique instance in Don's career when the words most definitely came before the music. It is the question all songwriters are most frequently asked, and he usually likes to have the music first, though he will often give the composers a title and two or three lines to work with. Not in this film. The producers felt that the lyric was all-important. 'The lyric', they told Don, 'is everything here.'

Don went off to write, and found what he regards as the single most important ingredient for a song: the universal thought that everybody can relate to. In *To Sir With Love* he found one of the most cherished of thoughts – that favourite teacher who influenced our lives. After Lulu contacted him, he came up with the finished lyric the very next day.

Those schoolgirl days,
Of telling tales and biting nails are gone,
But in my mind,
I know they will still live on and on.

But how do you thank someone,
Who has taken you from crayons to perfume?
It isn't easy, but I'll try.

If you wanted the sky,
I would write across the sky,
In letters that would soar a thousand feet high.
'To sir, with love.'

The time has come,
For closing books and long last looks must end.
And as I leave,
I know that I am leaving my best friend.

A friend who taught me right from wrong,
And weak from strong – that's a lot to learn.
What can I give you in return?

If you wanted the moon,
I would try to make a start,
But I would rather you let me give my heart,
To sir with love.

There followed a competition between rival composers to see who could set Don's lyrics to the tune that would end up in the film. Al Saxon wrote one version, Laurie Johnson another, but the commission went to a friend of Lulu's, Mark London (as far as Lulu was concerned, it was always going to).

The result is one of the most memorable movie songs of them all. London's nostalgically yearning, but playful melody perfectly caught the spirit of the lyrics, and set up the film's exuberance. 'I fell in love with it,' says Lulu. 'Everywhere I go in the world, people talk about that song to me, still.'

This time, not only was the film a hit, but the song shot to No.1 in the American charts and stayed there for five weeks. Lulu, whose screen-acting début had been well received by audiences and critics, was the first non-American female vocalist ever to have been No.1 in the States for that long, By November 1967, *To Sir With Love* had sold a million copies, and it has now sold many times that number. As I mentioned earlier, the song is now sung at graduation ceremonies across the US.

'It was a double whammy. I don't think it had ever been done before,' says Lulu, referring to her acting and singing success in the movie. 'That song not only helped to sell the film, it blew everyone's mind. I will never forget what Don did for me with that song and will always be grateful.'

Another hit came from a surprising source. Don and John Barry were hired by Sunsilk shampoo to write a song for their new television ad campaign. It drew from them a glorious song, which remains a favourite for its writers – 'The Girl With The Sun In Her Hair'. As the ads featured a girl with suitably lustrous locks running through cornfields and by the ocean, thousands of people around England began singing the song. 'Everyone was singing it,' marvels Don.

I'll wait a year for two weeks in July,
I'll fly to the sun, and my love will be there.
Wistful and warm as when we said goodbye,
The girl with the sun in her hair.

It never became a chart hit but was beautifully recorded by Davy Clinton.

In 1969, Don was asked to supply a couple of songs for a new film. It was to be a crime comedy, very English in feel, with some plucky British crooks taking on the might of the Italian mafia. Michael Caine was to star alongside Noël Coward, Peter Collinson was to direct. Don had no way of knowing what a great film *The Italian Job* would turn out to be, but he would have done the movie whatever it was, because the approach had been made by one of the classiest, and coolest, of composers – Quincy Jones.

Jones lived in central London, near Marble Arch, so Don went to see him and they discussed the plot, which all centred on our boys abroad in Rome, creating a huge traffic jam to outwit rival gangsters and the police. Don had a good idea, but the jazz legend was far from happy at being asked to write an Italian holiday song with a Neapolitan feel. 'He found it very hard,' says Don. 'As a sophisticated and brilliant musician, it went against all his instincts. The man had written these great things for the likes of Sarah Vaughan, and here he was being asked to supply an easy, flowing tune.'

Progress was painfully slow. One day Don arrived to see what Jones had composed, and there was nothing. He sat with him for two hours, during which Jones played a few notes on his piano, then relapsed into deep thought. 'I'll tell you what,' said an exasperated Don, with a flash of desperate inspiration. 'I'll give you a title. "On Days Like These".' He left him with the title and went for a long walk. By the time he came back the now-famous tune was waiting for him. Matt Monro sang it, and it became a vital part of the film's charm, rolling over the credits with delighted ease.

Quincy Jones had far more fun with the other song, an ego-swelling anthem for Caine's crooks. 'He loved the idea of Cockney rhyming slang and adored "The Self-Preservation Society".' The song had the barnstorming swagger and simple yobbishness of an English football chant, and is all the funnier in the film, where the gang end up forgetting all about their own welfare amidst the post-robbery celebrations, which is when we hear it. (And, just in case there is anyone out there who has not seen one of the best endings in cinema history, I'm not giving anything away here.)

This is the Self-Preservation Society,
The Self-Preservation Society.

Go wash your German bands,
Your boat race too,
And comb your Barnet fair,
We gotta lot to do.

Put on your Dickie Dirt,
And your Peckham Rye,
Cause time's soon hurrying by.
Get your skates on mate,

Get your skates on mate,
No bib around your Gregory Peck today, hey!
Drop your plates of meat,
Right upon the seat.

This is the Self-Preservation Society,
This is the Self-Preservation Society,

This is the Self-Preservation Society,
Gotta get a bloomin' move on.

Quincy Jones found that song great fun, and would chuckle his way through the lyrics. 'We got to know each other quite well,' remembers Don. 'We gave up smoking together. One day, when we were driving along Sunset Boulevard, I threw my Rothmans out of the car and he threw away his Lucky Strikes. I don't know if he kept to it!' It was 'a very happy gig' which turned into a classic film.

With *Thunderball*, *Born Free* and now *To Sir With Love* and *The Italian Job* under his belt, Don had status and a healthy bank balance. He and Shirley had moved from their small semi-detached house in Mill Hill to a nearby four-bedroom place. Now Don was finally able to indulge his great sporting passion – snooker. Since he first had the money and the space, a snooker table has been compulsory in the Black household. As well as being great fun (he is a keen amateur competitor), he finds it very therapeutic: whenever he gets stuck on a song, he pots a few balls and invariably the writer's block disappears.

And movie offers were coming in thick and fast. In 1968, when Paramount Pictures came calling, he was introduced to not only one of his regular collaborators, but a major figure in his life and one of his best friends.

Paramount were about to start filming *Where's Jack?*, about the 17th-century highwayman Jack Sheppard. Tommy Steele and Stanley Baker were lined up to star, and Paramount wanted a song from Don. 'Who's the composer?' he asked. The answer persuaded him to sign up immediately. To work with this guy was such a privilege that he would have done it whatever the film, because he was going to work hand in fist with one of the legends of the cinema, Elmer Bernstein. Black and Bernstein – to Don it sounded almost too good to be true.

That Don and John Barry had beaten Elmer Bernstein in the Oscars with 'Born Free' was of no consequence. That had been his fifth nomination. He won the year after, and he already had two Golden Globes and a shelfload of other major awards. Elmer Bernstein had written an incredible number of great – truly great – movie scores, over a dizzying range of styles. How could the man who summoned the heavens and the elements into his score for *The Ten Commandments* have also found a groove to accommodate the pulsing jazz of *The Man With The Golden Arm*, let alone that jaunty, optimistic march for *The Great Escape*? And then there was *To Kill A Mockingbird*, *Walk On The Wild Side*… The man had scored many of Don's movie-going nights, and he was over the moon at the prospect of being his writing partner. Bernstein was not.

'I knew who he was because of the Oscar,' remembers Bernstein. 'But suddenly I'm told he's *the* hot guy and he *would* do the lyrics. I wasn't consulted, and I was far from thrilled at working with a stranger. Songwriting is a very intense process and your relationship with each other is vital.' The composer was worried that he had been saddled with some young hotshot who would be full of himself and his Oscar, and would try to dictate the way they should go. That shows, of course, that he did not yet know Don.

When the songwriters met, the older man found to his delight that Don was overjoyed to meet him, and very respectful. 'I fell in love with him instantly,' says Bernstein, 'and we've been close ever since.'

Where's Jack? was not a classic, chiefly memorable these days for being the first film in which the actor Michael Douglas is credited (he played a police constable). The song sank without trace. But the next year Bernstein and Black worked together again, on a much bigger project, the John Wayne Western *True Grit*.

The movie, a big-budget revenge story, has John Wayne's character ride in to revenge a young girl whose family have been murdered. There was lots of action, but what won Wayne his Oscar was a real tenderness in his character's relationship with the girl, played by Kim Darby. Black and Bernstein picked up on that unusual combination of the paternal and the posturing, with a song that at once keeps to the conventions of the Western but also scats around with flecks of real sensitivity.

One day little girl,
The sadness will leave your face.
As soon as you've won
Your fight to get justice done.

Some days little girl,
You'll wonder what life's about.

But others have known
Few battles are won alone.

So you'll look around to find
Someone who's kind,
Someone who is fearless like you.

The pain of it,
Will ease a bit,
When you find a man
With true grit.

One day you will rise
And you won't believe your eyes.
You'll wake up and see,
A world that is fine and free.

Though summer seems far away,
You will find the sun some day.

Yes, there's the obligatory talk of fighting and vengeance, but 'Few battles are won alone', 'You will find the sun some day'. That's not fighting talk. There is, suddenly, the same passion for life that infused 'Born Free' and even – in a harsher way – 'Thunderball'. The viewer immediately understands that this film is a quest, not just for vengeance, but for freedom from the obsession with justice. The freedom to live. Bernstein's tune, all lilting country and western, similarly catches the harshness and the hopefulness of life in the West. The West can be wild, but it is also a utopia to be won.

John Wayne won an Oscar for that one, and the Duke would have enjoyed beating very actorly actors Richard Burton, Peter O'Toole, Dustin Hoffman and Jon Voight. Don and Elmer were nominated, but Burt Bacharach and Hal David got their revenge on the 'Born Free' writer with 'Raindrops Keep Falling On My Head' from *Butch Cassidy And The Sundance Kid*. Yet their nomination helped to solidify a partnership that over the years was to encompass (so far) eight films, one musical and a deep friendship.

'He's become a bit of a role model for me,' says Don. He's the kind of friend that makes you look at life differently. He wants to live, and he is tireless in his pursuit of a fulfilling life. Nothing puts him off. He gets in from LA and rings straight away to arrange dinner. Jet lag? He'll sleep when he sleeps! There's no sense of age about him at all.'

Bernstein remembers Don's initial reaction to his zeal for adventure somewhat differently. 'He thought I was mad!' he laughs. 'When we were doing *Where's Jack?* we were filming in Ireland and I rented a little car and dragged Don with me for hours on end to explore the country. He's not adventurous in the same way, but he came along anyhow.'

The two men will go to great lengths for each other. When Elmer Bernstein had his own star implanted on Hollywood's Sunset Boulevard, Don flew across the world to be with him for the auspicious occasion, just to give a five-minute speech in praise of his friend. When he was looking for a temporary flat in London, Don was there to co-sign the lease. And when Don was honoured by that Variety Club dinner, Bernstein travelled to London especially.

True Grit was their most successful collaboration to date. Don would have bet his shirt (luckily he didn't) on the chances of their 1970 project, an Anthony Quinn and Ingrid Bergman movie. The film was called *A Walk In The Spring Rain* and at last Don thought he had broken his jinx. It had become a rueful source of humour with him that he was always being given bad movie titles for his songs. It wasn't always true – there's nothing wrong with *Born Free*. But *True Grit*? *Thunderball*? They weren't exactly *Days Of Wine And Roses*! But *A Walk In The Spring Rain* was delicate, beautiful, and Don supplied a lyric he was proud of ('A walk in the spring rain/A time for reflecting/On our brief interlude/That's now become a memory'). Like the song, the film seeped romance, and Quinn and Bergman surely guaranteed the box office. The song was recorded by Michael Dees, who had so memorably sung 'Windmills Of Your Mind'. Nothing could go wrong. Except that nothing went right: the film crashed. And the song? Nobody even noticed it.

Still, that was better than their experience on *Merlin*. Friendships are sometimes cemented in adversity and that was certainly true of Elmer Bernstein's second musical (his first, *How Now Dow Jones*, had been a respectable success). To skip ahead – as it is such a wonderful illustration of their friendship – this was in 1983, by which time Don was writing a lot of musical theatre.

There was a popular American magician of the day named Doug Henning, who was very mysterious and a fabulous illusionist, occupying much the same sort of position that David Copperfield would in the 1990s. He had his own TV specials and even warranted a guest star slot on *The Muppet Show*, the height of success! It seemed logical that he would be the perfect star for a Broadway musical about Merlin.

Don and Elmer wrote the lyrics and the music, with a book by *Columbo* writers Richard Levinson and William Link. It was a talented team, and they had a fantastical, dramatic subject with vast appeal. After all, everyone likes magic, a lot of people love the Arthurian myths, and they had Doug Henning headlining, with the seasoned Broadway star Chita Rivera in support.

There was only one problem. They had Doug Henning headlining. 'Doug Henning', sighs Don, 'was an amazing magician, but he couldn't sing, dance or act. He was a triple threat.' Also, as they found, he was as mysterious off the stage as on. Either mysterious or just plain strange, depending on how you look at it.

Henning had stipulated in his contract that he had to be left alone for hours and hours to meditate. So he would join the rehearsals at 2pm every day, stay for about an hour and half, and disappear again for more meditation.

There was no shortage of enthusiasm, though. When Don and Elmer gave him songs, his eyes would light up and he'd say, 'Yes, that's so enlightening!' 'Spaced out', 'airy-fairy' – the two men have plenty of words to describe Doug Henning. After one particularly painful rehearsal, during which Henning must have mentioned 20 times how 'enlightened' he felt, a frustrated Don turned to Elmer: 'You know, we've got to get that boy a bottle of Jack Daniel's, make him drink it and get something out of him!'

They never got the chance. But their leading man did try hard, meditation allowing. He knew his voice was not the greatest, so he willingly went to a voice coach. He worked hard at the lessons and proudly arranged a day at his singing teacher's house where Elmer, Don, Link and Levinson could hear the results. The results were appalling, and even as they tried to murmur encouragement the atmosphere in the room sunk lower and lower. Afterwards, Elmer and the two book writers spilled out onto the lawn exhausted and depressed. They had no idea what to say to each other. It was Don who found the right words. 'We stood there in utter despair,' describes Bernstein. 'Don was still inside and we were anxious to know what he thought. When he finally emerged, he walked right past us, and as he left he uttered five words, "Which way to the airport?"'

It was that gallows sense of humour that Bernstein admired about Don. He recalls a similar situation when, before the press night, *Merlin* was clearly in trouble. The tricks were fabulous – Henning made horses appear and disappear, he made a girl turn into a panther and then back – but the magician was so bad at everything else the show was flailing. It had gone through several directors, beginning with the respected Englishman Frank Dunlop and ending with Jerry Adler, now best known as the Jewish gangster Hesh in HBO's *The Sopranos*. More than one choreographer had tried to work magic on Merlin's wizardry. Such chopping and changing is always a sign that a show is on the ropes. In desperation, the producers called in experts to make assessments – show doctors, in the same way Hollywood employs script doctors. Tommy Tune had a go, and Michael Bennett (the director of the smash Broadway show *A Chorus Line*) was brought in to give his advice.

Bennett sat through the show, making notes. Then he assembled the writers together for a meeting and went through his suggestions. 'He gave us a lecture which amounted to "rewrite the show",' says Bernstein. As they left the theatre, they were devastated. Months of hard work and now to be ticked off and told, effectively, to start again. Levinson and Link, newcomers to the theatre and by now completely stunned (nobody ever gave them these kind of orders on *Columbo*), stood at the street corner in utter misery. They and Elmer started hotly debating what should go where, beginning the hard business of enormous restructuring. Don came out a moment later. He walked up and gave it to them straight: 'I want my mummy!' The three men fell apart.

The show ran for ten months, so – while a failure – it was not an embarrassment. Chita Rivera, who played the wicked queen, threw fabulous parties at her house to keep everyone's spirits up. A pro to her fingertips, and a Broadway icon to rival Ethel Merman and Carol Channing, she never complained and was never a minute late. But the last time she and Don ran into each other, in London, they looked at each other and both began: "Don't mention it. Don't say a word!' *Merlin* has never been spoken about between them again.

The critics had their fun, with the all-powerful Frank Rich on the *New York Times* – the self-styled 'butcher of Broadway' – going to great pains to list all of Doug Henning's positive points, and then wittily ending his review with the comment that he could not act his way out of a paper bag.

Incidentally, the fate of *Merlin* was a picnic compared to another show Don tried to stage that same year – *The Little Prince*, with John Barry. Despite rumours of money troubles, all seemed to be going quite well with the show, which began previews. Then one evening Don was in his hotel room watching *Live At Five* when the announcer broke the news that '*The Little Prince* is going to close before it opens.' This was news to him. Apparently the producer Joe Tandet had run out of money and could not afford to open the show, so it simply never happened. (The producer later got some money out of the show's owners for renting the theatre to someone else, even though his own show had closed and, Don believes, made money out of the catastrophe.)

Back in the 1960s, however, after the success of *True Grit*, Don re-teamed with his other old friend. Black and Barry were back in business. And that business was Bond. A lot had happened to the secret agent since he and Don had last crossed paths: he'd faked his own death, got married twice and seen his true love shot dead before his eyes on the orders of his arch-enemy, Blofeld. Now Bond was returning, hungry for revenge.

It wasn't only Bond that was returning. Sean Connery had hung up his tuxedo and Walther PPK after 1967's *You Only Live Twice*, and declared that he was handing in Bond's licence to kill permanently. The trouble was that, whereas Connery's 007 was good at dodging bullets, his successor, Australian actor George Lazenby, walked right into a hail of them. From the critics.

Lazenby was so upset at the reaction to his spy that he refused to appear in any more Bond films. The series' production company, Eon, and the distributors, United Artists, were desperate to get Connery back. But to persuade him to take on the forces of evil for a seventh time, they had to tempt him with the biggest pay packet ever offered to an actor at that time: $1.25 million in cash, plus 12.5 per cent of the gross and guaranteed funding for two non-Bond movies, which he could choose. It was too good to resist, so Connery dusted off the dinner-jacket, refreshed his Martini and set off after Blofeld.

This was a vital film in the Bond saga. The series was under threat. For the first time, it had faced the problem of replacing the leading man and had failed with Lazenby (who turned out to be the spy who laboured). Connery was back, but the movie would have to be very strong indeed to keep the momentum.

One constant was the music. John Barry was still delivering superior scores, and Don was called back to supply the lyrics for the new film, to be called *Diamonds Are Forever*.

'The title songs are a vital part of the James Bond formula,' says Bond producer Barbara Broccoli (daughter of Cubby, who produced *Diamonds*). 'We have a pre-title sequence, as first clearly defined in *Goldfinger*, a little vignette which distils a day in the life of Bond. He plants some explosives, drinks a Martini, kisses a girl, kills somebody who was about to kill him, makes a funny remark. Then comes the song. Those two ingredients pull you in. They say, "Forget the rain, forget your mortgages, come and have fun in Bond's world. It's a vital transition; here are some graphics, here's a song."' If they get that wrong, she says, the film is in serious trouble. If they get it right, the audience is Bond's for the duration of the movie.

Diamonds Are Forever is not a bad title, certainly better than *Thunderball*, but for a thriller? John Barry gave Don some advice. 'Don't think of the song as being about a diamond,' he counselled. 'Write it as though she's thinking about a penis.' A penis? Well, Bond does move among crooks and murderers masquerading as polite society members.

'Seediness was what we wanted,' says Don. 'Sleaziness. Theatrical vulgarity. It had to be over-the-top with a dash of vulgarity.' What he delivered shocked co-producer (with Cubby Broccoli) Harry Saltzman:

Diamonds are forever,
They are all I need to please me,
They can stimulate and tease me,
They won't leave in the night,
I've no fear that they might desert me.

Diamonds are forever,
Hold one up and then caress it,
Touch it, stroke it, and undress it,
I can see every part,
Nothing hides in the heart to hurt me.

I don't need love,
For what good will love do me?
Diamonds never lie to me,
For when love's gone,
They'll lustre on.

Diamonds are forever, forever, forever,
Diamonds are forever, forever, forever,
Forever and ever.

Not so much about a penis, as a penis substitute – diamonds as dildos. And Barry's music is suitably raunchy, caressing the stave, teasing in the verses, hinting at what's to come, before the big ballsy climaxes.

Saltzman was aghast. 'Touch it, stroke it and undress it?' he protested. 'We'll never get away with it!'

But Black and Barry thought they would, and by this time nobody argued with them – particularly Barry – about Bond music. There remained the question of who should sing it. The composer, ever on the lookout for fresh names, wanted the beautiful Israeli singer Esther Ofarim. But Don pushed for an old favourite.

Don was a big fan of Shirley Bassey, who had enjoyed phenomenal success with 'Goldfinger'. She sometimes used to tour with Matt Monro, and Don would stay to watch her set. 'Matt would do the first half, Shirley the second half,' he remembers. 'It was amazing. She'd walk on, the band would play the first few notes of "Goldfinger" and she'd stand there for six minutes while the audience went mad. They'd be screaming her name before she'd even sung a note.'

Don pushed for Bassey. A previous Bond adventure, *You Only Live Twice*, had used Nancy Sinatra, who he felt sanitised the song. 'You need someone who sounds like she's been in some late-night situations. And Shirley Bassey has the perfect Bond voice. She doesn't sing the songs, she lives them. You go into the cinema, hear that voice and immediately think, "What on earth's going to happen here?" Something about that voice. It's come hither, come and see this world of James Bond.'

He did not have to push hard, for Barry was also a Bassey fan and had not forgotten the success of 'Goldfinger'. So in came Shirley Bassey, and she didn't raise an eyebrow when told by the songwriters to imagine she was singing about a penis. In the recording she positively glows at the thought, almost cooing that infamous line, 'Touch it, stroke it and undress it.'

As a child at the time, Barbara Broccoli was too young to get all the *double entendres*, and simply enjoyed it as a song about the glamour of diamonds. But, she laughs, 'As an adult I realise just how far they were pushing the envelope. Even today you wonder how they ever got away with that stuff.' She tells of a recent evening spent at a BAFTA (British Academy of Film and Television Arts) ceremony to honour the 40th anniversary of the James Bond films. Shirley Bassey took the stage to sing 'Diamonds Are Forever' and, giggles Broccoli, 'Everyone in the room sat there open-mouthed. The lyrics are still so provocative.' Mind you, she also sees a shocking subtext in 'Goldfinger'!

The song has become a classic. Years later, Don was at Andrew Lloyd Webber's apartment in New York working on the musical *Aspects Of Love* when Steven Spielberg, whom Don had never met, popped round to see his friend. Lloyd Webber did the introductions – 'Steven Spielberg, this is Don Black.' Spielberg gaped. 'You're not *the* Don Black, are you?' Now it was Don's turn to gape. He was never one to get star-struck, but this after all was the world's most famous film director. And Spielberg seemed to be in awe of *him*! 'I'll never forget that sentence,' he spluttered, between grins.

Spielberg shook his hand warmly, enthusing, 'You wrote my favourite title song of all time: "Diamonds Are Forever"!' He proceeded to discuss in great detail for a full five minutes both the lyrics and the minutiae of Maurice Binder's title sequence: 'Did you notice the way he made the light catch the diamond on the word "lustre"?' He went into forensic detail, while Don stood there in amazement.

The movie broke the Hollywood record for money taken in the first three days of release. Altogether it grossed over $116 million worldwide, on a budget of $7.2 million. The Bond franchise was back on track, and Don had cemented his position as one of its creative forces. Over the years he has now written five Bond songs, across the careers of three 007s (Connery – *Thunderball*, *Diamonds Are Forever*; Roger Moore –*The Man With The Golden Gun*; and Pierce Brosnan – *Tomorrow Never Dies*, *The World Is Not Enough*).

'Don's lyrics evoke the whole spirit of Bond, and that makes them commercial and artistic assets,' says Broccoli. But, she explains, he is also a member of the team. 'Don is very much part of the whole Bond phenomenon. We work with the people we like again and again, and as the key people work together regularly we tend to see each other socially. Don's such an entertaining, witty man and he developed a wonderful collaboration with John Barry, and also his successor in the series, Dave Arnold.' For all of his famed capacity to dodge speeding bullets and wield lethal gadgets James Bond has survived, she points out, because so many movie-goers feel so affectionately towards him. That is because the basic formula has stayed the same, and Don has been a source of continuity, from the early films to the most recent batch. He knows how Bond works so well that it is perhaps a surprise he was never considered for the part himself. On the other hand (as he himself would no doubt shrug), fighting, espionage, saving the world? It's no job for a Jewish boy, now, is it?

Immediately after *Diamonds Are Forever*, Black and Barry – who were by now known as a force separately and together in Hollywood – turned to a film of *Mary, Queen Of Scots*. It was a prestigious project, with Vanessa Redgrave as Mary and Glenda Jackson as Elizabeth I, with Patrick McGoohan, Trevor Howard and Timothy Dalton (a Bond in the making) in support. Mary had to sing a French song, 'Vivre et Mourir', whose original French lyrics had been written by Mary, Queen of Scots herself. Don was called upon to supply English lyrics, but he was not keen on writing a song for a mass audience about a woman who would rather not have her head chopped off. So once again he found a universal thought, and came up with 'Wish Now Was Then'. It drew from him some gorgeous imagery – 'I only fought the wind/And only answered to the sun/…Wish I could live those days again./Wish now was then.' – and remains genuinely touching. He also turned Barry's lazily romantic 'Mary's Theme' to make the song 'This Way Mary', originally sung by Scott Walker, and then recorded by both Johnny Mathis and Matt Monro.

Working with John Barry has been one of the long-running delights of Don's career. The two men have immense respect for each other. 'Don has a fine dramatic sense,' says Barry. 'My music is theatrical. I love responding to a script. Someone shows me *Out Of Africa* and I can't wait to react to it in my music. Don has that same instinct. It's more difficult than you'd think to stop movie songs from sounding corny, but he manages it.'

Black, who says much the same about Barry, adds, 'He's one of the few composers who has ideas for titles. A great reader, he is very lyric-conscious. He'll suddenly say, "I was reading a book of poetry the other day and picked up an idea." He likes simple titles, often about ordinary things.' He gives as an example a title Barry has recently suggested for the new show they are working on, *Brighton Rock*, in which the boy-gangster Pinky is romanced by a girl, Rose. Barry suggested 'I'll Never Let You Down'. 'It sounds nothing, until you hear it with his music,' says Don, 'and then you realise it's exactly right. It's what she wants to say. There's a great precision in his feeling for words.'

But there's a cold majesty to much of his music, and Don explains that this is a clue to deep shadows lurking in Barry's character. 'There is a dark side to John. He gets very depressed. He's a religious Catholic, and that spiritual side is a great part of him. He will slope off to a church every now and again without telling anyone and just sit quietly and contemplate life.' Does he like what he sees? 'John's view of life is not always happy.'

Being pushed around for years by the powers-that-be in Hollywood and by movie dictators has taken its toll, says Black. 'The world in which he works has increased his cynicism. Now he gets disillusioned easily, especially about people.'

Don remembers the filming of *The Prince Of Tides* as a particularly wounding experience for his friend. It's the story of a love affair between a football coach and his mentally disturbed sister's psychiatrist, and Barbra Streisand was to direct and star. Barry was looking forward to working with the great singer, but was to be deeply disappointed. 'He had so many rows with her,' says Don. 'He submitted various themes and she kept saying how marvellous they were. Next day, she'd have changed her mind totally and would ask for more. He'd submit those and the same thing would happen.' Streisand pushed Barry to breaking point, and he snapped. 'This', he snarled down the phone to her, 'has been the most joyless assignment of my life.' The movie went ahead without him.

Hollywood is a place where, more often than not, things don't happen and promises are not kept, and that gets to Barry. He is, says Don, happiest when he is working on movies. But times are changing. 'The music business has changed. Now composers use computers, the Hans Zimmers of this world, they're all into that. John doesn't work on computers, and I think he's depressed by the rise of technology and synthesised music in films.'

However, Black often sees Barry at his best – when he has just written a tune that he's proud of and delivered it to Don for the lyrics. 'At that point, it's all guns blazing. He'll have been up for weeks struggling with it, and I see him when he's just emerged clutching the unveiled piece. It's after that, when you can't get the artist you want or the producer didn't like the song that you loved – that sort of thing is hard.'

It is, he says, unsurprising that Barry is given to overwhelming mood swings. 'Who knows where that music comes from? You wonder how a guy like this can write *Dances With Wolves*. What does he know about frontier life in the Wild West? The guy comes from York, for heaven's sake. The answer has to be that there's a great depth of emotion in him.'

The two men do have their arguments. Barry once said to Black that 'Arrogance is not a bad thing for a writer to have. It's a bloody good thing.' And Don concedes that often that is true; a writer has to show confidence in his work. But there are times when he has to dig deep to convince Barry that something is not right. For *Brighton Rock*, Barry recently sent Don ten melodies and they were all melancholy. He reported back that they could not possibly have ten mournful tunes. 'It's not a fuckin' picnic,' growled Barry. 'It's about hell!' Patiently Don pointed out that even sad songs can have some anthemic quality. Barry was aiming at a Kurt Weillish darkness. 'But even Kurt Weill', argued Don, 'gave us *Mack The Knife*. That's about murder, but it's also fun!'

The arguments can be prolonged, but they are always constructive. Besides, Black is such a natural optimist, almost always cheerful and happy to accommodate other points of view, that they complement each other perfectly. 'I do have a dark side,' confesses Barry. 'That's part of being a musical dramatist. I have fed that darkness into scores like *The*

Lion In Winter, *Dances With Wolves* and *Out Of Africa*. All of those stories have darkness to them. Don balances that in me, which is why we're such a good team. But there's darkness in him, too – you can see it in one or two of his shows, and it's also in *Brighton Rock*.'

Barry is correct. It is in some of his shows – think *Sunset Boulevard* – but if Don has darkness in himself, it is well hidden. Of everyone I have spoken to, only Elmer Bernstein could remember ever having seen Don in a real temper: on *Merlin*, when a choreographer was being difficult and Don shouted at him and walked out. Bernstein followed him, and did not return to rehearsals for two days. With Barry, it could bubble to the surface if he was provoked. 'They say he can be a real scorpion,' says Don.

One night in the swinging 1960s, Don was working in Los Angeles and was invited to a party at fellow lyricist Leslie Bricusse's house. It was a star-studded occasion. Danny Kaye was there, and Julie Andrews. Don, an almost obsessively keen pool (as well as snooker) player, found himself racking up with Steve McQueen.

John Barry was also at the party. He'd had a few drinks and, according to Don, that can make him 'not nasty, but a bit verbose and outspoken'. Barry was sitting on a sofa, having a drink with the singer John Phillips, from the band The Mamas And The Papas. Phillips considered himself a devotee of Mahler, and as Barry was a composer he thought he'd love to hear about it. 'This guy', says Don, 'is going on in the kind of loud American twang which John Barry hates, about how wonderful Mahler is. Mahler this, Mahler that, and I could see John getting more and more annoyed. Phillips won't shut up, and John keeps shooting me looks to say how much this guy is winding him up.'

Eventually Barry could take no more. 'I've heard you talkin' all fuckin' night about Mahler,' he scowled, taking a wad of cash from his pocket and placing it on the table in front of them. 'I'll bet you this that you couldn't hum me two bars of Mahler. Not two fuckin' bars. You don't know what you're talkin' about!' The entire room went silent, everyone was riveted. Most embarrassingly, Barry had been right. Phillips couldn't hum him any Mahler.

'I think', said Phillips unsteadily, 'that we should settle this outside as gentlemen.' Barry leaped to his feet. 'Any time you're fuckin' ready!' And Phillips got up. According to Don, he 'just kept getting up'. He was incredibly tall, towering over John Barry, who exchanged glances with Black as if to say, 'Oh my God, look at the size of him!' Still, Barry was ready to launch himself at Phillips, and it took Don, Burt Bacharach and Henry Mancini to separate them. A classic John Barry moment.

However, Don relates all this with great affection. Barry is in his eyes a genius, and a very special person. He describes with glee the very singular experience of lunch with John Barry: 'He insists on going to the finest restaurants, and doesn't eat. I've been having lunch with him for 40 years, and the ritual is always the same. We go to Wilton's in Jermyn Street these days, a very high-class place filled with politicians and so on. And he cuts a fabulous figure as he enters – he goes to the sort of menswear stores where they have to buzz you in. He sits down and positively salivates, you'd think he was starving! He'll ask about the grouse or something with great excitement, and will really savour the thought as he orders. When the food comes he'll eat about a thimble-full, push it away and declare it to be "Excellent!"' There has never been a meal, Black reports, where the waiter has not worriedly scampered over to ask what was wrong with the food. That's the reason why Barry stays thin.

In the 1960s, drink was the larger part of the meal. 'He'd have a champagne cocktail to start, a glass of white wine with the crab, a nice claret with the grouse, and a large brandy afterwards. Back then he'd stagger out of the restaurant, Burke's was his favourite, always surrounded by a clutch of beautiful women.'

Another classic John Barry moment occurred one memorable evening when Barry and Jane Sidey, his wife at the time, were with Don and Shirley at the Factotum restaurant in Chelsea. Out of the blue, 'literally as he was passing the spaghetti', Barry casually said to Jane, 'It's not working out, love, is it?' And that was that. They agreed to get divorced as they ate dinner! 'It sounds horrible and cavalier,' says Don, 'but he did it with a smile. There was no bad feeling. That's what he's like.'

The marriage to Jane Sidey, which ended over spaghetti, only lasted for two years. (His biographer Eddi Fiegel calls it 'just another of those 1960s schemes that seem like an awfully good idea at the start, and then less so, soon after the event'.) John Barry has now found happiness with his fourth wife, Laurie, whom he married in 1978, though I wonder whether for the first few years she avoided Italian food.

For all the fast cars and gorgeous girls, for all the glamour and wealth he has enjoyed, Don insists that John Barry has at heart remained what he always was. He was born Barry Prendergast, a plain-speaking Yorkshireman. A good, if complex, man. And a great composer.

7 Premature Ejaculation And A Killer Rat

It was in 1971 that Don Black first dipped a toe in what was to become his first love – musical theatre. Well, perhaps a toe is not the most relevant organ. but whatever you want to say he dipped, his début stage show was a musical about premature ejaculation.

Just as there has been a recent flurry of dangly and fluffy bits in the West End in the early years of the 21st century (*Puppetry Of The Penis*, *The Vagina Monologues*, *The Blue Room*), genitals were 'in' in 1971. Only three years previously, the fleshfest that was the musical *Hair* had unveiled its assets in London and New York. In 1970, Kenneth Tynan's naughty nude revue *Oh! Calcutta* had put backsides (and more) on the front pages, and Philip Roth's now-famous best-selling novel about sex, *Portnoy's Complaint*, was published in 1969. So copulation was suddenly not just spoken about more openly than ever before, it was entertainment.

Don was approached by Lionel Chetwynd, an associate he knew from films who worked for Columbia Pictures. Chetwynd was later to become a prominent writer, especially of television drama (his credits now include *The Hanoi Hilton*, and *The Apprenticeship Of Duddy Kravitz*, a Richard Dreyfuss hit for which Chetwynd was Oscar-nominated). But at this point he was still looking to make it big in writing. And he knew Walter Scharf, a wonderful composer who had scored *Funny Girl*, a lot of the Elvis movies, the Martin and Lewis films, and was Jacques Cousteau's tunesmith of choice, and with whom Don was later to write one of his best-loved songs.

Chetwynd had an idea – a story about a guy who got overexcited in a way that led to problems in the bedroom. It is perhaps not such a surprise when you consider that Lionel Chetwynd's sister is Claire Rayner. I'm not implying here that Ms Rayner drives men to a state of uncontrollable passion (she may very well do, but I cannot claim any expertise on the subject), but she is Britain's best-known agony aunt, so premature ejaculation and similar troubles are her stock in trade. Ms Rayner probably knows how to deal with it, but her brother, Don and Walter Scharf certainly did not. At least, not in the form of a show. In the event it was called *Maybe That's Your Problem*, although the great lyricist Alan Jay Lerner told Black it should have been called *Shortcomings* (a joke which Black enjoyed so much he used the title for a song in the musical *Dear Anyone*, years later).

Black maintains that the idea was good and that there was some fine material, 'as well as some lousy numbers'. (There was one song he especially liked, 'A Night To Remember', which his sister Adele is given to singing around the house to this day.) The cast boasted the then-unknown Elaine Paige. Nevertheless, unlike the main character, the critics were able to contain their enthusiasm. 'A dismal piece', groaned one, when it opened at London's Roundhouse. The most premature thing about it finally was its closure, after only 18 performances.

Throughout Black's career, though, good things have invariably emerged from disaster, and after the opening night an elegant American man came up to him. After introducing himself as Alan Jay Lerner, he said, 'I like your wordplay. That bit where you rhymed "stamina" with the words "cram in a". That's good. Stay with that.' Black was staggered. Lerner was songwriting royalty. The man had written with Kurt Weill, the Gershwins and was one half of the Lerner and (Frederick) Loewe team behind *Brigadoon*, *Gigi*, *Camelot* and, of course, *My Fair Lady*. As far as Don was concerned, he was a lyrical genius. The two found a shared love of words and became dear friends, Lerner viewing the younger man as something of a protégé, and Black eager to learn.

'He had an old-world charm,' remembers Don affectionately. 'The kind of person where when you left him you would look back to see him waving goodbye. He was always dapper in his dress, but never flash. A real gentleman.'

Lerner was the right person from whom to seek consolation after the crash of *Maybe That's Your Problem*. He knew about flops, having endured his share of failures as well as successes. Big shows like *Coco* with André Previn, and starring Katharine Hepburn, and *1600 Pennsylvania Avenue* with Leonard Bernstein, had faltered or died. A version of *Lolita* with John Barry was a famous pre-Broadway disaster (it closed ignominiously in Boston before it ever reached the Great White

Way). His last show before he died, *Dance A Little Closer* – with Charles Strouse, the composer of *Annie* – flopped. He taught Don how to deal with the mistakes. With humour and good grace.

'I sent him a good-luck telegram for *Dance A Little Closer*,' says Don, 'and I got a letter back saying, "Don, I'll be home earlier than I thought. Hey-ho." There was a hey-ho quality about him.'

By the time Don knew him, Lerner was not well. It wasn't just that he was getting slower with the passing of the years. He had a phobia about ageing and, it is to be presumed, about death. In he went for cosmetic treatment after cosmetic treatment, somehow clinging to the belief that if he looked young he would stay young. He would have monkey gland injections to maintain his skin and the shape of his face. 'Forever Young' may be the title of a Rod Stewart song, but it is sadly a physical impossibility and, according to Don, all the cosmetic work was perfectly obvious from Lerner's appearance. It didn't look natural.

But he was young on the inside. If only he'd known that this was more important than anything. He adored musicals, and would solemnly tell Black to study the work of the greatest lyricist who ever lived, Larry Hart. These days Richard Rodgers' first writing partner is far less famous than his successor, Oscar Hammerstein. Say 'Hammerstein' and people think of a bright, golden haze on the meadow. Say 'Hart' and they think alcoholism and instability. They don't immediately think of his shows. But musical aficionados often go for Hart as their favourite, relishing his blend of wit and unsentimentality. The lyrics of 'My Funny Valentine', for instance, are at once hilarious and touching:

> My funny Valentine, sweet comic Valentine,
> You make me smile with my heart.
> Your looks are laughable, un-photographical,
> Yet you're my favourite work of art…

Is this a little cruel? No, not when you realise that the character is utterly under his love's spell. Wit is the only defence he now has, and to tell the truth it's no defence. Lerner loved that song. But beyond everything, Hart had one ability that no other lyricist he'd ever met could match. 'That man', Lerner would marvel, 'was the only genius in lyric-writing. Why? Because he could write completely pissed out of his head, and no

PREMATURE EJACULATION AND A KILLER RAT

matter what state he was in he would knock out gems.' Lerner would speak of Hart with extreme awe.

Maybe That's Your Problem had given Don a taste for musicals, but he also found them a very different prospect from one-off songs. From that show he learned some of what not to do. Lionel Chetwynd, a politically minded man, had tried to inject polemical references into it. 'He was determined to make the show a platform and say something *important*,' remembers Don. 'That's a common error in musicals. People think they have to try and make a point. Audiences and critics see through that stuff. No one comes out of a musical and says the arguments were clever.' Musicals, he decided, can make serious points, but they have to appear organic and natural, not sententious.

Chetwynd did not agree. During one meeting, his exasperated lyricist took issue with the fact that one character spoke of a 'puritanical backlash'. 'Lionel, this is an entertainment,' he protested, 'and you're giving us all these politically charged phrases which have nothing to do with it. It's a story about premature ejaculation, for Pete's sake!' Chetwynd, getting angrier and angrier, finally hurled a chair at the wall. There were crisis meetings and more crisis meetings as the team, aware that they were headed for the rocks, floundered to avert disaster. The entire experience was a nightmare.

What else did Don learn? That writing a musical is a phenomenally intense experience. The sheer length of the process, the days spent writing, the nights spent rewriting, the months and months of deep concentration – it all requires an enormous emotional and mental input.

So when the show closed after 18 performances, Don felt dejection almost beyond anything he had known before. It was as though he had simply wasted a chunk of his life. It was a terrible feeling.

'That show', says Don, 'taught me to try and be more selective about my choices. I did a lot of soul-searching and realised I could have done all that work with a better subject. Of course, you don't really learn, but that's what you tell yourself.'

There was also a happier lesson, though. Lerner recommended him all over town. One day he mentioned to John Barry, with whom he was also friendly, that if Barry ever felt like composing a stage musical, the lyricist who had served him so well in movies could be relied upon to provide something special. Barry did not forget those words, and his

85

first stage musical was written with Don, and became one of the big hits of the decade – more of which later. 'Even out of the worst failures,' insists Black, 'positive things happen.' He has been far more sanguine about his flops ever since.

The following year, 1972, Don did not have to worry about failures. Instead he was to have one of his most enduring successes, which did indeed come out of *Maybe*. Walter Scharf and his wife Betty – in her time a celebrated dancer – had discovered an instant rapport with Don and Shirley. They became great friends, a relationship between the four of them which lasted until Walter's death in 2003 (at the age of 92). So when the composer was offered a film called *Ben*, he naturally turned to Don.

Most people don't remember what *Ben* was about, but everyone knows the song. Well, some people know the basic fact that the film has something to do with a boy who makes friend with a rat called Ben. Sounds very sweet, doesn't it? Until you know the whole truth.

Ben was actually the sequel to a film called *Willard*, one of the commercial hits of 1971, about an office boy (Bruce Davison) who gets seriously cheesed off with his nasty boss (Ernest Borgnine), to the extent where he trains two rats to destroy Borgnine and his other foes. The rats, called Ben and Socrates, get a gang together and duly eat anyone their beloved Willard doesn't like. Things go wrong when Willard falls in love. The rats feel neglected, and rip him to shreds. There's probably a moral there somewhere.

As such movies go, *Ben* was well received, and its producers – you'll never believe this – Bing Crosby Productions, wanted to capitalise. So Ben, the cleverest and most dangerous rat, was to survive and have a sequel named after him. In it a lonely boy played by Lee Montgomery makes friends with him, despite the fact that he soon discovers his new pal to be the rodent ringleader of thousands of rats, who are waging a toothy war on mankind. And Don had to come up with a song for this?

Well, he had tackled lions before, so he decided that rats should not pose much of a problem. As he had with 'Born Free', Don opted to more or less ignore the specific context. There was no way that a song with the word 'rat' in it would sell. So, instead, 'Ben' became a song about friendship.

Ben, the two of us need look no more,
We both found what we were looking for,
With a friend to call my own,
I'll never be alone.
And you my friend will see,
You've got a friend in me.

Ben, you're always running here and there,
You feel you're not wanted anywhere.
If you ever look behind,
And don't like what you find,
There's something you should know.
You've got a place to go.

I used to say,
I and me.
Now it's us,
Now it's we.

Ben, most people would turn you away,
I don't listen to a word they say.
They don't see you as I do.
I wish they would try to.
I'm sure they'd think again,
If they had a friend like Ben.
Like Ben.

It is a haunting song of two misfits who find comfort in each other –
one who will now 'never be alone' and the other whom 'most people
would turn...away'. Don's approach was right: if one misfit had
mentioned in the song that the other was a killer rat, the listener's first
instinct would be to turn *both* of them away – sharpish!

But they still wanted a boy's voice. After all, early adolescence is
when many of us are feeling most lonely and misunderstood. They found
Michael Jackson, who was perfect, and as it turned out, sadly the lyrics
fitted his own life like a glove. (Don was to find out a great deal about
the young superstar when the two became close some years later).

The Jackson Five were under pressure at the time. MGM Records had just launched a rival sibling group, the Osmonds. Their strategy was simultaneously to push forward the 13-year-old Donny Osmond as a solo star. So Motown, the company behind the Jacksons, felt they had to answer the challenge and began finding vehicles for Michael. He had already scored big with the ballad 'Got To Be There' and the rock 'n' roll 'Rockin' Robin'. 'Ben' was a great tear-jerker, and could consolidate his emergence as the world's darling.

This was perfect. Fans like their child stars to be sweet, and Scharf's melody is plangent and moving. Jackson himself loved it, and has several times since said that 'I used to say/I and me/Now it's us/Now it's we' are his favourite lines from any of his songs. Even then there seemed to be something lonely about Michael Jackson as he sang alone to the microphone, and his rendition melted hearts around the world. The film did OK. The song was a smash, going to No.1 in America. It was lucky that it worked, because the songwriters had taken a low salary to accommodate the star, anticipating that a big hit would result in lucrative royalties.

Black and Scharf were Oscar-nominated, and this year the field did not seem so tough: Fred and Marsha Karlin were there for 'Come Follow, Follow Me' from *The Little Ark*; Maurice Jarre with Marilyn and Alan Bergman, for 'Marmalade, Molasses & Honey' from *The Life And Times Of Judge Roy Bean* (not one of Jarre's more famous efforts); Al Kasha and Joel Hirschhorn, for 'The Morning After' from *The Poseidon Adventure*; and Sammy Fain and Paul Francis Webster for 'Strange Are The Ways Of Love' from *The Stepmother*.

Though Jarre and Webster were never to be underestimated, 'Ben' was the clear favourite. And this time Don brought Clive and Grant as well as Shirley. The grown-ups went off to the Dorothy Chandler Pavilion, while their children waited expectantly and full of excitement in their hotel room. Peter Noone – a member of the popular 1960s band Herman's Hermits and a family friend – had agreed to babysit, and they all munched burgers and chips as they watched the ceremony on TV.

The category came up, the envelope was opened, and *The Poseidon Adventure* won. The song about a rat had been sunk by a disaster at sea. 'Back in the room,' says Grant, 'we nervously wondered how Dad would deal with it. "Ben" was such a clear favourite that year. It had been a huge record.' But when their father returned, his reaction was characteristic. A shrug, a smile, and 'Sod it. Put the kettle on.'

However, not getting the Oscar was the only bad thing about *Ben* (and getting the nomination was nothing to sniff at). It was a wonderfully happy experience.

The same year as *Ben*, Don and John Barry were invited to work on a film musical, a big production, of *Alice's Adventures In Wonderland*. The cast was packed with famous names – Michael Crawford as the White Rabbit, Peter Sellers as the March Hare, Ralph Richardson as the Caterpillar, Dudley Moore as the Dormouse, Spike Milligan, Flora Robson, Robert Helpmann, Michael Hordern. It was hyped to the sky.

The only trouble was that, according to its songwriters, it was a bore. At the Royal Première for the Queen in Leicester Square, Barry looked across at Her Majesty and whispered to Don, 'I'm amazed she's stayed awake!' Don always thought that it had too many stars for its own good: every one of them had to be given a decent role, which meant that an already episodic story got stretched to the point of tedium.

The songs went over well, though, with 'The Me I Never Knew' and 'Curiouser And Curiouser' successfully recorded by Matt Monro. There's a rather fun number (though it goes on too long, until the groans become irrepressible) called 'The Pun Song', in which Peter Sellers maniacally cackles his way through a series of puns – 'A riddle or a pun can provide a piece of fun/The worse they are, the better they are/It's hard to find a rotten one…Where was the Magna Carta signed? It was signed at the bottom!… How do you find out the weight of a whale? Tie him to the nearest whaleway station!' (It sounds better than it reads.)

By Don's standards, 1973 was a relatively quiet year. He worked on three films. There was *Cahill – US Marshal*, in which he and Elmer Bernstein once again worked on a John Wayne Western. If Wayne was shooting with less than all six barrels in this one, *Cahill* was solid enough entertainment, with an interesting plot that involved Cahill's sons plotting a bank robbery, which their marshal father must investigate. Needless to say, things go wrong and a lot of people get killed.

The year also brought *Walking Tall*, the real-life story of a Tennessee sheriff called Buford Pusser (played by Joe Don Baker), who set out to crush all crime in his county by the use of truth, justice and a very big stick. After his wife is murdered by the bad guys, Buford goes berserk and sets out after them. Pusser became a cult hero after this movie, which grossed a surprise $17 million-plus on its release, spawning two sequels and a TV series. Johnny Mathis sang the title song.

By way of contrast, James Hill and Bill Travers – the director and lead actor of *Born Free* – were reuniting on a film called *The Belstone Fox*. It was about a fox who is much cleverer than the dogs tracking him (sound familiar? The story was later remade by Disney as *The Fox And The Hound*). They called in Don to see if he could recreate his *Born Free* magic, though this time he was working with Laurie Johnson, the British TV theme king behind *The Avengers*, *The Professionals* and *Jason King*. Don was pleased with his song – called 'Going Back', and sung by Roger Whittaker – but the film, critically admired, never did big business.

It was hardly an inactive year. Don was already hard at work on making another dream reality – stage musical number two. And this one was going to be a hit.

8 The Battles Of *Billy*, And A New James Bond

The story of *Billy Liar* had been one of the defining tales of 1960s Britain. It began its life as a best-selling novel by Keith Waterhouse, then became a play by Waterhouse and Willis Hall, with Albert Finney in the lead. In 1963, it emerged as a landmark British film of the decade, starring Tom Courtenay and Julie Christie.

A kind of *Peer Gynt* for its time, it tells of young Billy Liar, trapped in a (literally) dead-beat job for a company that sells 'funeral furnishings', and crowded by his family and the two girls who want to marry him (he is engaged to them both). To escape, Billy goes on flights of fancy, imagining that he is king of a make-believe world, Ambrosia. A compulsive liar, as his name suggests, he cannot help but spout untruths – most of them whoppers, as when he tells one girlfriend that he can't come out with her that night because his dad has had his legs amputated. These eventually start to catch up with him, and as he tries to extricate himself the lies get bigger and bigger, until he is forced to make a choice. He can leave his small Yorkshire town and run away to London with the only girl he really admires, the free-spirited Liz, and become a scriptwriter, or he can stay and face the music. And that is the crucial added dimension that really makes you care. Can Billy muster the courage to turn his dreams into reality? Imagination by itself is not enough.

This was the dilemma facing Britain in the 1960s. The nation's youth was struggling to shrug off the strait-jacket of the social expectations of older generations. They needed to seize their own music, their own clothes, their own lives. The empire had been lost, World War II had led to economic depression, but if they had the courage Britain could find a new type of greatness.

Which is, of course, exactly what happened. From The Beatles to the young guy in the street who was suddenly wearing clothes and sporting haircuts that would shock his parents, they were all Billy Liars. Except that, unlike Billy, they lived their dreams. And Cool Britannia had its first hoorah.

John Barry had grown up in postwar Yorkshire. In a way, this was his story too. And he felt deep empathy with the character: 'My Dad owned cinemas around the north of England, and I used to visit all of these northern cities with him. So I knew about Billy's world. If you went to Leeds or Manchester at the end of the war, they were dark, grey places. Leeds was so depressing. The only leisure on offer was the football matches and pub life. I could understand Billy wanting to get out, as I did. But I could also understand why he doesn't. The north/south cultural divide was much stronger then. Everything was different. Even the favourite northern comedians like Albert Modley would have died in London. It was only the television age that eventually ironed out the differences. Now we can all laugh at the same TV shows.'

Billy Liar had all the makings of a first-class musical. Billy's fantasy life would give plenty of room for big production numbers and would allow Barry to throw in a variety of musical styles. His enthusiasm grew. But before he decided on a lyricist, he needed something even more vital – a producer. As Ira Gershwin famously replied when asked whether the words or the music come first, 'The cheque.'

Barry turned to the big American agent Peter Witt. 'Peter', he laughs, 'was one of the great characters in our business. He was Berlin-born, and came to America in the 1930s where he made his fortune and handled really important stars like Lauren Bacall and Lee J Cobb. But he always had an extremely strong accent. He had a plane crash at one point. It was a small private plane, but it had one of those boxes which records everyone's conversations. At the enquiry, they played it back and all a startled Peter kept saying, in his heavy accent, was, "I didn't vealise I hat a German accent!"'

Witt had never produced before, but was a great lover of the theatre. Barry took the idea to him, and he was enchanted – 'I vant to do it!' Now they set about assembling the team, and he had not forgotten Alan Jay Lerner's advice about Don Black being perfect for a stage show. He telephoned his old friend.

Don loved *Billy Liar*. 'The story propels you, there's so much feeling in it. You can relate to it on every level. And all it boils down to is, will the poor bugger make that train to London or not?' Don, as the boy from Hackney who wanted to go to Broadway, knew that feeling. But, he insists, so do we all. 'Whatever we all want to do, you have to make that leap. You have to leave home, and Billy can never quite bring himself to do it. And everyone in the audience knows that feeling. When you reach that threshold and have to decide whether or not to take the risk.'

Don was on board, and after him came the rest of a talented bunch. The book writers (responsible for the script outside of the songs) were Ian La Frenais and Dick Clement, who sealed their place in TV history with a string of classic series, such as *The Likely Lads*, *Porridge* and *Auf Wiedersehen Pet*. Patrick Garland was to direct, and Onna White, veteran of the *Oliver!* movie and the Broadway shows *The Music Man* and *Gigi* was the choreographer. The cast reunited Don and fellow *Maybe That's Your Problem* veteran Elaine Paige as Billy's sexy girlfriend Rita, with Diana Quick as his other, classier girlfriend Liz. And for the crucial role of Billy? There was a natural choice – Michael Crawford.

If Crawford eventually found superstardom in a mask and a cape when he played Andrew Lloyd Webber's *Phantom Of The Opera* in the mid-1980s, *Billy* helped to consolidate his emergence. A naturally appealing screen and stage presence, there was something about the young Crawford that suggested he needed mothering. An innocence, a gawky naiveté. At the same time, he played earnestness very well, so the qualities combined made for some terrific comic turns, on stage in shows like Peter Shaffer's *Black Comedy* (a farce in a blackout – his 1967 Broadway début), and on screen in films such as Stephen Sondheim's *A Funny Thing Happened On The Way To The Forum*, in which he plays a rather fey hero called Hero.

He'd had a rocky few years. When Gene Kelly cast him in the extravagant movie musical *Hello, Dolly!* opposite Barbra Streisand, it had seemed like the pinnacle of good fortune. Suddenly Crawford had second billing alongside Walter Matthau in a cast that included Tommy Tune and Louis Armstrong. And this was a *big* production. One of the gowns Streisand wore reportedly cost $8,000 (in 1969!). But the film fell to earth with a resounding thud that effectively buried the entire genre of musicals on film for years to come.

It took Crawford's career several years to recover, but two farces were his salvation. Actually, they were the making of him. The first was a stage show, *No Sex Please – We're British*, which many had thought an odd choice for an actor of Crawford's calibre (sex farces were going out of fashion, but Crawford liked the script and, besides, at this point he was desperate for work). It was a hit, and ran – even after Crawford had left – for more than eight years.

Meanwhile, in 1973 Frank Spencer burst onto British TV screens, and proceeded to wreck everything in sight. The well-meaning but hopelessly clumsy and dim protagonist of *Some Mothers Do 'Ave 'Em* made Crawford a household favourite and remained his defining role until *Phantom* came along. One suspects that, for all the maturity of that famous performance, it's still Frank that most people love him for. Frank was a man who had his dreams, the courage to give them a try, but nowhere near the ability to achieve even the simplest of them (apart from one, his family, which was of course the most important). In that sense he was the flip side of Billy Liar, who probably does have the ability to make it as a scriptwriter in London but not the requisite courage and sense of self-worth.

Some Mothers Do 'Ave 'Em began airing as *Billy* went into rehearsals, and commercially Michael Crawford was suddenly looking like a very good bet indeed. He was perfect for the character – innocent, poetic, lovable – and a consummate performer. 'He danced to die for,' marvels Black. 'What a tap dancer. Danced till his feet bled, almost. He was so dedicated. There was nothing this guy wouldn't do. And it showed.'

Recordings of *Billy* (sadly and inexplicably hard to get hold of these days) reveal a very different Crawford than the heavier-voiced performer who starred in *Phantom*. Then, he had a very high and light baritone, flexible and pretty. His lyricist admired it greatly: 'It was so natural. Now he's had all these lessons and you can hear that the teacher has instructed him where and how to use his diaphragm and how to give it weight. But then, it was a natural outpouring.' If you can get hold of the cast recording of *Billy*, listen to its star's sensitivity in the dreamy 'I Missed The Last Rainbow', and then his smile-inducing exuberance in the rocky 'Girl From LA'. Crawford is one of America's most popular singers today, but there are those of us who think that his craft today does not begin to compare with the instinctive art of his singing in *Billy*.

However, Crawford may have been dedicated, he may have been brilliant in the part, but he was also a handful. 'He was so difficult,' groans John Barry. 'Once he got the show under his belt, he became a monster.' The show began playing in Manchester, so the (then) traditional regional run-in could help it prepare for the West End. Once the Manchester run opened, to wild acclaim, Crawford began questioning everything in the show, from the director to the script. Don remembers several occasions when he changed some of his dialogue without telling anyone. At other moments, he told people exactly what he thought. John Barry felt the responsibility keenly. It had been mainly his call to bring Crawford in, and he saw it as his job to keep him quiet. They would have terrible arguments. 'Don't be such a fuckin' idiot. Listen to the director,' he would tell his star.

Crawford continued to throw his weight around, however, and it came to a head in one rehearsal, when he was giving Patrick Garland a particularly difficult time. 'John thought he was being horrible,' remembers Don, who was watching from the stalls, 'and told him to shut up. Michael puffed himself up, and replied, "You don't realise how important I am to this production!" Well, no one says that kind of thing to John Barry. So John stared straight back at him and said, "If you're so important, why am I telling you to fuck off?" And, as far as I remember, Michael did fuck off for a bit.'

Elaine Paige well remembers being in the firing line of her co-star's perfectionist temper. 'Michael was quite intense as an actor. You could see everything had to be perfect with him,' she recalls. 'He would throw his weight around. He was the star, and he expected us all to treat him as such. There was a tension. You could feel it.' She refused to 'take any nonsense from him', however. In one early rehearsal, after finishing a scene with Crawford, Paige went to sit with the director and began unravelling a sweet while the actor continued rehearsing. 'The sweet wrapper was louder than I thought it would be,' she laughs, 'and suddenly Michael stopped rehearsing and threw an absolute fit at me. "How dare you! What the bloody hell do you think you're doing?" he screamed. I was so shocked. The tantrum was so out of proportion to my crime that I actually wasn't sure if he was joking or not, though I later realised he was serious. My reaction was to tell him to shut up and throw the sweet paper at him. It hit him dead on the nose and everybody laughed. He had to, as well, and it relieved the moment. After that I never had any trouble from him. Others did, though. There were tears and all manner of things.' Nevertheless, Paige adds, she would stand in the wings and watch him perform, in amazed admiration of his talents as a comic actor.

'He behaved like an absolute prima donna,' says Barry, 'having a go at everything and everyone.' For the London opening night at the Theatre Royal, Drury Lane, Barry devised a witty plan. Some days earlier he had visited London's exclusive Asprey's store, where he was a regular customer. Asprey's of Bond Street is not your usual shop. It is one of the city's most distinguished vendors of 'articles of exclusive design and high quality, whether for personal adornment or personal accompaniment, to endow with richness and beauty the tables and homes of people of refinement and discernment' (as the founder Charles Asprey said at Prince Albert's Great Exhibition of 1851).

An extremely courteous, elegantly tailored salesman approached Barry, who was looking at the watches section. 'How may I help you, sir?' he asked, with the utmost politeness and grace. Barry pointed to a magnificent gold watch. 'I'd like to buy that, and I'd like it engraved please. It's a gift for Michael Crawford.' The assistant recognised the name and smiled, 'Oh, of course, for Mr Crawford, sir. What would you like us to engrave?' Barry looked at the salesman unflinchingly. 'I would like it to read, "Cunt, thank you for Billy".' The salesman's eyes widened. Clearly this was not a request Asprey's of Bond Street had encountered before. '"Cunt", sir?' Barry, deadpan, began to spell it. 'Yes, "cunt". C…u….' The salesman's eyebrow shot up as he interrupted, his politeness fraying at the edges. 'I do know how to spell it, thank you, sir.'

Opening night came, 1 May 1974, and there were the usual nerves and jitters. But everybody knew, they could smell, that they had a hit. Barry knocked on the door of Michael Crawford's dressing room. 'Come in.' He entered, all smiles. 'I wanted to wish you good luck and I've got a present for you, Michael.' Crawford was charmed. He opened the package and saw the watch.

'John, that's fabulous. You—'

'Turn it over.'

Michael turned it over and read the inscription. '"Cunt, thank you for Billy".'

Crawford saw the funny side and gave a sensational performance. 'He was just so marvellous,' says the composer. 'He even looked right, slim and gangly. He was just *it*.' Drury Lane is a famous musicals theatre,

Moris and Betsy Blackstone outside their Hackney home: 'Humble, but to them it was a palace.'

Cassland Road School, Hackney. Top row, third from the right, grinning, a future Oscar winner

All those hours watching films weren't wasted. A teenage Don wins first prize as a Robert Mitchum lookalike in a *Hackney Gazette* competition

Engaged in one of his favourite
pastimes, Don pores over his
collection of 78s in the Hackney flat

'With one look': Don and Shirley, dating
and in love, 1957

NME gave 16-year-old Don the chance to meet the biggest star in the world when
reporter Mike Butcher allowed him to sit in on an interview with the great Nat
'King' Cole

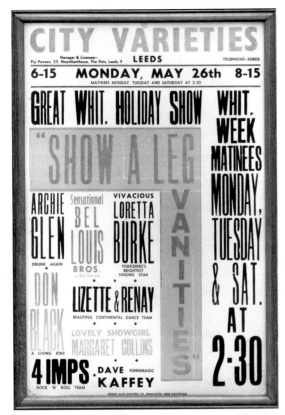

Don Black, 'a living joke', tries to get a laugh. According to his brother Michael, Don was unofficially known as 'the shoe comedian': 'He walked off to the sound of his own footsteps'

Don and Matt take Time Square in the Big Apple for Matt's first New York engagement, at the Plaza Hotel

The big night: *Born Free* wins Oscars for Don and John Barry, and a sober Dean Martin hands them over

Black, Jones and Barry at the famous 'Thunderball' recording session. Tom Jones blacked out on the last note

Don with singing legends Matt Monro and Gordon McRae at a Capitol recording session

'70s Bond boys: Don and John Barry working on 'Diamonds Are Forever'

Jule Styne takes a break from placing bets to write *Barmitzvah Boy*

Don takes tips from mentor and friend, Alan Jay Lerner

Don and Mort Shuman at work on the ill-fated Adam Faith show, *Budgie*. Writing it was fun; reading the reviews was not

Pals: Downtime with Elmer Bernstein at his California home

One of Don's favourite people, Bernadette Peters won a Tony for *Tell Me On A Sunday*

A perfect couplet: Don and fellow lyricist Tim Rice

Barbra Streisand consults *Sunset Boulevard* scribes Don and Christopher Hampton in between recording songs from the show

Amigos Para Siempre: Don and Andrew Lloyd Webber at a Variety Club dinner

'He said it was the best night of his life': *Bombay Dreams* composer AR Rahman meets his hero John Barry

The family. L-r: Don, Adele, Cyril, Nita and Michael

Don and his sons Grant (left) and Clive (right) at the 2003 opening of *Tell Me On A Sunday*

Tom Jones at a 2002 concert with his new backing singers, Don's grandchildren Martha and George

Don and Shirley at the *Bombay Dreams* opening

Two surprises in one night: A Lifetime Achievement Award at a BMI dinner and that famous red book

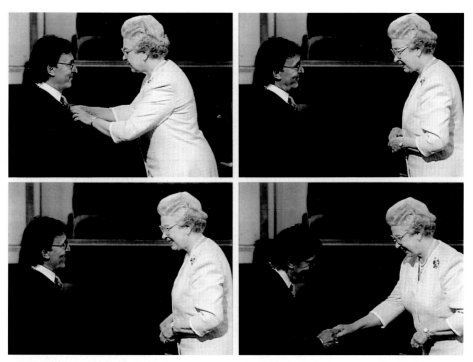

From Ma'am with love. Don receiving the OBE in 1999

Don helps celebrate Michael Jackson's career at a gala dinner in Hollywood, along with Petula Clark and Sophia Loren

A Mexican peasant, sketched
by budding artists Michael
Jackson and Shirley Black

Michael Crawford, sensational but
hard to work with in the hit
musical *Billy*. 'He became a
monster', says John Barry

Passion and pain:
Marti Webb in *Tell
Me On A Sunday*

Michael Ball in *Aspects
Of Love*. 'Love
Changes Everything'
made him a star

'With One Look': Glenn Close's brilliant Norma Desmond in *Sunset Boulevard*

Salaam Bombay! Bringing *Bombay Dreams* to life

'Hang on…I've got an idea.' Michael Caine leads the Self-Preservation Society in *The Italian Job*

Gambling that they'll get away with the risqué lyrics: Sean Connery rolls the dice in *Diamonds Are Forever*

The Bond formula: Pierce Brosnan's pre-credits boat chase in *The World Is Not Enough* precedes the title song

and has seen the London premières of classic shows like *My Fair Lady* and *Camelot*. *Billy* was not felt to have disgraced that illustrious line.

The opening night was attended by stars, including the British Prime Minister Edward Heath. And the reviews were almost all fabulous. Jeremy Kingston in *Punch* celebrated the arrival of 'An unmistakeable, joyous hit'. Irving Wardle's review in *The Times* declared 'Waterhouse's anti-hero lying in style'. Milton Schulman in the *Evening Standard* called Crawford 'a cracking Billy Liar' and Don's lyrics 'sharp and bright'. 'It will', he wrote, 'undoubtedly pack them in for a long time.' Best of all was Michael Billington in the *Guardian*, who found it 'sumptuous... a pleasure to watch. Michael Crawford's lean, spindly frame suddenly takes on the elegant flowing line of a mock-Astaire or the gyrating bum-rolling frenzy of a fantasy Presley... This takes the curse off the British musical that seems to have surrounded it ever since the palmy days of *Oliver!*'

'It was a fantastic show,' explains Elaine Paige, 'and Don's lyrics were brilliant. He has the knack of capturing characters in his words so vividly. My character in *Billy*, Rita, had lyrics that were rightly hard-edged ("Any minute now, that git will show up") and really encapsulated the feeling of the north of England at that time. It was also very funny, because Don's a very witty man. Often, when I'm touring a concert and I get stuck for a funny line, I'll ring him and he'll give me some one-liners.'

Billy ran for 904 performances – almost three years. Had Crawford stayed for longer, it could have carried on. But his replacement, Roy Castle, though he was talented and played the trumpet and drums on stage, was not the draw that Crawford had become. Crawford was *such* a sensation in it that he became the show. He *was* Billy Liar.

Don and Barry had written the most successful musical of that year and the next, and they were both now established as masters of the stage musical as well as pop and movie songs (and, of course, scores in Barry's case). Crawford's career took another leap forward and he later went on to have hits in *Barnum*, *Phantom Of The Opera* and his very own Las Vegas showcase, *FX*. Despite everything, he and John Barry stayed friends and Barry is godfather to Crawford's daughter, Emma.

Don believes that Michael Crawford has never bettered his work in that musical. 'All that trouble we had with him emanates from his commitment. He's a driven man. And he does have the talent. In certain roles, he's great. He was brilliant in *Phantom*, he was great in *Barnum*. I still think he was best of all in *Billy*. He's a great comedic actor, and *Billy* was the only one of his big stage roles where he's been able to be funny. And he was – hilarious. He brought the house down every night; they'd be screaming with laughter.' Sadly for Crawford fans, it seems as though one of the most naturally gifted comic actors his country has produced now feels obliged to appear in inflated 'event' musicals worthy of an ex-*Phantom*. His much-heralded return to musical theatre (after those years spent raking in the money in Las Vegas), 2002's *Dance Of The Vampires*, was a case in point. The critics swiftly put a stake through its heart, but not until the *New York Times* had criticised the actor's 'taxidermic variation on his *Phantom* persona'.

Billy, meanwhile, had another success story. Elaine Paige scored one of her early successes as the lower-class Rita. Theatrical folklore has it that musical theatre's biggest UK draw was plucked from obscurity in 1978 to star in Andrew Lloyd Webber's *Evita*, which made her an overnight star. It's a cliché which suggests that she had spent her previous years working in a completely different area, but *Billy* got her some good notices, and her class was evident. Don was to get to know her well, from *Maybe That's Your Problem* to *Billy* to (years later) his musical *Sunset Boulevard*, which saw her belatedly conquer Broadway.

'She'd had a small part in *Maybe* as one of the disappointed girlfriends of the guy with the sexual problem. *Billy* gave her a chance to show us what she could do.' Recalls Don, 'Rita is very common – not a slut, but mega-common. It's all the short skirt and "Where's me bleedin' ring you promised me?" She loved it. She also had some of the funniest lyrics. All the three main girls get a different variation of the song "Any Minute Now" and she had to sing, "Any minute now that git will show up/ Any minute now or I will throw up"! She's even said that if we ever did it again she'd love to come back and be in it for six weeks.'

Yet, for all her talent, Black feels that Paige's personality has held her back from the crown that was rightfully hers. 'She still hasn't reached the heights that were within her grasp. She's fabulous in every role, but there's something in Elaine's character that stops her wanting to sacrifice everything.' It is not laziness, he insists, and points out that she has been in a lot of shows. But at the end of her 2001 run of *The King And I* at the London Palladium, she confessed to Don, 'I'm shattered. What do I want to do eight shows a week for at my time of life?'

That, says Don, is not enough for the highest level of showbiz fame. 'It's bloody hard work doing a musical. But you have to have burning ambition all the way through your career if you want to become a legend.' So Paige has made her money and her fame, but Black believes she will never be spoken of in the same breath as Ethel Merman, Judy Garland or Elaine Stritch – simply because she does not possess the same drive that Stritch and her predecessors had. When I mention that most of those legends self-destructed, perhaps consumed by the same flames that burned with ambition, he concedes the point. 'Who's to say that Elaine is right or wrong? Those legends do often destroy themselves. But they also reach icon status. They leave a legacy. And Elaine Paige is very nice and down-to-earth and that's how she approaches her work. She just happens to have a great talent.'

That talent still has Don in awe. 'All my life I've been amazed by certain people who have this God-given gift for no reason. They just have it. That's the simplest way of putting it. Elaine Paige has this incredible vulnerable quality in her voice that lets her tear your heart out. As well as that, she feels songs, she lives them. There's an intensity to her and you have to go with it. With other stars, you say, "They're fine." But she's more than fine. She's special.'

But, he continues, she finds it a battle. The whole business, the fighting for roles, the obligatory and seemingly endless interviews, the recordings. She finds it a drain. And there is, says Don, something else missing: 'Elaine has never really had a man in her life as part of a long-term relationship. There was the affair with Tim Rice, and I think that's the closest she got. I believe she misses that part of her life. I wonder whether she feels that she's already given too much to the theatre.' It's an interesting thought – an artist who has given too much of her life to the stage to be happy, but who is not willing to put that final drop of her pain into her art and career to become a legend. So she misses out on the best of each. Sounds like a subject for a musical? Except that in the musical she would finally give everything for one last great role, become an icon, then die just as the man she has always loved proposes. Forget musicals: it sounds like an opera!

There were two more treats in store for Don in 1974: another date with 007, and another Oscar nomination. Both featured Roger Moore.

The Man With The Golden Gun is one of the most underrated Bond movies – sinister (despite the second-half high jinks), and with a great Bond villain in the ruthless, utterly unfeeling Christopher Lee. Not for nothing was Lee the most renowned screen nasty of his day (and still, in his Indian summer, playing both the devious wizard Saruman in *The Lord Of The Rings* trilogy and the twisted Count Doku in *Star Wars* Episodes 1 and 2. Lee's malign presence as Scaramanga, the assassin hunting Bond for sport, infects the film.

And it begins in style with perhaps the best of all the Bond opening sequences (mind you, the anti-terrorist strike in *Tomorrow Never Dies* runs close). We see Scaramanga's righthand midget Nick Nack (a terrifically unsettling, giggly Herve Villechaize) welcome a smug hoodlum onto his boss's island retreat. Once the fly is in place, an unarmed, dead-eyed Lee is set to defend himself, and the two of them play cat and mouse in Scaramanga's nightmarish fairground labyrinth. At last Scaramanga gets to his famous golden gun, shoots the guy right in the forehead, and then whips round to deliver five more shots in a pop-up statue of – guess who? Cue the titles.

Barry delivered a fast, rather intense theme – a bit of a cross between *Thunderball* and *Goldfinger*. It is chase music, but with a hint of seductiveness. This time Don could write about the villain, and he had fun with those lyrics:

> He has a powerful weapon,
> He charges a million a shot,
> An assassin that's second to none,
> The man with the golden gun.
>
> Lurking in some darkened doorway,
> Or crouched on a roof top somewhere,
> In the next room, or this very one,
> The man with the golden gun.
>
> Love is required whenever he's hired,
> It comes just before the kill.

No-one can catch him, no hit man can match him,
For his million dollar skill.

One golden shot means another poor victim,
Has come to a glittering end.
For a price, he'll erase anyone,
The man with the golden gun.

His eye may be on you or me,
Who will he bang?
We shall see. Oh yeah!

One golden shot means another poor victim,
Has come to a glittering end,
If you want to get rid of someone,
The man with the golden gun,
Will get it done.
He'll shoot anyone,
With his golden gun.

Clever and, to borrow a John Barry phrase, 'right on the money'. The lyrics actually set up Scaramanga as an inverted, perverted Bond (so does the film, for that matter). 'He has a powerful weapon' – the sexual resonance is unmistakable, and it's appropriate, given that we later hear that Scaramanga's distinguishing feature, a third nipple, is 'in some cults...a symbol of invulnerability and great sexual power'.

Still, a powerful weapon sounds threatening. In an unforgettable but brief scene, Lee returns from a kill exultant and caresses his lover's face with his gun. It makes you wonder just what, for some women, is the attraction of the assassin we all know already, James Bond?

As for the murderer lurking in doorways, crouched on a roof, in the next room or – scariest of thoughts – the same room, since few people know what he looks like; that's stylish. It's hewn from the same dark stuff as *Mack The Knife* ('On the sidewalk...lies a body oozin' life/Someone's sneakin' round the corner...could that someone be Mack the Knife?').

Lulu supplied the vocals, and went right along with the 'powerful weapon, seductiveness of power' theme. There was a thrill in her voice.

And, she says, this song had an unexpected benefit years later. 'When my son's friends got to the age of about 9, they became obsessed with Bond. And when they found out that I sang "The Man With The Golden Gun", I was suddenly cool! I was the coolest mum in the school!'

Don almost did not get the call for this Bond. As a matter of fact, Alice Cooper presented a version. 007's last outing had been in *Live And Let Die*, for which Paul McCartney and Wings had favoured a rockier-than-usual sound. It was, and remains, one of the all-time favourite Bond songs. So Cooper took his lead from McCartney and decided to get even rockier. This is his version, which comes across as obvious and trite after the Black/Barry job:

> The man
> With the golden gun
> Is waiting
> Somewhere
> Out there
> For you.
>
> The man with the golden
> Gun in his pocket, oh, oh,
> The man with the golden
> Gun in his case, oh, oh,
> The man with the golden
> Gun in your face.

That same year, a different Roger Moore film was to bag Don his fourth Oscar nomination. In *Gold*, directed by Peter Hunt, Moore was no secret agent, but the determined foreman of a South African goldmine. Thoroughly nasty businessmen led by John Gielgud are planning to flood the mine to manipulate the world price of gold, and it is down to Moore to stop them.

Wisely, Don and Elmer Bernstein decided not to write a song about international gold markets and came up with a number called 'Wherever Love Takes Me'. It took them back to the Academy Awards, where they lost out to 'We May Never Love Like This Again' by Al Kasha and Joel Hirschhorn, written for one of the year's huge hits, *The Towering Inferno* (although it would probably have been more fun to have lost to another of the nominees, 'Blazing Saddles' by John Morris, from the off-the-wall Mel Brooks comedy).

The year 1974 had been a great one. Another year, another nomination. Another year, another Bond. *Billy* had given Don back his pride after the catastrophe of *Maybe That's Your Problem*, and he felt he was riding the crest of a wave. And if he wanted to surf it all the way to the beach, he knew where those golden sands were. In those days, all waves led to one place. The Black family were about to move. From Mill Hill to Los Angeles. Hollywood...

9 Hollywood Bullshit And Getting Close To Michael Jackson

For a member of the showbiz community, there are two ways to enter Los Angeles. You can move there quietly, hopefully putting down roots and praying that the harsh LA sun (heat generated by thousands of agents, producers, the ever-churning Hollywood machine) will help you grow and flower rather than wilt, because there is little so depressing as being ignored in Hollywood. Or you can have your arrival announced, come out as a showbiz grandee in imperious fashion. Another landmark on the LA horizon. Hell, you're not there to seek favours from the Hollywood set. You *are* part of the Hollywood set!

Elmer Bernstein knows how it works and he also knew that Don was far too modest to blow his own trumpet. So he decided to do it for him: 'I thought if he was going to live here he should meet the people.' The call went out – 'Elmer Bernstein invites you to meet Don and Shirley Black' – and when Elmer Bernstein throws a party the big guns show up. He gave over his ranch in Topanga Canyon to a fabulous, glittering evening.

To the Blacks, it was like something out of a Edith Wharton novel, or *The Great Gatsby* – the ranch was full of big-hitting producers and directors. As he walked in, Don spotted *In The Heat Of The Night* and *The Thomas Crown Affair* director Norman Jewison, the great composer Henry Mancini, *Laura* composer David Raksin, and at the piano was Meredith Wilson, the famous writer of *The Music Man*. Everyone was delighted to meet the new arrivals. It was all smiles, kisses and 'Welcome to LA's. The Hollywood hierarchy had accepted their English guests as two of their own. 'We knew nobody there,' says Shirley. 'For Elmer Bernstein to announce our presence really meant something in that community. Don got to meet the people who counted out there, and they wanted to meet him. Elmer brought us into the network.' The Blacks had arrived. And whenever Don looked over at him, Elmer was beaming.

Buying a house in Hollywood is unlike anywhere else in the world. Estate agents are a different breed there: in London, the agent points out the fittings; in Hollywood they concentrate on the neighbours. 'I would be shown a place and tell the agent I didn't really like it and he'd feign surprise and say, "Really? That's funny because it was always one of Marilyn Monroe's favourites," or, "Well, when Frank Sinatra lived here he was very happy with it." And you are impressed by all of that, because who wouldn't be?'

They eventually settled on a house in Bel Air. 'It was very nice,' says Shirley. 'We had a pool, but it wasn't over-the-top. It was all on one level, mostly open-plan, a really pleasant family house. Of course the first thing Don did was buy a snooker table, which arrived the day we moved in.' And they had their share of famous neighbours. Fred Astaire lived at the end of the road. The jazz star Cannonball Adderley was next door. Tony Curtis was also nearby.

Clive and Grant were seriously impressed with their new surroundings. 'We were never particularly in awe of the people Dad mixed with in London – the John Barrys and the Shirley Basseys – because we grew up seeing them around the house,' says Clive. 'But when we got to LA there were suddenly all these cinema icons everywhere. I was able to tell my old schoolfriends that I lived in the same road as Fred Astaire!'

They went to see Elvis in his last ever concert at the Las Vegas Hilton (they went backstage and Elvis gave Clive a scarf he was wearing), and at the première for the movie *The Champ* Clive remembers standing centimetres away from Muhammad Ali while he arm-wrestled *The Six Million Dollar Man* Lee Majors (Ali won, of course). He even got to swim with Olivia Newton-John in her Malibu swimming pool.

Grant points out another advantage to LA. He had not been thrilled to leave London, having to leave behind friends and his girlfriend. 'But I got there and it was amazing, paradise. American girls loved our accents! You only had to say, "Hello, love" and they'd be all over you.'

It is, reflects Grant, demystifying after a while to live among the stars. Soon enough, Fred Astaire and Tony Curtis became simply Fred and Tony the neighbours. He has never been star-struck since (a quality he has found useful of late, as a songwriter for pop stars such as Holly Valance and Dido).

Talking of stars, one morning Henry Mancini phoned Don. If it sounds like one of those name-droppy statements – 'I was out in the garden this morning and was disturbed by Henry Mancini on the phone', where the phonee would be all exaggerated casualness to show that, hey, Mancini's a friend and why on earth *wouldn't* he call? (After all, the man's got to call *somebody*, right?) – you've got Don wrong. It's not that he gets star-struck, exactly. He is not impressed by celebrity itself. I remember recently seeing him at the Leicester Square première for the movie *Chicago* and then not being able to locate him at the ultra-chic after-show party. When I phoned Don the next day, it turned out that, rather than hang out with the likes of Richard Gere and Renée Zellweger (yes, well spotted, that's me being name-droppy), he and Shirley had gone home for a cup of tea and an early night.

However, Don is deeply impressed by talent. 'Dad', says Clive Black, 'idolises people like Sammy Davis Jr. Because to him these people have got it. They're magical. He worshipped the British songwriter and star Anthony Newley – when he was with Newley, he'd be just blown away, he'd act about 8 years old!' At his bar mitzvah, Clive joked that he thought of his father as a best friend – 'a younger best friend'.

Don also greatly admires composers like Elmer Bernstein, John Barry and Andrew Lloyd Webber. 'I get a real thrill,' he says, 'at being able to work with these people. Sometimes I get home and there's messages on my answerphone from Andrew and John Barry, and I say to Shirley, "We should keep the tape!"' He recalls being taken out for lunch by Lloyd Webber and Tom Stoppard for discussions about writing the long-rumoured *Phantom Of The Opera II*: 'The fact that you're there, having lunch with those two guys, does a hell of a lot for your confidence. I've worked with the top people, but these guys are special.'

So when the call came from Mancini, he felt a thrill. A Mancini doesn't call every day and he definitely belonged in the 'special' category. This was the guy who wrote 'Moon River', for Pete's sake! The 50-something Mancini's immensely distinguished career had included Orson Welles' *film noir, A Touch Of Evil, The Glenn Miller Story*, the famous jazz score for the TV series *Peter Gunn*, and – perhaps most famous of all – the score for *The Pink Panther*. And the great Mancini wanted to meet with Don Black.

Over pasta at one of Mancini's favourite Italian restaurants, Mateo's, he told Don about the project. Mancini had an ongoing collaboration with the film director Blake Edwards. The two had already done the huge Peter Sellers hit *The Pink Panther* and its sequel *A Shot In The Dark*. The bumbling Inspector Clouseau became the brilliant Sellers' defining role and Edwards wanted to try something new with him. The idea they hit upon was called *The Party*.

Sellers was to play an Indian extra on a film set, the clumsy Hrundi V Bakshi. He's supposed to get fired, but some names get swapped around and instead he lands on the invitation list to an exclusive Hollywood party. By the end of the evening, Bakshi has accidentally ruined the party and practically destroyed the house. It's mostly slapstick and, for an actor with Sellers' timing, a gem. If it's mostly slapstick, that's because the cast worked from a story outline, shot the film in sequence, devising each new scene as they finished the last one. The experiment worked and *The Party* became a cult hit.

Don supplied two songs for the movie – a theme song, and a love song for Claudine Longet to sing called 'Nothing To Lose'. Blake Edwards loved the Langet number. He played it to his wife, Julie Andrews (the same 'little Julie' Andrews Don had watched on those afternoons with his mother at the Hackney Empire), and she adored it. 'Nothing To Lose' became one of her favourite songs. 'I was proud of it. It was a bloody good, classy song,' says Don. The pity, from his point of view, was that in the movie it is sung by Claudine Longet, while Peter Sellers is literally bringing the house down around their ears, so nobody noticed the song, as they were too busy laughing at the mayhem.

Don was also proud of his association with Henry Mancini – Hank to his friends. Mancini became a dear family friend of the Blacks. They would frequently have dinner at Italian restaurants, since Mancini was inordinately proud of his Italian heritage (though he was born in Cleveland, Ohio). 'He was a gentleman with a twinkle in his eye,' smiles Don. 'But that's the thing about composers. They all have a twinkle. A look about them that says they're still young inside.' Unlike some composers, Mancini was also a terrific pianist and would leap to a piano with pleasure, at the slightest invitation. (In cotrast, Richard Rodgers always protested he was only average and hated giving public recitals, while Lionel Bart could not even play or read music.)

Mancini and Edwards were so pleased with Black's lyrics for *The Party* that they recruited him again for their next Sellers film, the latest *Pink Panther* sequel. This one, *The Pink Panther Strikes Again* (ignoring the fact that the panther of the title was actually originally a precious stone), was to be the best of the lot. Clouseau's boss, former Chief Inspector Charles Dreyfus (a gloriously twitchy Herbert Lom), can take no more and decides to kill Clouseau himself and, while he's about it, take over the world. The hilarious hero is his usual idiotic self and Black and Mancini were to score his big 'love scene'.

They devised a straightforward, if deliberately over-smooth, love song called 'Come To Me'. Bringing in the sexiest male voice around – Tom Jones – for the vocals, they set it against Clouseau trying manfully to entice a girl into his bed. Sellers trying to be seductive is hysterical, especially when set against Jones's crooning: just as he is about to succeed, his karate-happy manservant Cato leaps from his hiding place for a sparring match. Priceless. And, icing on the cake, the song won an Oscar nomination (in the event losing to Barbra Streisand and Paul Williams' enchanting 'Evergreen', from *A Star Is Born*).

So far Los Angeles was treating Don well. But there are some strange characters in the film industry, and half the time they're full of – to use the lyricist's choice term – 'bullshit, pure Hollywood bullshit'. It was with Peter Sellers that he had one of his most remarkable encounters with Hollywood bullshit.

After the huge success of *Billy* in London, Don and John Barry were looking for a big project to follow up. Black happened to mention this to the film producer Jerry Weintraub, whom he knew from his days working as an agent with Vic Lewis. Weintraub had executive-produced Robert Altman's hit comedy *Nashville*, and was later to do the *Karate Kid* films and the George Clooney vehicle *Ocean's Eleven*. The archetypal Hollywood producer, he always wheeling and dealing. He owned a lot of pies and those he didn't own he had his fingers in. He was a big fan of *Billy* and came up with an idea.

'Come and do a big film musical for me!' he demanded excitedly. 'Is there something you've always wanted to do? We'll do it!' As it happened, there was one project that Don had long treasured. He told Weintraub he wanted to do *Ruggles Of Red Gap*. He pitched the story.

Ruggles Of Red Gap was an old 1935 movie ('a wonderful, wonderful film', enthuses Don) starring Charles Laughton, and had a great opening. Laughton played Marmaduke Ruggles, a dignified butler. One day his aristocratic English employer calls him in and asks, 'Ruggles, how are you with shocks?' Ruggles isn't sure how he is with shocks, but his employer tells him that he's about to find out because he lost him in a card game the previous night to a wealthy Texan. So the old-style butler is uprooted to Texas and has to learn how to cope with the vastly different world. It had long been one of Don's favourites. Not his, but Lionel Bart had once optioned it and even taped a batch of songs for it (but typically, and despite having interested a Hollywood studio, he proceeded to lose the tapes, so never bothered to pursue it).

'I *love* it!' declared Weintraub, beside himself with delight. 'But it needs a big star. Tell you what – you and John know Peter Sellers, don't you?' Don confessed that, yes, they did know Peter Sellers. 'If you can get Sellers, I'll produce your *Ruggles Of Red Gap* as a big movie.'

Sellers was known to be very choosy about his film projects, but it was worth a shot. Black and Barry went to see him, and told him the story. He adored it, punctuating their commentary with cries of 'Marvellous, marvellous!' When they had finished the tale, he declared that it was wonderful and he would love to play Ruggles. The writers left Sellers in buoyant mood. It was in the bag.

They reported back to Weintraub who, if anything – and understandably, now they had hooked one of the world's leading comic actors – seemed even more ecstatic than before. 'Leave it to me,' he bubbled, and started the wheels turning. There were meetings and more meetings, arrangements, ideas, plans. Dick Clement and Ian La Frenais joined the writing team. At each stage Weintraub was saying how excited he was, over the moon. 'It's going to be terrific!' he kept insisting.

After many meetings, during which everything seemed to be going amazingly well, the producer invited the creative team round to his house to have dinner with him and his wife, the singer Jane Morgan. He lived in a magnificent home, and Sellers, Don, John Barry, Dick Clement and Ian La Frenais duly turned up and were welcomed by their hosts like royalty. The solid-gold cutlery had been brought out for the evening and, despite the welcome, Don felt that a point was being made. It all seemed very ostentatious.

Still, the conversation was enjoyable. They naturally talked about the project and how 'terrific' Jerry Weintraub thought it was going to be. After a while, the doorbell went. It was one of Weintraub's neighbours. They had heard that the great Peter Sellers was round for dinner and couldn't resist coming to ask for an autograph. The assembled diners chuckled politely. It wouldn't happen in London, thought the Brits, but, well, this was Hollywood. Sellers took the interruption in good part and obliged,

Some minutes later, the doorbell rang again. Here were some more neighbours, and they had come round for the same reason. There were raised eyebrows, but again Sellers politely signed. After a while there was yet another ring.

It turned out that Weintraub had boasted to everyone he knew that Peter Sellers was coming to his house for dinner. Throughout the meal, there was a non-stop procession of his friends and neighbours, who had all dropped by to get Sellers' autograph. If his guests seemed a trifle embarrassed and not a little startled by the arrivals, their host was obviously bursting with pride. Clearly his social standing had been elevated a good few notches.

Sellers remained charming throughout, and in the end everybody enjoyed themselves. The next day Don had a call from John Barry. 'Don, have you heard from Jerry about the contracts yet? We haven't signed anything and I think we should get it down.' Don told Barry he was worrying unduly. 'Give him a bit of time, John,' he laughed. 'We only finalised everything last night!' He left it a day or two, then phoned Weintraub's office. He got the secretary. 'Hi, it's Don Black here. Could you just ask Jerry to give me a call? We should start thinking about getting these contracts out.' Nothing. So he tried again. And again. He must have called around 100 times and never once received a reply. To this day he has never heard another word from him. It was enormously embarrassing. Sellers kept asking, John Barry kept asking and Don had to keep saying that he had not, in fact, heard a thing.

He could not understand what had gone wrong. They had been so far down the line. Dozens of long phone conversations and meetings. They had even cast the lead.

Finally, he figured it all out. 'I think Jerry must have engineered the whole thing just to get Peter Sellers to his house for dinner. It was all done so he could show off to his friends.' Black never spoke to Jerry Weintraub again. He grimaces. 'Bullshit Hollywood.'

You can, as Don found out, never have a bad meeting in Hollywood. They don't exist, or at least he never came across one. They are all intensely pleasurable experiences during which you are flattered to high heaven and your ideas gratefully received like holy benisons. And then, more often than not, you're out in the cold.

Don had the best meeting of his life during his time in Hollywood. The James Bond producer Harry Saltzman had come up with an idea for a children's movie called *Sherlock Holmes And The Case Of The Missing Santa Clause*. He brought it to Don and to the composer Charles Strouse, who wrote a batch of songs. Don was deputised to set up a meeting with Hanna-Barbera, home of Scooby-Doo and Yogi Bear. He went, he pitched. They *flipped*. 'It's brilliant!' the execs almost yelled in delight. 'Two of the most famous characters in the world, and you're bringing them together! Why haven't we thought of this before? It can't miss!' So excited were they that they called their boss into the meeting. Then *he* got really excited and called in Bill Hanna himself. Everyone waited to hear what Hanna would think, as a by-now-none-too-steady-voiced Don Black began his pitch for the third time. Hanna listened, and loved. 'It sounds fabulous,' he opined.

Don walked out of that meeting with a verbal agreement to do the movie and, man, were they all fired up about it! He couldn't wait to get home to tell Shirley, so he called her from the freeway. 'I've never had a meeting like it!' he gabbled with excitement. 'They say it's going to be really big!'

He never heard from them again. Not a note, not a phone call. They never even let him know that they had changed their mind. It was as though the meeting had never happened and Don Black did not exist. 'That's Hollywood,' he says. No such thing as a bad meeting...

It was around this time that Michael Jackson came back into Don's life, and into the lives of his family. They had stayed in contact since the mega-success of 'Ben', and Don had a soft spot for the boy celebrity. Now that he lived nearby, Michael used to come over to Don's house regularly, to play with the boys, to shoot some pool and to swim.

Of course, he would not just wander over. A limo would pull up in the Blacks' drive, out of which would pour a clutch of burly minders, and finally – in stark contrast to the heavily-built bodyguards – little Michael. He'd ring on the doorbell and politely ask whether Clive or Grant were in. Clive was the one he was closest to (even though Michael was 19, while Clive was only 13) and it was usually he that ended up spending time with the soon-to-be King of Pop.

Clive liked Michael, but after months of frequent visits began to tire of him. 'He was nice, but he was older and at that age you really want to hang out with guys of the same age. We used to have swimming races and play pool, but he was too easy to beat, and I got bored.' One day Clive was busy with homework and looked out of his window to see the usual limo pull up. He bolted downstairs and hurriedly shot instructions at his mother. 'Mum, Michael's here, but I've got too much homework to do and I really can't be bothered to see him. Will you tell him I'm not here?' He ran back to his room, closed the door, and hid.

Shirley relayed the message, but Michael was prepared to wait until Clive came home. Not wanting to seem rude, she let him come in for a bit. At the time Shirley was taking art classes and was halfway through a charcoal drawing. Michael, who was good at art, asked if he could help. So there they sat happily for several hours, totally absorbed and at work on this drawing of a Mexican peasant. Shirley, much to Clive's exasperation, had totally forgotten about her son hiding upstairs. Finally, looking very sheepish, he could stand no more and came down. Clive still has the drawing, signed by Shirley Black and Michael Jackson, to this day. Don says if he could only erase Shirley's signature it would be worth a fortune!

'Back then he was just a lovely ordinary boy,' says Shirley. 'Despite the bodyguards who were so big they didn't even fit in the chair, Michael seemed to have that ordinariness about him. I don't know what happened to him along the way.'

After some months, things suddenly turned sour. Michael, as has been well documented, had a very controlling father called Joseph, and he did not take kindly to any unauthorised friendships with his son. He called Don at home. 'Mr Black, this is Joseph Jackson. I understand you've been getting very friendly with Michael.' Don bristled at Jackson's bully-boy tone: 'What do you mean "getting very friendly"? He just comes over and we talk, that's all.' Jackson started to get angry. 'No,' he said. 'This stops now. Everything has to go through me. Everything. If you want to see Michael, you have to arrange it with me. Don't call him. If he wants you, he'll call you.' Don put the phone down, angry now himself. He was not about to phone Joseph Jackson for the privilege of seeing Michael. It soured what had been a very happy friendship.

The relationship between the Blacks and Michael Jackson reveals a great deal about Michael's character. 'He liked us. He liked spending time in our house,' says Clive, 'because he loved spending time with a normal family. His family, especially his father, were far from normal. We were very down-to-earth, and all very close to each other and he wished he could be part of that environment. He loved nothing better than to get some biscuits from the tin and some milk from the fridge and flop down with us in front of the TV. And we'd talk about snooker trick shots – I was a very keen snooker player – or about movies.'

Put in the context of Michael Jackson's life then and since, it's an almost tragic image. When he and Don spoke, much of their conversation was about Don's relationship with Grant and Clive. He wanted to know more about how a functional father–son relationship works.

Don did see Michael again after being warned off by his father, but years later. Around 1995, Walter Scharf called his 'Ben' collaborator. Michael had been in touch and wanted some new songs, for a children's project, so the pair wrote six children's songs. Nothing came of it in the end, although Jackson paid a lot of money for them and said that he loved them.

But Don (with Scharf) was asked to go and see Michael, by now one of the biggest stars in the world, in a recording studio where he was working. Though the two had spoken on the phone a few times over the years, they hadn't met since those days in LA.

'He wore that quasi-military uniform that you often see him in on TV,' remembers Don. 'The one that makes him look like he's in a marching band.' As he went in, he noticed a solitary figure killing time and looking very bored. It was José Feliciano. 'He was just hanging around for whenever Michael was ready!'

Michael was delighted to see his old friend again. It turned out that, not only was he was a big Matt Monro fan, he was also best friends with the son of Monro's musical director, Johnny Spence. 'I love these songs,' said Jackson, 'but Don, I want to talk to you about Matt.' They talked for half an hour about Matt, about his drinking, about his past as a bus driver, and Jackson was enthralled.

Soon Michael turned the conversation to musicals and his favourite songs. He said he loved *Hans Christian Andersen*. His favourite number was 'Inchworm'. And, much to Don's amazement, this world superstar best known for funky hits like 'Bad' and 'Beat It' launched into a rendition of 'Inchworm'. 'Inchworm, inchworm, marrying the marigold', he sang, sweetly and softly.

He asked about the boys, and was eager to know how often Don spoke to them. 'Every day?' he asked, incredulous. It was obvious to Don that the wounds inflicted by Michael's own father had never healed.

'All mega-stars are a bit strange,' he says, 'and Michael more than most, because of what we all read about. And the plastic surgery and all that stuff. But he sings to die for, and the songs I wrote for him and he loved were sweet, innocent, childlike songs. That shows you where his head is. He's a child, living in Never-Never Land.' It was quite obvious to Don that Michael had never found what he was looking for when he would come round daily to sit with the Blacks, to hang out with the boys and, once, to draw with Shirley. He had never found a normal life.

LA introduced Don to a man who was to have a great impact on both his and Matt Monro's life – an extraordinary gentleman by the name of Leonardo Schultz. Although he was no longer managing Matt on a day-to-day basis, taking him to each concert and holding his hand (John Ashby in London now did that), he was still guiding his friend's career. And he took a long-distance call from Buenos Aires from this South American agent, Leonardo Schultz, who wanted to bring Matt to South America. Don was interested, and asked Schultz to write to him, giving him his LA address.

Some weeks later the doorbell rang. When Don answered it he saw this little Jewish man who, with a smile and a half-bow, introduced himself. 'Ah, Mr Black. I am Leonardo Schultz.'

Don was aghast. Schultz had misunderstood and thought that Don wanted to see him in person, and he had turned up at a dreadfully inconvenient moment. Don was entertaining Vera Lynn's daughter Virginia, and had promised faithfully to take her to Disneyland that same day, but he also felt an obligation to make this unexpected guest feel welcome. Schultz's English was halting, and it took Don quite some time to explain that he would like to invite him to Disneyland.

He was not quite sure whether to be pleased or not when Schultz eventually understood and agreed, but off the unlikely trio set – Don, Virginia and this man that neither of them knew and whose English was not the best. It turned out to be a lovely day. Leonardo and Don had much in common. They were roughly the same age, and Schultz was a singer himself. Like Don, he loved Al Jolson and did a fabulous, if heavily accented, Jolson impression. Like Don, he had seen *The Jolson Story* hundreds of times. He was even a songwriter, though in Don's opinion not a good one. Most important, he was a genuine, good-natured man with a deep enthusiasm for his work. They hit it off immediately and, as they browsed through the rides and shook the hands of various oversized Disney characters, they discussed songwriters and singers with joyful fervour.

It was Schultz's idea to get Matt Monro to sing in Spanish. There was, he insisted, a vast untapped market that would really go for him. Leonardo translated lyrics into Spanish (some from Monro's existing repertoire, and some new songs which Don wrote), Matt recorded the songs and they were released as the album *Alguien Canto* (*Someone Sings*). It was a smash in South America, and shot straight to No.1. They released single after single from it and each one was a big hit. Matt, who learned the songs phonetically, became an enormous star out there – as big as The Beatles. In fact, it was *Alguien Canto* that became his first ever platinum disc.

Other Spanish albums followed, such as *En España* (*In Spain*) and *Un Toque De Distinción* (*A Touch of Distinction*). They could not get enough of him, and Monro mania was everywhere – especially in the Philippines. On his first visit there, when the plane landed, Matt saw crowds of people screaming adoringly. He wondered who on earth they could be there for, until he disembarked and saw a welcome mat embroidered with the words 'Welcome Matt'. There were flowers everywhere, cheers, smiles – and all because of Leonardo Schultz.

'There weren't many agents in South America who you could trust,' says Don, 'but you knew where you were with him. We loved this man, and were so glad he had come into our lives.' In 2000, Don was called up by Leonardo's son. His father, he explained, had just died. Leonardo had been out running to try and lose weight, and had suffered a heart attack. Don was deeply upset.

His time in Hollywood was not one of Black's busiest periods. 'He didn't like living there,' says Shirley. 'It was very easy living, a slow pace of life. And Don likes to stay busy and have meetings which actually lead to things. It was like a prolonged holiday for him; he couldn't stand waiting for the phone to ring.'

John Barry, who now lives near New York, was never inclined to move out west. 'It's a great place to go and work, the level of expertise is phenomenal. But you just can't come from Yorkshire and go and live in a place where it's always sunny.'

Similarly, Black found he could not, after a lifetime in the hustle and bustle of London, put up with the relaxed Bel Air lifestyle for long. It simply wasn't him. 'It doesn't work like in the old movies. A Ziegfeld doesn't phone you with offers. You usually have to be your own catalyst, come up with ideas yourself. It's a funny life out there. I used to look at my diary and say to Shirley, "Not this Thursday, but next Thursday, I've got a meeting with Henry Mancini." It might be ten days away and that would be my only meeting in that fortnight.'

He stuck it out for a year, whiling the days away by writing songs, thinking of ideas, playing with the kids. He even wrote a screenplay about Svengali, which he planned to do with Olivia Newton-John (the two had scored a hit with the song 'Sam'), but never showed it to anyone.

There were movies, notably (wait for it) *Won Ton Ton: The Dog Who Saved Hollywood* with Elmer Bernstein, and a film musical of *Gulliver's Travels* with Michel Legrand. *Gulliver's Travels* starred Richard Harris, and for the first and only time Don wrote the screenplay as well as the lyrics. It was not his cup of tea. Or, rather, it didn't leave enough time for cups of tea.

'Writing a screenplay is very grown up,' he grins. 'You actually have to sit down and plot and scheme. It's too much like hard work!' Don submitted his script and lyrics alongside music by John Barry, yet director Peter R Hunt loved the words but not the music. Barry was replaced by Legrand – not a situation he has often found himself in.

After giving Los Angeles a prolonged shot, Don decided that he was most productive in London. He has always been happiest working on several things at once, with other projects lining up to start. Bel Air just wasn't the right environment.

'Hollywood,' he concluded. 'You mix in the star-studded fraternity, you drive around, you do the odd bit of work. That's the life.' It was not a life he was comfortable with, so the Blacks packed up, sold up and came home.

10 Jule Styne And The Demolition Of A Musical

When Don got back to London, he bought a smart flat in Basil Street in Knightsbridge (one of central London's most desirable areas), and found the stage calling him once more. Now that he was back, *Billy's* producer Peter Witt wanted him to come up with a follow-up musical. After the bullshit and boredom of Hollywood, the lyricist fancied getting back to the grit and grind of the theatre. 'I've got the perfect subject,' he told Witt. 'A fabulous play by Jack Rosenthal called *Barmitzvah Boy*.'

Although Don had empathised with *Billy*, it had been set very much in the world in which John Barry grew up. *Barmitzvah Boy*, on the other hand, spoke about a society which Don himself was part of. Rosenthal's terrific 1976 play tells of a boy about to have his bar mitzvah, the time at which Jewish boys take a formal part in the reading of the law in synagogue to symbolise their ascent to manhood. It is customary for the children to learn a section of the Torah in Hebrew, but it is also too often a showcase for the parents. Rosenthal cleverly depicts a nightmare family in which the boy, Eliot Green, himself feels surplus to requirements.

At the climactic moment, when he is called to read the law in synagogue, Eliot leaves his seat, strides towards the scroll, then past it and out of the building. He flees to a park and recites his portion to a friend while standing on his head. All of his family's manic fussing over his bar mitzvah has brought to the surface his greatest fear. He sees his father as unfeeling, his grandfather as trivial and self-indulgent, and his sister's fiancé as weak. So what's so wonderful about becoming a man? Eliot worries that if he says his piece and joins their ranks, he might become like them.

'It's a great story for a musical,' says Don, 'and we messed it up.' He's right, it is, and by all accounts they did. The ingredients all seemed right. *Barmitzvah Boy* offers all the elements a good musical needs – a society and locality with a strong individual flavour, an uncertain central character facing a moment of life-changing revelation, and plenty of strong supporting roles (all the family members, plus vivid local characters, such as the hairdresser, the rabbi, and plenty more). There were also three writers who knew exactly what it was like to go through a bar mitzvah. Witt persuaded Rosenthal to write the book, though Rosenthal had never worked on a musical before; Don was on the lyrics; and – as an amazing coup – the legendary American composer Jule Styne agreed to supply the music.

In the hierarchy of musical theatre, Styne is at the pinnacle. There are others there alongside him, but not many. He may have been born in London, emigrating with his family at the age of 7, but he was the epitome of the self-made American. After early ambitions to be a concert pianist failed because his hands were thought to be too small, at the age of 16 he had put together a band that included Benny Goodman. Styne went on to be one of the greatest of songwriters, composing classic after classic – 'Let It Snow, Let It Snow, Let it Snow!' was his, as were 'Three Coins In The Fountain', 'Time After Time', and dozens of others. When he turned his considerable powers to Broadway musicals, he came up with *Gentlemen Prefer Blondes* (a big hit for Carol Channing that included that most seductive of numbers, 'Diamonds Are A Girl's Best Friend'), *Bells Are Ringing*, *Gypsy* and the Streisand career-maker, *Funny Girl*. There was much, much more besides.

Styne was a powerhouse on Broadway. As well as being a composer, he was also a producer. And he was a larger-than-life character. He loved to gamble, was almost obsessed by it. Don would visit him in his office above the Mark Hellinger theatre and the scene would always be the same. He would be at his desk, smoking, old copies of *Variety* magazine strewn everywhere. His secretary Dorothy Dicker would be running in and out as he swore at her, 'Get that fuckin' thing in here!' And he would be on the phone every few minutes placing bets. Don would try and focus his mind on the show, suggesting, 'We've really got to write this song for the end of Act I,' and Styne would reply, 'Yeah, OK, Don. We'll do it right away. This minute. Hang on one second,' and pick up the phone, into which he would bark, 'Five bucks either way on Brown Boy. Yeah, that's it. And three to one I'll take Hallelujah. Sweetheart on the fifth.' Without pausing, he would slam down the receiver and jump to the piano. As soon as he started work, he would be called back to the phone to talk to some famous showbiz personality. 'It was', says Don, 'absolute chaos. An overwhelming atmosphere in which to try and write a song. But yet this was the guy who wrote "Everything's Coming Up Roses"!'

Styne always claimed to Don that the gambling kept him going. 'I may have lost four or five million dollars over the years,' he would shrug, 'but it's kept me alive. Every day is exciting.' And it was. He would get incredibly motivated, even for a $5 bet. Mid-song, he'd rush over to the intercom: 'Dorothy, what the fuck's going on with Hallelujah? Any news on Brown Boy?'

Predictably, Styne and Black became fast friends. Styne loved to tell stories about his mother, and Don loved to hear them and reciprocate with stories about his own mother. There's a book in there somewhere – *Jewish Boys And Their Jewish Mothers*.

Styne's mother lived in Chicago, and there was a period when her son did not see her for some years. He had gone off, become a huge and very busy success with *Gypsy* in New York and, he felt, neglected her. She kept herself well occupied. Five nights a week she would go to her beloved Yiddish theatre. It was her home from home. Meanwhile, *Gypsy* was coming to Chicago, and Styne decided to come with it and see her. He told her, 'Mum, I'm coming to town. I'll take you out anywhere you want to go. The best restaurant in Chicago, you name the place.' She replied, 'I want to go to the Yiddish theatre.' Her son was aghast, 'Mum, you go there every night!' 'Yes,' she said, 'but not with you.' So they went to the Yiddish theatre, and she showed off her son. And Styne would relate this story with tears streaming down his face.

The funniest tale about Jule Styne and his mother concerns her incredible salad dressing, for which she kept the recipe a strict secret. So marvellous was this that the whole neighbourhood knew about it. Styne had the idea that he would get this terrific concoction sold in the shops, so he spoke to someone he knew in the salad dressing industry – a real mover and shaker. The composer sold him the idea of 'Styne's salad dressing' and he was interested, then the two men went round to see his mother, he tasted it and was convinced. They would do a big deal, and Styne's dressing would hit the high streets.

'So, Mum,' asked Styne. 'How do you make it?' With great glee she revealed her method. There were plenty of herbs and spices, mixed in a certain way, but the most essential, secret ingredient was…Colman's mustard. She had not realised that it was illegal to market a dressing if its main ingredient was already on the market!

Jule Styne was a great composer, but he was wrong for *Barmitzvah Boy*. Both he and the American director Martin Charnin, fresh from directing *Annie,* were too New York. Too Broadway. *Barmitzvah Boy,* the play, is a London story. It is straight-talking, short, and gets to the point. It is also somewhat understated and deliberately claustrophobic. Styne and Charnin saw it as a big extravaganza.

'They brought to it this New York veneer, this show-stopping polish, that was wrong for it.' So big production numbers were the order of the day. There was one song called 'The Barmitzvah Of Eliot Green' which featured dancing caterers and huge piles of mushroom vol-au-vents. Even the poster was busy – it looks like a messy fridge-door display, with a big calendar, badges emblazoned variously with the Chelsea Football Club crest and Darth Vader – even darts.

Styne made an effort to get to know the world Rosenthal was writing about. He had been born in London's East End, but had moved to America while still a baby, so he asked Don to drive him to see it. They drove to the Bethnal Green house that had been Styne's first home, and then on to Hackney to see the flat where Don grew up. 'Always remember this place, Don,' counselled Styne. 'You'll never get where you're going if you forget where you came from.'

But Rosenthal and Black knew that with the musical things were not right. It was a story about ordinary Jewish lives, about families much like their own (if a little exaggerated), but Styne and Charnin decreed that it had to be big, had to be spectacular. And the Brits allowed themselves to be overawed. After all, Rosenthal had never written a musical before, Don had only worked on two, while Charnin had just directed the biggest musical hit in the world. Styne was, well, Jule Styne.

At least Don and Jule Styne liked each other. As fellow songwriters they had a natural bond. Jack Rosenthal never fitted in. He was not, as he soon discovered, a musicals kind of guy.

Big musicals have a lot riding on them. They get noticed, they are expensive, so reputations and fortunes are very publicly made and broken. They also require several disciplines to mesh – dance, song, acting, the whole shebang. Hence, writing a musical is not like writing a play. You write a play on your own, or with a partner. And even through the rehearsal process the playwright retains a great deal of control. Musicals are written by committee. You have the composer, the lyricist and the book writer. You frequently need a strong guiding hand to unify these forces, so the director and/or producer will take a very active role.

This means that nobody has total artistic control. The buck stops with the producer, but as the writers are usually the first component to slot into place it is very rare that the producer will replace one of them, though directors can be an endangered species. Everyone is expected to swallow their pride and hack away at the great edifice until the perfect sculpture emerges, which can often mean rewrite after rewrite. Rosenthal was not used to working this way. And Jule Styne did not mince his words. 'When can we get some flesh on these fuckin' characters?' he would growl. 'Jack had to keep rewriting and rewriting,' says Don. 'He was mortified. It was a nightmare for him. I knew it's all part of musicals, but he wasn't used to it.'

Rosenthal also had no idea how to take Jule Styne. The composer was exuberant, brash, foul-mouthed – in fact, the clichéd Broadway showman. It was not Rosenthal's scene, though he did try. Even his best efforts were doomed to failure, however. On one unforgettable occasion the trio were preparing the London production of the show in Styne's New York apartment.

'Jule had a habit of announcing songs, and building them up,' laughs Don. 'He'd burst into the room, proudly saying, "Are you guys ready? Are you guys *ready for this*?"' Rosenthal was never sure how he was supposed to react, and his usual discomfort around Styne increased on these occasions. Should he tell the truth? Should he just agree adoringly? On this night in Styne's apartment, the composer announced at high-decibel volume, 'I've gotta tell you guys, this is probably the best *motherfuckin'* song I've written in my entire *fuckin'* life!' Rosenthal looked startled, as Styne sat at his beautiful Bosendorff piano and began to play, demanding that they 'Just listen to this!'

Rosenthal rested his gin and tonic on the piano and really tried to get into the music. Styne was putting his soul into the piece. Veins were popping up on his forehead, his face was red with emotion. And, just as he reached the crescendo, Rosenthal knocked his gin and tonic into the piano. Styne stopped and glared as the deeply embarrassed Rosenthal stammeringly apologised, simultaneously trying to say how marvellous the tune was and clean up the G&T dripping through the instrument.

Rosenthal was thoroughly miserable. 'It was', he said, 'an utterly grim time.' He was so scarred by the whole experience that he later wrote a play about it, called *Smash*. And boy does he get revenge on Styne! Although Don emerges as the play's most likeable character, thinly disguised as an easygoing, wise-cracking lyricist called Mike, Styne is rechristened Bebe. And Bebe is one nasty, foul-mouthed piece of work. At one point, when Bebe yells at the Rosenthal character (feminised as an English novelist called Liz working on her first musical) at their first meeting, the playwright's fury at Styne comes across loud and clear: 'BEBE: You know what'd please *me*? Knowing how to put flesh and blood into those cardboard asshole characters of hers! *She* got any ideas? 'Cause sure as hell *I* ain't!... Twenty-eight Broadway shows, so what's a shmock like me know? Twenty-eight Broadway smasheroos. How many *you* done? Two? Three? So that gives you the right under the Constitution to wear a scarf down to your ankles and tell me to simmer down? I did not get no first draft delivered! I got a fancy packet of *crap* delivered!'

Although the play makes clear just how miserable Rosenthal was, Don could not be happier. He was pleased with his own work, and takes little responsibility for its eventual failure. 'I loved working on it, because I knew it, I knew the people. I can write about Jewish people, easy. I can write a song about Jewish caterers because I know what they're like.'

The opening night, on 31 October 1978 at Her Majesty's Theatre, was a distinctly Jewish affair. The songwriter Tony Hiller (who wrote 'Save All Your Kisses For Me') has said, 'I'll never forget the opening night of *Barmitzvah Boy*. Full of Jews, and no one was at the bar but everyone was eating bridge rolls!' It was what Don describes as a 'wonderful Yiddisher opening', with ample supplies of bridge rolls, bagels and smoked salmon. Sounds a bit like a bar mitzvah kiddush (after-synagogue buffet), in fact!

Sadly, a good spread does not a hit show make, and *Barmitzvah Boy*, starring Harry Towb, Joyce Blair, and Barry Angel as Eliot, flopped. 'Wisecracks and unmannerly bustle displace the humorous exactitude of the original,' frowned John Barber in the *Daily Telegraph*. 'The main sensation of the evening was of strenuous effort, towards a result which is too big and noisy for what Mr Rosenthal has to say,' agreed Irving Wardle in *The Times*.

Not everyone was so damning. The *Financial Times*'s BA Young called it 'uniquely enjoyable among recent musicals', and the cast recording reveals an uneven but jauntily tuneful score with some fabulous numbers (and others that are obviously trying to be big, Broadway-style show-stoppers). One in particular, the catchy 'Thou Shalt Not' – where Eliot and his friends discuss the reality of bar mitzvahs and adolescence – finds Black at his sharpest, with its witty semi-talmudic lyrics.

ELIOT:
Thou shalt not do this and thou shalt not do that,
And thou shalt not get in the way.
And thou shalt never bother thy father
When he's reading the news,
Or when he wants a little snooze.
And thou shalt not waste food,
Or let thine hair grow long,
And thou shalt sit up straight in every chair.
And thou shalt never answer thy parents,
When they're talking such rot.
Thou could, thou would,
But thou shalt not.

Thou shalt not cause any aggravation,
Thou shalt not expect consideration.
I'm tied in lots of little thou shalt nots.

Thou shalt not show off, and thou shalt listen more,
For thou is only the barmitzvah boy.
And thou shalt not plan anyone's murder,
Though thou easily can.
Thou might, when thou becomest a man.

FRIENDS AND ELIOT (VARIOUSLY):

Thou shalt not smoke pot and thou shall not get drunk,
Or share thine self with lots of boys.
And thou shalt not play rock n'roll music when Dad's trying to think,
Or leave thine stockings in thine sink.

And thou shalt not take pills,
Or wear thine see-through blouse,
And thou shalt not pretend that thou is old.
And thou shalt stop thy flirting with teachers when thou's taking
    exams.
Or thou may soon be buying prams.

Thou shall not be cruel to baby brothers,
Thou shalt leave thy bathroom fit for others.
Thou shalt use shoe polish on thine shoes.

Tis written thou shalt not go out,
And thou shalt not sleep late,
And thou shalt always act as children should.
If thou shalt do whatever's expected,
Then thou wilt be adored, and loved,
And thou shalt also be bored.'

It closed after only 77 performances. And with a reported £350,000 budget, that was no joke. Peter Witt was quoted in the London *Evening News*, moaning that 'The show has bled me to death.'

It was very far from what Black and Rosenthal had envisaged. And when, in 1987, a production was mounted at New York's American Jewish Theatre on 92nd Street, the show came no closer. An American journalist, Martin Godfrey, was brought in to help Rosenthal with the book, but it was, says Black, 'even more New York – they tried to make it more Neil Simonish and even more of an event'. In America, the bar mitzvah scene itself became a vast extravaganza. There was a brutality of truth in the play that was entirely missing from the show. The great temptation in musicals, as Black found, is to glamorise the story in a way that removes it from the initial thought. Styne, irrepressible as ever, always loved the show. 'Mind you,' says Don, 'he always loved everything that he wrote.'

It flopped in New York, too, but some good came out of the bad. The lyrics were generally liked, and after the London opening Black received telegrams of praise from two stars of the Broadway theatre world – Hal Prince and Michael Bennett. Prince's telegram read, 'Impeccable work. Bravo!'

Don remained friends with Jule Styne. They never worked together again, but often on trips to New York Styne would take him to ice-hockey matches at Madison Square Garden. And, of course, he would always have money riding on the outcome.

11 Meeting Lloyd Webber And The Birth Of
Tell Me On A Sunday

There was another benefit of *Barmitzvah Boy* – one that would have lasting impact on Don's life, his public profile and, not least, his bank balance. It brought him to the attention of Andrew Lloyd Webber.

The 1970s were the decade when Britain finally overtook Broadway as the world centre for musicals, a success that was consolidated with the four blockbusters of the 1980s: *Phantom Of The Opera*, *Les Misérables*, *Miss Saigon* and *Cats*.

I ought perhaps to pause here and – mindful of the time Claude-Michel Schönberg (the decidedly Gallic composer of *Les Mis* and *Saigon*) phoned me from JFK airport to say how upset he was that I had written that his shows were 'English' – make myself clear. What my editors on that occasion had cut was my explanation. I know that Schönberg and his librettist Alain Boublil are French and, as he pointed it out to me, I now know that they had lunch with the Queen as representatives of French theatre. But the truth remains that *Les Mis* would probably never have become the phenomenon it is had it not been for the expert guidance (leading to substantial reworking) of producer Cameron Mackintosh, director Trevor Nunn and English lyricist Herbert Kretzmer. Had *Les Mis* not gone the international route, who knows whether we would have had a *Miss Saigon*? So, in that sense, those shows are as English as fish and chips (the plaice may have swum all the way across the Channel, but it's still regarded as an English delicacy when it's wrapped in newspaper and drenched in vinegar).

Yet it was a pair of ex-Oxford University students who paved the way for this success. Andrew Lloyd Webber and best chum Tim Rice had penned *Joseph And The Amazing Technicolour Dreamcoat* for a London primary school, then moved on to Broadway success with the visceral rock opera *Jesus Christ Superstar*. After *Superstar* created a sensation, they soon revived an expanded version of the ultra-ebullient, zestful *Joseph*, and then eschewed the Bible for politics. They did the unthinkable – creating a musical from the life of Eva Peron. *Evita* was phenomenally successful, making an 'overnight star' (so the papers claimed, though we know better) out of Elaine Paige.

After *Evita*, though, Lloyd Webber and Rice split. They have never admitted to any big argument, and the general opinion is simply that their personalities clashed. The composer solved the problem of finding a new lyricist by writing his next show around the verses of a dead poet. TS Eliot's *Old Possum's Book Of Practical Cats* thus became the worldwide sensation *Cats*, which soon dug its claws into dozens of cities around the world.

Cats saw the emergence of another great force in musical theatre, the 35-year-old producer Cameron Mackintosh. Don had known Mackintosh for some years, and vividly remembers offering consoling words and encouragement to the down-on-his-luck producer in a Covent Garden bar. Mackintosh's latest show was struggling, and he was determined to find the cash to keep it running – 'I've got to find another £30,000', he worried. But, says Black, he already had the reputation of being a superb producer, with great integrity, and that is why Andrew Lloyd Webber chose him for *Cats*. The composer's track record already spoke for itself. Still, an entire musical just about cats, based on some old poems? To most, it seemed ridiculous.

As anybody remotely interested in theatre now knows, *Cats* became the world's longest-running musical. After marking its territory at the New London Theatre in 1981, it stayed there for an incredible 21 years. And Mackintosh took it global, so that to date it has played in over 250 cities around the world, taking over $2 billion. Noël Coward and Ivor Novello had put British musical theatre on the international map, Lionel Bart had helped to keep it there, but when Lloyd Webber and Mackintosh came along they bought the map. With *Cats* purring its way around the globe, Lloyd Webber needed a new librettist to replace Tim Rice.

Don knew Lloyd Webber slightly. He had met him at the launch of a concept album for a show about an agony aunt, called *Dear Anyone*, which he had written with Geoff Stephens. (Concept albums were then a recognised route to attract investors and an audience, one that *Jesus Christ Superstar* had followed to spectacular effect.)

It is one of the few great pities of Don Black's career that *Dear Anyone* never had a successful stage production. One of his own personal favourites, it is also one of mine, and well worth taking a moment to discuss briefly. (Who knows? Maybe some enterprising producer will be inspired.)

Dear Anyone is about an agony aunt, Dear Pandora, the troubled correspondents who write for her advice, and her own inability to deal with her emotions. There are some of the same preoccupations that inhabit Stephen Sondheim's great musical *Company* – emotional isolationism, and at the same time a deep need for the central character to have 'someone to miss me too much', as Sondheim's Robert puts it.

Black's Pandora, in the tender title song (buoyed by Stephens' gently strumming melody), puts it in the form of a letter – only, since she's the agony aunt, the cry for help is addressed to anyone and everyone:

> Dear anyone,
> Anyone will do.
> Don't care who saves me,
> Or whose hand I hold on to.
>
> Don't let me fall.
> Turn on the light,
> Somewhere for me.
>
> Dear anyone,
> Someone must be there.
> Why don't you answer?
> Do none of you care?
>
> I need you now.
> I'm where you used to be.
>
> Each day,
> I found the right words to say.
> I took all your problems away.
> And I ignored my own.

And now,
Looking at my life right now,
I am the loser somehow,
Ending up alone.

Dear anyone,
Where do I begin?
If you think you know,
Send your letters in.

Dear somebody,
Dear anyone,
Help me win.

Beautiful, insightful stuff. The show finds Black on great form, and Alan Jay Lerner's suggested alternative title for *Maybe That's Your Problem* was finally used in the song 'Shortcomings' – in which an impotent man complains to Dear Pandora that:

Nothing is growing, no cock is crowing,
I always feel such a fool.
Cause every sick dame calls me by my nickname.
I'm known as Peter-No-Tool.

There's nostalgia, too, in the tale of the sad old man who used to be a big-shot in vaudeville, who now bores his nephew by telling him the same stories again and again. 'Don't stop him if you've heard it,' appeals Pandora. 'He only wants to make you smile, and get back in the spotlight for a while.'

My favourite line comes from the man who loves Pandora, who asks himself why she has got him into such a panic. After all, he sings, 'She's just a person.' Then it hits him. 'But so', he concludes sadly, 'am I.'

For all their finery (Norma Desmond), extravagant dreams (Billy Liar) and wealth (the *Aspects of Love* crowd), underneath their masks Don Black's characters always remain exactly that. Just people.

The concept album had two great benefits. It gave the group Hot Chocolate a Top 20 hit with the single 'I'll Put You Together Again'.

Both Lloyd Webber and Rice were fans of the album, and at the launch they introduced themselves to Black and told him so. That was his first meeting with Lloyd Webber. Not long afterwards, the composer decided to become a member of SODS.

SODS is more correctly known as the Society Of Distinguished Songwriters. Its membership consists mainly of songwriters who made their names in the 1960s – from Les Reed, who wrote 'It's Not Unusual', to Mitch Murray, who penned 'I Like It'. They meet four times a year to have dinners in fine hotels (three stag dinners and a ladies' night), swap funny stories and reminisce.

The new recruit was not comfortable. 'It's a real silly boys' night out,' says Don. 'People tell dirty jokes, all that kind of thing. Andrew comes from a different background to these guys. More upper class. He was sociable, but I think he felt awkward in that scene. He never swears, and you never hear him tell a dirty joke.' After a few SODS dinners, Lloyd Webber stopped attending.

However, he and Black saw each other from time to time and the composer professed himself a great admirer of the *Barmitzvah Boy* lyrics. For his part, though he was still more part of the film world than the theatre scene, Black had been stunned by *Evita*. 'It was all so different, dramatic and new. Fresh. What he did with that story was amazing.'

Don was intrigued to get an invitation to lunch from the composer. They went to a restaurant on Walton Street, now Scalini's, and over the meal Andrew said, 'I've been thinking that we may do something together.' Lloyd Webber loved writing for female voices, and – with a readiness to experiment that has characterised his career – wanted to write a one-woman show. He had come up with a couple of tunes, and was eager to play them to Don. So Don invited him back to his Knightsbridge flat. Lloyd Webber sat at Don's piano and played two tunes.

'OK, let me think and see what it could be,' responded Black. He duly delivered lyrics for both of the melodies. One was called 'Come Back With The Same Look In Your Eyes' and the other was 'Tell Me On A Sunday'.

Lloyd Webber was delighted, Black was hired and a new partnership had begun. Media interest was sky-high – had Lloyd Webber really found a replacement for Tim Rice? Lloyd Webber replied that he had lost his Larry Hart but found his Oscar Hammerstein.

These days Lloyd Webber, who now matches lyricists with projects (though Don remains his most regular collaborator), plays that down. 'There wasn't really that expectation,' he says. 'In the first place, I had only written three shows with Tim, and Hart wrote about 30 with Rodgers, and I had also done the unsuccessful *By Jeeves* with Alan Ayckbourn. Actually, many people say my finest ever lyrics are by TS Eliot!'

A one-woman show was an ideal format for Don. 'There's an expectation with musicals that, if the audience are paying £40 for a seat, they want to see a big show. But I like writing about people, about personal emotions and feelings. If someone asked me to do a musical of *My Dinner With André* I'd be very interested, as opposed to a suggestion like "Let's do *Spartacus*". So a one-woman show was a gift.'

After the misplaced razzle-dazzle of *Barmitzvah Boy*, the new show was a gift in other ways too. 'It was just Andrew and me. No directors, no choreographers. It was just him popping round to the flat, playing me a couple of tunes. And it was one of the happiest working periods of my life.'

Lloyd Webber agrees, adding, 'I was my own producer on that, so there was nobody else. All musicals come down to a few people around a piano, but then the record companies and producers and everyone else come crashing in. This was small and very enjoyable.'

Black had been struck during his time living in LA by the number of English girls who had moved out there by themselves, hoping to embrace a new life (and maybe a new man) in the New World. Lloyd Webber had a friend at the time who had just been through that experience, so it was decided that they would make the show about an English girl who goes to America.

'It's always nice to write what you know about,' says Don. 'I know about America. I knew about the Hollywood phoniness and the sourness beneath the suntans. So I was on firm territory.'

The show took form, and took the title of the song around which its structure pivoted. It's a song of a romance that will inevitably break up, where all illusions have already been dispelled – 'Tell Me On A Sunday'.

'Don't write a letter when you want to leave,
Don't call me at three a.m. from a friend's apartment.
I'd like to choose how I hear the news.

Take me to a park that's covered with trees.
Tell me on a Sunday please.

Let me down easy, no big song and dance.
No long faces, no long looks, no deep conversation.
I know the way we should spend that day.

Take me to a zoo that's got chimpanzees,
Tell me on a Sunday please.

Don't want to know who's to blame,
It won't help, knowing.
Don't want to fight day and night,
Bad enough you're going.

Don't leave in silence, with no word at all.
Don't get drunk and slam the door, that's no way to end this.
I know how I want you to say goodbye.

Find a circus ring with a flying trapeze.
Tell me on a Sunday please.

Because the show was a song cycle, the songs themselves dictated the story and the pace. As well as the romance and yearning of songs like 'Come Back With The Same Look In Your Eyes' and 'Tell Me On A Sunday', there was humour (the much-admired 'Capped Teeth And Caesar Salad') and there was anger ('Take That Look Off Your Face', which was to become a chart hit). And the recurring motifs of a messy, bitter argument – 'Wait, let me finish' – and letters home to Mum became clever linking devices.

Fascinatingly, Lloyd Webber tells how he taught Don some of the techniques of musical theatre. 'Because of his background in Tin Pan Alley and films, he is very accommodating – he can deliver things quickly, and that makes him a joy to work with. But, although *Billy* had been fresh and good, he was not yet completely versed in stage musicals, not at least in my world of sung-through musicals. Suddenly I had presented him with a 45-minute, sung-through show with only one character, so *Tell Me On A Sunday* was in part a baptism by fire for him. It was an experiment and even I wasn't sure it could be done. But I was introducing him to that world, to my world of through-composed musicals. Both of us learned a lot. And it solidified our friendship.'

In the finished piece, the girl goes through four relationships and an emotional progression. She begins by getting herself out of an affair that isn't working. Then there is a glamorous but neglectful agent, a toy boy and a married father. By turns she is dazzled, touched, and finally cynical (singing sardonically that she 'won't look crushed when you say your wife is pretty.. I won't cry at all when you walk right by me'). And back and back comes that harrowing conversation which recurs in so many relationships – 'Let me finish, you must let me finish'.

Tell Me On A Sunday drew from both Black and Lloyd Webber some of their finest work. Don's lyrics for 'Tell Me On A Sunday' and 'Come Back With The Same Look In Your Eyes' (a beautiful, tender idea for a song), in particular, strike right to the heart. 'Capped Teeth And Caesar Salad' was his chance to get witty revenge on the Hollywood bullshitters:

Capped teeth and caesar salad,
Good old Beverly Hills.
With every deal that's done,
An award is won.
You can rent a car or rent a star.

Sun tans and Sunday brunches,
Sprinklers sprinkle away.
It's like a fairy-tale,
Long as you don't inhale.
I'll call you back and
Have a nice day.

Capped teeth and caesar salad,
Spotless Beverly Hills.

If someone takes a walk,
All the neighbours talk.
Every man and beast came from out East.

Egos and valet parking,
Cameras rolling away.
Survival's very hard,
Without your Diner's card.
I'll call you back and
Have a nice day.

Capped teeth and caesar salad,
Prime-time Beverly Hills.
The cost of land's so high,
You can't afford to die.
When you feel bad there, you dial a prayer.
Earthquakes and English muffins,
Ulcers popping away.

Careers are being hyped,
Before the scripts are typed.
I'll call you back and
Have a nice day.

One wonders if Jerry Weintraub flinched at all if he heard the lines 'Careers are being hyped/Before the scripts are typed' – at least Black resisted a couplet along the lines of 'Sellers wined and dined/Before the contract's signed'!

'Come Back With The Same Look In Your Eyes' contains, for my money, some of Don's most moving lyrics, both truthful and direct. ('A lot of Don's best work is in that show,' says Lloyd Webber.) They blend perfectly with the composer's greatly affecting melody: fluent and bravely optimistic, in each verse it pulls itself up for the vulnerable payoff line:

I will see you in a week or two,
It's late, you'd better get going.
Take care of yourself,

And call anytime you feel that you're missing me.
I can only say,
What I always say at these goodbyes.
Come back with the same look in your eyes.

I know you've got your work to do,
And I know how much you love me.
But sometimes a friendly face,
Can look good to you on a lonely night.
If there comes a time,
Just remember I'm the kind that cries.
Come back with the same look in your eyes.

Everything we want we find in each other.
We would be fools to let love slip away.
Everything's so right I'm scared,
That we might lose it one day.
We could never keep things from one another,
You know all the feelings that are in my heart.
It's not easy, it's not easy,
When you have to be apart.

So I'll see you in a week or two,
It's late, you'd better get going.
You'd think that by now,
We'd know how to handle this, but we never will.
When you are away,
Every day I pray that nothing dies.
That you'll come back with the same look in your eyes.

Beautiful. And the song is followed by the stark reality of 'Take That Look Off Your Face', where the girl learns the truth of her lover's infidelity. She gets a rough ride, and the audience comes face to face with the truth of failed romance and disappointed adventure – something everyone can empathise with.

The choice of singer was desperately important to the show. Lloyd Webber plumped for Marti Webb, a respected but not yet famous musical actress who had succeeded Elaine Paige both as Evita and as Grizabella in *Cats*. 'This girl', he informed Don, 'has got great range.' He then introduced her to Don, who instantly knew she was right: 'She was so down-to-earth, which is the quality I wanted in the girl. It needed someone who seemed like she was from Muswell Hill. The character was just an ordinary girl who went to America to sort herself out. That's all it was.'

He and Webb became fast friends, and her conversations came to influence some aspects of the show. 'She can talk for hours about the most boring everyday things, like the gas bill or insurance! So I liked that, and came up with the idea of having the girl write letters home to Mum as a way of helping to narrate the storyline. And I put in lines that were typical Marti, like, "Mum, you must stop Cassius barking" and "That picture of Aunt Edna is absolutely lovely."'

Tell Me On A Sunday was premièred to a rapturous reception at Lloyd Webber's Sydmonton Festival (a weekend he holds at his mansion near Newbury, when new shows are tried out in a converted chapel in his garden). It was ready for the public.

The subject matter was not the composer's only experiment. He decided that, as a musical in close-up, as it were, it would make a smashing television show. Black was startled by the power of the man – he only had to pick up the phone to get a prime-time television slot for his new show! 'The BBC producers came down to Sydmonton to see it,' remembers Webb, 'and they started fighting amongst themselves as to who should have it. Andrew gave it to BBC 2.' So an album was recorded, and a live one-off performance at London's Royalty Theatre in January 1980 was broadcast by the BBC.

'It was fantastic on television,' says Don, 'because it was almost all filmed in close-up on Marti Webb's face. Every eyebrow raised, every look registered. It was a brilliant piece of TV, like one of Alan Bennett's *Talking Heads* series, but sung.'

Webb recalls her nervousness at the recording. 'I was used to singing it with Don and Andrew there, but this was only the third time I had sung it without them near me. In the TV studio, I suddenly felt very alone and scared. But Ron the cameraman stuck a sign on his camera that read "Good luck!", which made me feel much better. Then, at the end, he changed it for one which read "Well done!"'

The broadcast picked up an enormous number of viewers as it progressed. There was a football match on ITV, and during the breaks people were turning over and staying with *Tell Me On A Sunday*. Since so many missed the beginning, the BBC was inundated with requests for a repeat showing, so it was broadcast again three weeks later. 'None of us guessed how successful it would be,' says Webb. 'I got the *TV Times* award for best female singer on TV, and the show was broadcast around the world. It was the No.1 album in Germany and South Africa. But then those songs are just so great, each has its own value and style.' Don's lyrics, she adds, caught the female perspective with startling accuracy: 'I was amazed that a man wrote those lyrics; they say so much about women. There are even lines that I wish I'd used in my relationships. We had so many letters from people who felt that it was personal to them. One guy had been chucked by his girlfriend and had put the tape of the show through her door. They got back together because listening to the tape convinced her that he knew how she felt!'

The show propelled Webb into the limelight, and she needed a good manager. Don took her on at Lloyd Webber's suggestion, and looked out for her interests between 1979 and 1990, until he was working on *Sunset Boulevard* and was simply too busy. At that point he found her a new manager, and they have stayed close. She even refers to him as 'Uncle Don': 'Uncle Don and Auntie Shirl have always been there for me.'

The TV broadcast was to have been the triumphant end of *Tell Me On A Sunday*, but Cameron Mackintosh had an idea. At three-quarters of an hour long, it was too short to be staged in a theatre on its own. But there was another new Lloyd Webber piece around. After losing a bet with his famous cellist brother, Julian, Andrew had composed a piece for him, the catchy *Variations*, based on Paganini's *Caprice in A Minor*. It was written for cello and orchestra, but Mackintosh saw no reason why it shouldn't be perfect for a dancer. So, taking a line from *Tell Me On A Sunday* ('no big song and dance'), *Song And Dance* was created, with *Tell Me On A Sunday* lengthened to 50 minutes and *Variations* comprising the second half. As the *Song* part of the evening focused on one woman, Mackintosh balanced it by showcasing one man in the second. He did not have far to look, for one of the great successes of *Cats* had been the ex-Royal Ballet star who set the stage alight as Mr Mistoffelees – Wayne Sleep.

Song And Dance opened to ecstatic reviews at the Palace Theatre on 26 March 1982, where it remained for two years. The cleverest thing about the show was the balance. The first half was all intimacy and emotions, the second was flamboyance, glamour and pizazz.

Being Andrew Lloyd Webber's new lyricist, after he and Tim Rice had become the most successful double act British musical theatre had ever known, brought its own special challenges for Don. The media interest was intense; there was interview after interview, television and radio appearances. 'After he did *Cats*,' explains Tim Rice, 'Andrew became mega-famous.' And reporters wanted to know all about anyone he worked with.

Not that Don was phased. This was not remotely as bad as what he had faced working at the strip clubs during his early days as a comedian. At least the reporters actually *listened* to what he had to say. 'Having been a comedian, I'm not afraid to stand up and do all the interviews, which was a great relief to Andrew,' he says. 'It's important to do the publicity rounds when you're promoting something. Tim was always good at that, Andrew wasn't. He got better, but he was always very nervous. He's self-conscious in those situations.'

Don, who was to work with Lloyd Webber a great deal over the years, knows the composer very well – so well, in fact, that in 1992 he became godfather to the composer's son Alistair, going to the hospital when he was born. Since *Tell Me On A Sunday*, says Don with affection, he and Shirley have grown up with Andrew and his wives. Their lives have been intertwined.

'Andrew', he reflects, 'is a wonderful talent. When he plays me his new songs, I'm just gripped, every time. The way he uses the music, the key changes, are so unexpected and theatrical. It's not predictable, it's never safe. Sometimes you listen to music and feel that there was no blood or sweat in its creation. With Andrew, some of those expansive melodies, you really feel a heart at work.'

Lloyd Webber is also, according to Don, a complex character. Sometimes amusingly so. 'He's full of contradictions. After that initial meeting at my flat, he invited me to his house at Sydmonton. Shirley and I drove down there in the most horrible weather, all fog and rain, and you know what Jews and maps are like! Normally I'd have called it off, it was such a long way, and terrible travelling conditions. But it was Andrew and it was important, so we got into the car and set off.

'Andrew came out to greet us, and I couldn't believe it – he was in his shirt sleeves! It was winter beyond belief, Shirley and I were covered up in scarves, hats, you could hardly see us. And out he bounded with a cheery "Oh, hello!" as if it was a beautiful day. Oblivious to the freezing cold!

'Then there was another time in New York, when it was gloriously hot and we had an important meeting lined up. We stepped out the hotel, he stopped, registered the heat and said, "This is just not on." And he went back inside to the air conditioning, and *they* had to come to *him*!'

But the composer, reveals Black, has greater worries than the weather. 'Because of who he is, there's a forensic department waiting to dissect everything. He's very conscious of that, and often, when he plays me a tune, he'll ask in a worried way, "Does it sound like anything else?" I'm sure he has sleepless nights. That's his nature – to worry and to struggle with melodies.'

What is not often talked about, he stresses, is Lloyd Webber's knowledge in areas besides music. 'You can talk to him about gardening and you'd be amazed. At his place in the south of France he would take me around the garden and tell me all the names of everything. In Latin. Then he'd talk about the Budget, and say, "Well, of course clause 3E is ludicrous." He knows about banking and economics. He knows about architecture, about art, about wine. If he wasn't a composer, he could run the Bank of England, or be something at the Tate Gallery. He's a very well-read, learned guy.'

These days Lloyd Webber is much more than a composer. His company, the Really Useful Group, jointly owns around half of the major theatres in London, including the Palladium and the Theatre Royal, Drury Lane. It has record and magazine divisions. Lloyd Webber himself is now a peer (Lord Lloyd-Webber of Sydmonton – he was only allowed to keep the double-barrelled surname if he hyphenated it when using it with the title). To spin all these plates, Black says, he has developed the knack of getting to the point of an issue and making a decision fast. 'He's not long-winded. You can have a three-minute meeting with him and get it all done. It'll be, "Hello Don, coffee?", and then, "Right, this is it." And then it's done in minutes. Being a lyric-writer, that's what I like – compression, getting right to it.'

Of course, with such a high-pressure lifestyle comes great stress, and the composer is known for not being reticent if he thinks things are wrong. 'There is that side to him. I've seen him be furious with people,' admits Don. 'If things aren't ready, or a table hasn't been booked, he can really snap. He expects his office to run like a Rolls-Royce operation. He has people there to arrange these things, and doesn't want to have to worry about them. They're not what matter to him, so if they're not done he can really go for someone.'

As a lyricist, Black manages to avoid any encounters with the Lloyd Webber wrath. 'I've heard of instances when it's been said that he's threatened to withdraw his score if it's not being played properly. I've never wanted to get involved in that side of Andrew. Other people have to, directors like Trevor Nunn and Stephen Pimlott have to. But as a songwriter, well, he might argue about a couple of lines but that's his job as the composer, and it's not a matter for fire and brimstone.

'Other people have said to me, "Don't go near Andrew today because he's going mad. He's furious because the arrangement's not right, the orchestration's not right, he's saying they've misunderstood his score." And you realise that Andrew does have an empire, a global, far-reaching organisation. I write songs with him and we're friends, but he's got a lot of lives. Knowing when to leave is also very important.'

There has always been a great deal of press comment on Andrew Lloyd Webber, and the more hurtful remarks upset Black very much. 'When Frank Skinner said he was ugly on TV, or when some years ago Malcolm Williamson said that Andrew has never written eight bars of original music in his life. Scathing and horrible. And you often hear things like that, lacerating stuff to be said about any human being. And I have seen him when he is shattered by these things. But he hides it well, and friends and family are there to help him through them.' It is, Don feels, in Lloyd Webber's music that the pain comes through. 'Music is where he pours his heart out. His emotions come through then. You cannot write melodies like those in "As If We Never Said Goodbye" or "All I Ask Of You" unless you are feeling pain.'

However, Lloyd Webber also has a pronounced, sometimes quirky sense of fun. Once, on Concorde (he denied this story to me, but Don assures me that it is true), he comically pretended to be very upset that there was none of his music on the in-flight entertainment. Don laughed and then fell asleep. When he woke up, Lloyd Webber presented him with a letter he had written to the TV show *Jim'll Fix It*, asking the host Jimmy Savile to arrange for Concorde to start playing his music! It is, says Don, typical of his sense of humour.

There are the odd moments of unintentional humour, too. Don has never forgotten the time when, on completing the score for *Aspects Of Love*, Lloyd Webber suggested that they 'get a few mates around to hear it'. Don asked who he was thinking of, and his friend reeled off a few names – David Frost, the famous television personality, John Selwyn Gummer, the Conservative MP, Geoffrey Howe, then one of the most powerful members of Margaret Thatcher's Cabinet. Don said, "Fine, but what good will that do?" "Well," replied the composer, "at least we'll find out what Joe Public thinks of it."'

Song And Dance was going strong in the West End, and several actresses replaced Webb, including Gemma Craven and Sarah Brightman, who was later to become Andrew Lloyd Webber's second wife. (When she joined the show, she was given the gorgeous emotional number 'Unexpected Song', one of the best songs the pair ever wrote.) There was also Liz Robertson, Alan Jay Lerner's eighth wife. She was to be the final wife of the man who once told Don, 'I've supported more women than Playtex.' Lerner adored her, and went to every single performance that she did of *Song And Dance*. And at every single one of those performances he would sit and watch, and cry his eyes out. 'He was also very proud of *Tell Me On A Sunday*,' remembers its author. 'Very proud that I had gone from *Maybe That's Your Problem* to a hit of that magnitude.'

The decision was made to take it to New York. And as far as Don was concerned, it was the same old *Barmitzvah Boy* story all over again.

Richard Maltby was brought in to work with Don to expand the lyrics, and it was decided to use an American voice for the American audiences. Black was not happy. What had been his and Andrew's baby, raised and nurtured in their homes, with just the two of them, was now being pushed into a rebellious adolescence.

'I was very unhappy about what we did in America. But Andrew and Cameron thought it should be bigger, and should have an American in the lead, to tailor it for the Broadway audience. So you listen, you listen and you wonder, "Why do we need that – it worked so well in London?" But you do it, because the powers that be decide that's the way it should be. But in America the vital ordinariness went out of it.'

For the girl in *Tell Me On A Sunday*, the choice fell upon Bernadette Peters, an immensely appealing actress on her way to becoming the biggest box-office draw for musicals on Broadway, and the Great White Way's leading musicals diva. Don was not convinced. 'Suddenly we had Bernadette Peters, gorgeous to look at, but it was suddenly A Broadway Show. It had that glitzy veneer, which I hated because this was about a girl from Muswell Hill. And they all said, "She's gotta do something. Let's give her a job –she's a milliner!" So now she's selling hats to big stores and she's successful. They kept saying, "American audiences love a winner." And I kept thinking, "This is terrible, terrible." It became hokey. *Tell Me On A Sunday* is, at heart, honest. This wasn't.'

Peters won a Tony Award for her interpretation and the show ran for a very creditable 474 performances. It was a success, a big success, but Peters is not generally thought to have been as thrilling and as touching as Marti Webb in the role. Don certainly thought that, and was not surprised.

'I knew something was wrong at the beginning, when Bernadette – one of the nicest women I've ever met; she still asks after my children by name – asked me to show her Muswell Hill. I asked why. "Because I want to see where this girl comes from," she said.' The trip turned out to be an instructive, and rather off-putting, lesson in the American tendency for actors to research their roles deeply (some might say to within an inch of their lives). Don arranged for the actress Maureen Lipman, Jack Rosenthal's wife and a resident of Muswell Hill, to take them on a local tour.

'We spent the day there, and she kept asking things like, "What does the character's Dad do?" And I'd say, "Well, we don't talk about her Dad." She needed to know. "Could he have owned one of those sweet shops? How about that sweet shop?" she'd persist. I'd say, "Er, yeah." And she'd reply, "Great. That helps me." That's when I realised: she was having to consciously motivate herself to get the character. Call it method acting. Whatever. Marti never asked any of that. She *was* the girl, and that was it, and that was why there was a truth to it with her.'

In 2003, *Tell Me On A Sunday* was again expanded, to 80 minutes. It was updated – there are now lines about email, speed-dating, and 'Capped Teeth And Caesar Salad' has new targets, like Botox and plastic surgery ('When her bosoms droop 50 surgeons swoop') – and revived with five new songs in London's Gielgud Theatre, starring the popular TV star Denise Van Outen. More glamorous than Marti Webb, Van Outen still has that down-to-earth London character. 'With Denise,' says Don, 'the show has truth again.' Truth, yes, but with Van Outen's poster-girl looks it's also sexier. As the Really Useful Group's marketing people like to put it, it's more '*Sex And The City*' (when the show opened, some critics even felt that the star was simply too sexy to credibly have such a blighted love life).

For years there had been talk of reviving *Tell Me On A Sunday* in some form or another. There was even a mad-sounding rumour that it was to be expanded into a full-scale musical, with extra characters added. But it remained one of the composer's favourites among his shows, and needed only the right girl to come along. Van Outen came to Lloyd Webber's attention when she sang 'Take That Look Off Your Face' at the 2001 Royal Variety Show. In stark contrast to the enormous hype that been generated by the news that she was taking to the boards, the actress had made a lukewarm impression in her first West End leading role (in *Chicago*), but Lloyd Webber was impressed. So was his influential creative director at Really Useful, Tris Penna. 'She's a now-girl,' he enthused. 'She's just what we need.'

Black and Van Outen spent time together, so that he could try and personalise the show for her, just as he had with Marti Webb. 'Tell me about your love life,' he suggested. And out came all the stories about her partner, the Jamiroquai singer Jay Kay, what he was like to live with, the joys and the frustrations. 'Don and I had the whole tears-and-laughter experience as I told him about my entire life,' says Van Outen.

She told Don about Jay Kay's drink problem. And some of the images from her domestic life with him found their way into the show: 'You're asleep all day and you're up all night watching gangster films... You're a different man when you stop drinking. You can afford the Priory, why don't you go?'

Van Outen admits to an eerie symmetry between work and life. 'I had just finished a relationship with someone famous, and we were very much in the public eye. And now I was enacting aspects of that relationship in front of an audience every night. So it really got to me. I was in tears at the first preview and didn't know how on earth I'd manage 16 weeks of this. But the show is so good, it pulls you through.' Her on-stage emotions, she insists, were genuine. And with a modern girl in the updated show, it became about women of today.

'Denise is a completely different person to me,' says Marti Webb, 'and as times have changed, girls have changed. And the show has changed to reflect all of that. My girl had a bloke in America already when the show started, and she tended to fall into relationships. For Denise, it has become much more about a girl who actively goes out looking for dates. That's what girls do now.'

'I am Miss *Tell Me On A Sunday*,' enthuses Van Outen, 'just as every girl is. Flocks of twenty-somethings have come to me after the show and they've all identified with it. It's everything that women care all about. Every girl has dreams of a fairy-tale life, and a fairy-tale love.'

There are plans for the show to tour Australia, America – perhaps other territories. Denise Van Outen has put aside a year to work on it. *Tell Me On A Sunday* refuses to lie down, and it looks like someone, somewhere, will be making a song and dance about it for years to come.

Back in 1985, if Don was not happy with *Tell Me* on Broadway, it was still a success as far as audiences, critics and the moneymen were concerned. And that made it his first Broadway hit. Which was something. Something big. And it was not lost on him.

'When you come from where I come from, and you're walking around those numbered streets, and you're eating lunch at Sardi's, every day has a romantic strain to it. When they say, "Your show's a hit", you think, "Hey, I'm a hit on Broadway!" I feel like Mickey Rooney in those movies. Suddenly every day is an adventure, and it covers up all the scars from when things aren't going right.'

Given the success of *Tell Me On A Sunday* and the enthusiasm Andrew Lloyd Webber had displayed for their partnership, it came as a disappointment to Black when Lloyd Webber worked with another lyricist, Richard Stilgoe, for his next big musical, *Starlight Express*. After the departure of Tim Rice, in fact, the composer became famous for frequently changing lyricists, matching them to the projects in hand. It has become a standing joke among his writing partners. Don was once in his car on the way down to Sydmonton with Richard Maltby, and they saw a long traffic jam snaking in the opposite direction. 'Well,' remarked Black, 'it's just a bunch of Andrew's other lyricists.'

Even though Black has now written more with the composer than any other lyricist, apart perhaps from Rice (it's very close between the two), he still pines for the kind of long-standing relationship that Rodgers enjoyed with Hart and then Hammerstein, that John Kander has had with Fred Ebb (resulting in *Cabaret* and *Chicago*, among others), and that Lerner had with Loewe.

'Alan Lerner once said to me,' says Don, '"When you work together with the same person you know their strengths and their weaknesses, and it's better."' And he had known success with other people; he wrote *On A Clear Day You Can See Forever* with Burton Lane. I think if I had written everything with Andrew Lloyd Webber after *Tell Me On A Sunday*, or if after *Billy* I had stayed with John Barry and written ten shows with him, it would have been fascinating. As it is, I've written with over 100 people. So there's a kind of promiscuity to it, and there's positives and negatives to that. I've had success with people whom I would never otherwise have met. But to explore a creative partnership with someone over, say, four shows in a row – who knows, maybe we'd find something.'

The regular-partnership idea has, as he says, its pluses and minuses. Apart from anything else, personalities cannot help but come into it. Richard Rodgers had enormous stress dealing with the drunken antics of Larry Hart. Tim Rice saw his successful partnership with Lloyd Webber dissolve, but he later went on to write *Chess* with ex-Abba members Benny Andersson and Bjorn Ulvaeus, and *The Lion King* with Elton John, and he is sanguine. 'I seem to be permanently associated with Andrew because we started together. My initial thought for quite a while after splitting with him was that it was really bad. We had a good thing going and we could have been like Gilbert and Sullivan. But as the years have gone by I've worked with other people of that calibre. Had we stayed together, it probably would have got worse. A partnership is like a marriage, and it can get very tense.'

The Gilbert and Sullivan reference is telling. Those two gentlemen may have been England's greatest ever musical partnership, but they were frequently at loggerheads (each always believing that the other grabbed more of the headlines), and although they stayed partners for many years, Sullivan became increasingly unhappy frittering away his time on what he considered to be trivial comedies unworthy of his higher aspirations.

Elmer Bernstein, however, agrees with Don. He also would have liked a long-term partnership, one that was not merely on an ad hoc basis. However, he is practical. 'I'd absolutely love to have done that,' he says. 'We could have pushed each other and got better and better. Working with lots of different people keeps you on your toes, but for stage musicals particularly, a partnership is very healthy. However, today a Broadway musical can cost upwards of $10 million. So doing show after show is a thing of the past for most of us now. And to make the partnership work, you have to. The Gershwins, Rodgers and Hammerstein, all of those guys did show after show. Kander and Ebb may have had two big successes with *Chicago* and *Cabaret*, but they did one show every four years.'

So, while with *Starlight Express* Stilgoe joined the Lloyd Webber librettists' roll call (a list that was also later to include Charles Hart, Ben Elton and Christopher Hampton), Black got on with other projects. In 1983 he wrote a hit Christmas show with Abba's Benny Andersson and Bjorn Ulvaeus, called *Abbacadabra*. Featuring Abba songs with a new story line by Alain Boublil and new lyrics by Don – the plot is about a boy who gets sucked into a computer – this was a forerunner of the catalogue musicals which now so dominate the West End.

(In the last few years, the good citizens of Theatreland have variously been able to enjoy, or had to put up with, Queen's *We Will Rock You*, Abba's *Mamma Mia*, *Our House* from Madness, *Cliff – The Musical* and there are plenty of others in the works.) That same year the Birmingham Repertory Theatre mounted, finally, the first production of *Dear Anyone*, the album of which had so attracted Lloyd Webber. Jane Lapotaire starred as the agony aunt and, although not a long-runner, the soulful number 'I'll Put You Together Again' became a UK Top 20 hit for Hot Chocolate.

The mid-1980s saw a musical phenomenon of the small-screen kind. Soap opera stars suddenly all began revealing, in breathless profiles and interviews for teen mags like *Just Seventeen*, that all they ever wanted to be were pop idols. They were just lumbered with the acting as a way to make a crust, it seemed, and wouldn't somebody please help them to realise their *true* dreams by spending small fortunes on their heavily marketed albums. It did not work for everyone, thankfully. Stefan Dennis, who played the *Neighbours* bad (well, baddish) boy Paul, flopped with a leather-jacketed soft-rock single called 'Don't It Make Ya Feel Good?' EastEnders leading lady Letitia Dean never quite made the jump from Walford to long-term chart glory, despite singing 'I'm Your Venus' on *Top Of The Pops*.

But other *Neighbours* imports, Kylie Minogue and Jason Donovan, made it big. So, for a month or two, did *EastEnders*' Nick Berry (remember 'Every Loser Wins'?). And it had occurred to record-industry bosses that, not only did they have instant audiences by promoting soap stars, they were also sitting on some of the most recognisable and loved melodies in the country. OK, they were theme tunes, but with some decent lyrics and singers they could be hits.

Don was approached first of all to write words for Simon May and Leslie Osborn's tuneful, if by now over-familiar, *EastEnders* theme. What he came up with was a clever idea that encapsulated the idea of the programme – 'Anyone Can Fall In Love'.

Anyone can fall in love.
That's the easy part, you must keep it going.
Anyone can fall in love.
Over the years it has to keep growing.
Sun and rain,
Joy and pain,
There's highs, there's lows,
We've no way of knowing.

Anyone can fall in love.
That's not hard to do, it isn't so clever.
Anyone can fall in love,
But you must make the love last forever.
Who can say,
Love will stay?
It's up to you,
Don't hide what needs showing.

Anyone can fall in love.
That's the easy part, you must keep it going.
Everyone can fall in love,
But you must make the love last forever more.

It's a skilful job, skilfully packaged by the programme's bosses, who picked the show's biggest draw, Anita Dobson (who played the volatile pub landlady Angie Watts), to front it. At that stage Dobson could just have hummed the tune and it probably would have done pretty well, but the show's fans (which then numbered the vast majority of the British population) bought the single in droves and it made the Top 5. Soon Anita Dobson was the only pub landlady in the country to star on *Top Of The Pops*. Not that she was any stranger to the pop music scene – she was shacked up with Queen's shaggy-haired guitarist, Brian May.

The pop world almost always does business by following the latest craze (occasionally someone will come along and start a craze, but then everyone will follow them for the next year and a half). So it was only natural that, where *EastEnders* had led, rival soap *Howard's Way* would follow. Its theme tune was also by the *EastEnders* composer Simon May and, since Don had done such a professional job for the first record, it was he who was approached for the follow-up.

Sung by Marti Webb in 1986, 'Always There' (as the *Howard's Way* theme became in its pop incarnation) reached No.13 in the charts. Again, Black did a clever job, using images of seafaring(the series centres around a boat), and manages to stay the right side of cheesy – just. But then it was a cheesy phenomenon.

TV themes were bigger then: every record store would sell compilations of them, and these programmes were the biggest things on the box. After the inflated pomp of *Dynasty* and *Dallas* the kitchen-sink realism of *EastEnders* and, to a lesser extent, *Howard's Way* caught the public's imagination.

Don, Shirley and the boys were now living in a plush four-bedroom flat in Basil Street, in London's luxurious Knightsbridge area. Comfortable, even luxurious, they had completed the cliché of 'rags to riches' from their early days. Yet they never lost touch with their roots. However, a partnership from those earliest days was about to come abruptly to an end. Matt Monro was ill. He was dying.

12 Farewell To A Friend, And On To *Aspects*

In 1985, a chapter of Don's life closed. Matt Monro, comrade-at-arms and dear friend since those first days in Tin Pan Alley, died aged 54.

The previous year Matt had been diagnosed with cancer of the liver, and with characteristic courage he continued to work. 'I've never met anyone braver than Matt,' says Don. 'Even after the diagnosis, for a long time he never missed a show. Until it caught up with him.'

Matt's doctors decided to try a liver transplant, so he checked into Harefield Hospital in Cambridge. His wife Mickie was with him. Don and Shirley went to visit. As they entered, Matt was his usual self, looking up at them and cheerfully enquiring, 'Hello son, how you doing? How was the traffic – all right?' Don said that they had popped by to wish him luck and that they would stay a minute and then let him rest. Matt looked astonished. 'Where are you rushing to?' He insisted that they stay for a chat. So this man, who was about to undergo major surgery, laughed and joked with them as though he had not a care in the world.

After some time a nurse came in to administer the premed. It was almost time. Affably, Matt took the pills the nurse gave him and swallowed them, then turned to Don. 'Now look, son,' he said, 'they say this operation will take about six or seven hours. So there's no point in you both hanging about here. Why don't you go home, and I'll give you a shout when I get up.' Don was amazed. 'I couldn't believe how casual he was. He was about to have a liver transplant and he was acting as if he was having a haircut!' At one point, Matt began talking about plans for a six-month holiday in France, something he wanted to do when the operation was over. They continued talking and laughing, until the pills took effect, and in mid-sentence Matt fell asleep.

Don, Shirley and John Ashby, who had also come to visit, walked across the road to the University Arms pub for something to eat. And something unforgettable happened. As they sat down, Don's eyes widened and he said, 'Listen to that.' The speakers in the restaurant had started to play one of Matt's biggest hits, the heartbreaking song of farewell, 'Softly As I Leave You'. The quiet, tender lyrics and the voice they knew so well floated across the room:

Softly, I will leave you softly,
For my heart would break if you should wake and see me go.
So I leave you softly, long before you miss me,
Long before your arms can beg me stay,
For one more hour or one more day.
After all the years, I can't bear the tears to fall,
So softly as I leave you there.

Don froze. They all did. 'I felt a cold shiver run through me, we all fell silent and tearful. It was a terrible moment,' he says. 'A hell of a moment.'

'I don't know if it was to the exact second or not,' adds John Ashby, 'but during the operation they opened Matt up and found he was riddled with cancer. Removing the liver would have been useless. They left it in, and he died about six weeks later.'

The operation was aborted after seven hours. When he woke up, his first words to Mickie were, 'What's it like having a hero in the family?' The doctors had told her to wait before revealing that the operation had failed, but eventually, of course, she told him the truth.

Knowing he had only weeks left to live, Matt went back to what he loved most – singing. His last concert was at London's Barbican Centre. He gave it everything he had left, and the audience responded with a long standing ovation. 'People still talk about that concert,' says Don. 'He looked so pale, but he was fantastic.' It was a fitting curtain-call for one of the country's best-loved entertainers.

His last days were spent in the Cromwell Hospital in Kensington. Don went to visit him, and at this point they all knew it was really just a matter of time. 'I opened the door, and he was in bed smoking a cigarette and watching Steve Davis playing snooker on the TV. He looked terrible, but cheerfully said, "'Allo, son. Watch this." We sat watching the snooker together.

'After a while, the comedian Bernie Winters, a great friend of Matt's, came in and joined us. And there we sat with him, for hours. At one point Bernie and I were chatting in the hall while Matt slept. The nurse went to check him, came out and told us that he'd just gone. Bernie went in to see him. I couldn't bring myself to do it.'

He was buried at Golders Green Cemetery in a showbiz state funeral. There were hundreds of people there, including dozens of stars, all gathered to pay tribute to this man who gave his life to the joy of song. There was a real sense of bereavement among the show-business community, and the messages flooded in – from Tony Bennett, Bing Crosby, Paul McCartney, Michael Jackson, Quincy Jones, Shirley Bassey. Frank Sinatra wrote that 'If I had to choose three of the finest male vocalists in the singing business, Matt would be one of them…. He will be missed very much not only by myself, but by his fans all over the world.' Sammy Davis Jr – who had taken to paying tribute to Matt in his concerts by singing one of his favourite of Don's songs, 'If I Never Sing Another Song' – wrote, 'He was my friend and he was one of the best singers I have ever heard. From my point of view in both categories he was very special.'

And Don? Hardly a week goes by when he doesn't talk about Matt. Hardly a day goes by when he doesn't think about him. The rest of us? It's a cliché to say that the singer will sing on through the wonderful recordings he left us behind. It's also a truism to say that the world would be much the poorer if he hadn't.

The years 1987 and 1988 constituted one of those patches people wisely call 'a learning experience'. Except that when you've had success and things drop off a bit, you are not really in the mood for a lesson. It's not that the work was drying up – far from it. But stage musicals are, as Don had already found, notoriously difficult to get right. How do you get them to work? What are the rules? Who knows? Not Cameron Mackintosh (don't mention *Moby Dick* to him), not Don Black, and certainly not me. Some people, like Mackintosh, get them right more often than they get them wrong, but (as they will tell you) it is often as much a matter of pure instinct as of following any guidelines. 'All you can do', says Don, 'is make certain that you don't repeat yourself. Always try and do something different.'

Does a revival count as repeating yourself? Not if the show was never right in the first place. Then a revival can afford an opportunity to revisit, rework and get it all right. Mackintosh did that with *Martin Guerre* (too late for the vast commercial success of its writers' previous shows, *Les Mis* and *Miss Saigon*, but the critics were convinced). The revival of *Barmitzvah Boy* got it all wrong. (Or, rather, as I mentioned in Chapter 10, they made the same mistakes they had almost ten years earlier, but on a larger scale. And in New York.)

So it was a disappointed Black who returned home. And if *he* was disappointed, imagine how Jack Rosenthal felt, enduring as much verbal abuse from Jule Styne this time around as he had in London. Don was not to find relief with his next show.

Budgie, based on a hit TV series starring Adam Faith as a Cockney conman, had great credentials. Faith agreed to reprise his role, the *Billy Liar* team of Keith Waterhouse and Willis Hall wrote the book, and the composer was the popular American songwriter – of dozens of classics such as 'Save The Last Dance For Me', 'Can't Get Used To Losing You' and 'Viva Las Vegas' – Mort Shuman. Don not only wrote the lyrics, but he also co-produced (with Laurence Myers).

Adam Faith, who died suddenly in 2003, was not easy to work with. Don liked and respected him, but as a producer he was often frustrated. 'He worked hard on the show. But when it came to promoting *Budgie*, Adam was difficult. He used to have this expression. Every time I asked him to do an interview somewhere, he would say, "I run my life on the credo, 'What would Marlon Brando do?'" And usually he concluded that, "No, love. Brando wouldn't do it, would he?"'

One day Don joked that Brando was on breakfast television. They both laughed, but Don was feeling the frustration.

It reached fever pitch one night during previews. Tension was riding high and the pressure of getting the word out about the show was immense. A charity night for Princess Anne was a much-needed shot in the arm in terms of publicity. However, when the cast lined up on the stage to be introduced to the Princess by Don, he was told that Adam Faith would not come out of his dressing room. It was not an anti-monarchist statement; he just did not like the idea of waiting in line to meet Princess Anne. 'If she wants to see me,' he told Don, 'she can come to my dressing room.'

This was a delicate moment. If word got out that Faith was refusing to come out, it would be all the over the next day's paper. Publicity like that the show did not need. Don made up an emergency toothache and told Princess Anne that he had rushed off to hospital, news she received graciously (though one wonders whether she could possibly have believed it). But Faith's stubbornness created a lot of bad feeling. 'He was a lovely fella most of the time,' says Don, 'but he had these funny ways of looking at things.'

Budgie opened on 18 October 1988 at London's Cambridge Theatre, and three months later it closed. One or two decent reviews and some good songs (the toe-tapping 'There Is Love And There Is Love' among them) were not enough to save it. The reported losses were in the region of £1 million.

At this point, there was one man who could meaningfully claim to know the rules, the only composer who could credibly convince a bank manager that one of his shows was a sure investment. That man, of course, was Andrew Lloyd Webber. But even he had not been completely untouched by failure. His only pre-*Evita* stage work away from Tim Rice had been 1975's *By Jeeves*, based on the PG Wodehouse stories he so loved. Alan Ayckbourn had penned the lyrics, but the show had limped to a close a mere 38 performances after it had opened. It had greater success in a decently received 1996 West End revival, but despite high hopes its Broadway début in 2001 was not auspicious. Sometimes, a show that's broke just can't be fixed.

Next to his few failures, however, Lloyd Webber's financial success dwarfs that of any other composer. While Don was toiling to save *Barmitzvah Boy* and *Budgie*, his *Tell Me On A Sunday* collaborator was enjoying the biggest hit of his career to date – for that matter, the most commercially successful musical in history. On 9 October 1986, Her Majesty's Theatre in London saw the opening of *Phantom Of The Opera*. The venue is still selling tickets for the show 17 years later.

Phantom – here come the statistics – has grossed over $3 billion. It has been seen in more than 91 cities. It has taken more than twice the amount of money taken by the highest-grossing film ever, *Titanic*. The album has sold over 25 million copies, to say nothing of the other merchandising spinoffs – T-shirts, jumpers, mugs that suddenly sport a *Phantom* mask when you pour hot liquid into them. All of which is mightily impressive.

These days Don is sanguine about the fact that he was not asked to write the lyrics for *Phantom*. He was, he says, 'disappointed'. In a rather theatrical irony, Lloyd Webber picked the 25-year-old Charles Hart, a writer Black himself had discovered when he chaired the Vivian Ellis Award for young talent in musical theatre. Don recommended this youngster to the composer, and suddenly Hart had been given the break of his life. It's almost right out of *A Star Is Born*, except that Black and Hart were not sleeping together (James Mason and Judy Garland, they are not), and neither of their subsequent lives has turned out the way they would in a musical.

Charles Hart, who should have gone on to great things, did a few shows and then has been little heard of since. On the other hand, *Phantom* has ensured that he never needs to work again if he doesn't want to, which reminds me of a remark Stephen Sondheim once made about someone whom I thought could be 'the future of musical theatre'.

'He's too rich to be the future,' replied Sondheim. To achieve it, you have to really want it. And often that means really needing it.

Don, on the other hand, had much of his best work still to do. And some of it came in his next show. He was called back into the fold for Andrew Lloyd Webber's follow-up to *Phantom*, which was to be a musical of a little-known novel by David Garnett called *Aspects Of Love*.

This was a surprise to most theatre-lovers. *Phantom* was a show on a scale to match its success. Gaston Leroux's novel, from which it was taken, is a classic – it's Gothic, set in the vast underground labyrinth of the Paris Opera House. The lead characters are an opera singer and a monster with the heart of an artist. Lloyd Webber had supplied a show that was more opera than musical. Hal Prince conjured up a magical production with grand masquerades, clouds of atmospheric dry ice and, famously, a chandelier which threatens to fall on the stalls. Before the audience members even got into their seats, they were bombarded with stalls full of merchandise (*Phantom* was the first show to fully realise the potential of this area, thanks to the marketing brilliance of its producer, Cameron Mackintosh). It was seen as big, outsize, an event.

Even before *Phantom*, though, Lloyd Webber's shows had become events. *Jesus Christ Superstar* had been a big, and controversial, rock opera. *Starlight Express* featured actors on roller-skates racing around the theatre! *Song And Dance*? Well, even though *Tell Me On A Sunday* was intimate, the idea of a one-woman show coupled with a dance extravaganza was novel.

But *Phantom* topped the lot. Consequently, whatever Lloyd Webber chose to do next was expected to be of a similar magnitude. The papers were full of speculation as to what it would be. Another famous novel (*Les Misérables* had opened the year before *Phantom* so classic books were the thing)? A theme-park experience to rival *Starlight*?

With a defiance of expectation that has characterised his career, Andrew Lloyd Webber decided to go intimate – with a book precious few of us had ever even heard of.

Garnett's novel tells of the romantic entanglements between a teenager (Alex) and the actress (Rose) who captivates him. Things get complicated when Alex's wealthy, worldly uncle George also takes a shine to her.

If Don was surprised at the choice of subject, once he read it he saw what had drawn the composer to it. 'It's set in Montpellier and the south of France, and Andrew's childhood was spent in all of those places. It was a very personal story to him. And it is very Andrew, when you know him. It uses his language. The Bloomsbury set and all that, that's all very him.'

There were early plans for the director Trevor Nunn to write the lyrics (it was Nunn, after all, who had come up with verses for the only song in *Cats* not taken from the original poems – 'Memory' was the biggest hit of the show). Scotching these plans, Black was asked how he felt about working with Charles Hart. Naturally, Lloyd Webber wanted to return to the partner who had helped him to create such a hit with *Phantom*, but this piece was about love on a domestic scale – something he knew Don Black does better than everybody.

That was not all. Don also knew how to deliver hits that would work outside of the show. As Lloyd Webber says, 'I didn't think that Charlie Hart could do that kind of lyric, the kind that works outside of the theatre. It was Richard Stilgoe, not Charlie, who came up with a lot of the memorable titles for *Phantom*, though Charlie then shaped them. And I wanted to keep Charlie on board because, just as I knew these characters from my upbringing, so did he.'

'I met Charles,' says Don, 'and, apart from the fact that he had never heard of Frankie Laine, we got on very well. We had a laugh.'

The two worked well together. He adds: 'Working with anyone on lyrics is a very strange process. You have to be a certain type of person to do it, and not many people are like me. I'm a very open person. You have to learn to think aloud. I said to Charles at the beginning, "I'm going to say some things that are absolutely diabolical. And vice versa. The first rule is absolute honesty. If you think it stinks, you've got to tell me.'"

He tried hard not to impose his own technique on the younger man, wanting to catch 'a boy's effervescence and enthusiasm and natural outpouring'. It was a telling insight, considering that *Aspects* is about love at two stages of life – youth and middle-age. As the two male characters discover love from the perspective of their two different generations, so did Hart and Black write the show from theirs. They also found complementary strengths. Don concentrated on the big songs, coming up with the titles and the ballads, while Hart pushed the drama forward. And there are some wonderful lyrics in the show. Rose's moment of revelation, when she shows how scared she is of being alone, is elegantly caught in 'Anything But Lonely'.

Anything but lonely,
Anything but empty rooms.
There's so much in life to share,
What's the sense when no-one else is there?

Anything but lonely,
Anything but only me.
Quiet years in too much space,
That's the thing that's hard to face.

And you have a right to go,
But you should also know,
That I won't be alone for long.

Long days with nothing said,
Are not what lie ahead.
I'm sorry but I'm not that strong.

Anything but lonely,
Anything but passing time.
Lonely's what I'll never be,
While there's still some life in me.

And I'm still young don't forget,
It isn't over yet,
So many hearts for me to thrill.

If you're not here to say,
How good I look each day,
I'll have to find someone who will.

Anything but lonely,
Anything but empty rooms.
There's so much in life to share,
What's the sense when no-one else is there?

Nunn, returning to his familiar role, agreed to direct. Michael Ball – who had been so impressive as the romantic male lead Marius in Nunn's production of *Les Mis* – had caught the composer's eye even more when he moved to the cast of *Phantom*. There was one question. Alex was a complex role. Could Ball act?

'I had to audition for Trevor Nunn,' says Ball. 'Actually we workshopped, he made me do sections from *Henry V* and *Romeo And Juliet*. It was a fascinating experience. He wanted to see whether I could take direction.' The director was convinced, and Ball's name went on the cast sheet.

For George, Nunn needed someone urbane, sophisticated and attractive. Who better than the most sophisticated of James Bonds, Roger Moore? Moore had never previously acted in a musical, and the newspapers were delighted with the casting coup. In *Phantom*, Lloyd Webber had turned Michael Crawford into a singing star. (He, of course, had been in *Billy* and Cy Coleman's *Barnum*, but that was as an actor with an attractive voice; but for *Phantom* he developed a fuller, richer sound, and Crawford afterwards was in great demand to give concerts, especially in America.) Would *Aspects* do the same for Moore?

The casting of Rose was crucial. Auditions were held, and Lloyd Webber tells the story of one young hopeful who caught the judges' eyes. In fact, she was so stunning that they could not take their eyes off her. As Catherine Zeta-Jones confidently walked into the room and stood before Black, Hart, Nunn and Lloyd Webber, they were struck by her beauty. She started to sing and, as the movie *Chicago* has now made evident to millions, displayed a gorgeous, strong voice. She had just finished a London production of *42nd Street* where, as second understudy to the lead, she had been required to go on for the two ailing girls. The producer had been in that night and, amazed, promoted her to the main role for the rest of the run. Now *Aspects* could be the show to launch her officially. Hurriedly, the men huddled in whispered conference. It was obvious they were watching a born star. They did not want to let her go. 'We've got to sign her up,' said composer and director. Don shook his head. 'Why not?' asked the astounded Lloyd Webber. 'She's perfect! She sings, she acts, she looks unbelievable!' Patiently, Don explained that the entire plot depended on this woman being left alone at the end, on Alex leaving her. 'If you cast Catherine Zeta-Jones,' he said, 'the entire audience will be thinking, "Go on, Alex. Are you mad? Give her one!"' Reluctantly, his colleagues agreed. *Aspects Of Love*, meanwhile, went ahead without her and Ann Crumb landed the part of Rose.

While the show was still being written, Michael Ball and Sarah Brightman were touring the UK with an Andrew Lloyd Webber greatest-hits concert. I went to see it the night it reached Bournemouth's International Centre. At the end, Ball raised his arms to stop the applause and held up some loose sheet music. 'This', he announced, 'is a song from Andrew's new show, which will be called *Aspects Of Love*. I've only just got the song, so it's hot off the press, and this will be its world première.' Holding the sheet music in front of him to read the words, he began to sing 'Love Changes Everything'. By the time he reached the final B flat, the audience were on their feet, cheering and calling for an encore. Ball looked round, clearly moved. Standing near the entrance I spotted Lloyd Webber, and he was smiling.

'That B flat wasn't originally there,' remembers Ball. 'We'd only just got the song, and when I rehearsed with Andrew and Don it simply ended on a low note. I said to them, "It's got to have a bigger ending." So Andrew played a B flat on the piano and said, "Do you think you can get up there?" "You bet!" I replied, and sung it straight out.'

As soon as he heard it, Ball knew that 'Love Changes Everything' was a winner. 'I couldn't get the tune out of my head. And the lyrics were exactly right. Simple, almost childlike and precisely what was needed for this teenage boy.'

'Love Changes Everything' was to be the making of Michael Ball, and the show's hit song. Don had delivered the chart hit that Lloyd Webber so wanted.

Love,
Love changes everything.
Hands and faces,
Earth and sky.
Love,
Love changes everything.
How you live and,
How you die.

Love,
Can make the summer fly,
Or a night,
Seem like a lifetime.

Yes, love,
Love changes everything,
Now I tremble,
At your name.
Nothing in the
World will ever
Be the same.

Love,
Love changes everything,
Days are longer,
Words mean more.
Love,
Love changes everything,
Pain is deeper,
Than before.

Love,
Will turn your world around.

And that world,
Will last forever.

Yes, love,
Love changes everything,
Brings you glory,
Brings you shame.
Nothing in the
World will ever
Be the same.

Off,
Into the world we go.
Planning futures,
Shaping years.
Love,
Bursts in and suddenly,
All our wisdom
Disappears.

Love,
Makes fools of everyone.
All the rules
We make are broken.

Yes, love,
Love changes everyone,
Live or perish,
In its flame.
Love will never,
Never let you
Be the same.

'Love Changes Everything' took Michael Ball to No.2 in the British charts (rather cruelly, it twice touched No.1, but midweek, so it did not show on the weekly chart update), and made him not only a household name, but one of British musical theatre's few genuinely bankable stars, alongside Michael Crawford, Elaine Paige and, perhaps, Jonathan Pryce. Only these four performers can guarantee a good box-office advance purely on the strength of their name (not counting pop or TV stars, who are often short of stage experience, moonlighting on the strength of their celebrity).

'When the song came out, Trevor took me aside,' says Ball. 'He said, "You've got a choice. You can either be a singer and make records, or you can go into the legitimate theatre. But not both. The public won't let you. You'll be pigeon-holed." He said it was either the theatre career or the fame and glory of singing. So I went for the fame and glory! Cheap turn that I am!'

There was no time for that pursuit just yet, however. 'Love Changes Everything' hit the charts during rehearsals when, on top of all the media scrutiny, a crisis broke.

Roger Moore was quitting. And Michael Ball, who had become close friends with Moore, was the first in the company to know. 'I could see it coming. Roger was badly handled by the production team. He was a huge star, who was taking an enormous risk that he had no need to take. He had never done a musical before, hadn't even been on stage since his very early years. And I could see his confidence gradually eroding. He was floundering and was not being helped. There was so much pressure on all of us and rewrites flying around everywhere. Everyone was taking care of their own little areas and ignoring Roger's distress.'

Ball remains convinced that Moore would have been ideal as George, but however much he tried to convince him the older man had made his decision. In his own mind he was not up to the part. 'Opening night was not that far off. We were already into the technical rehearsals,' says Ball. 'It knocked us all for six.'

It was a blow to lose their major star, but Kevin Colson stepped into the breach and delivered an assured, dignified performance. Assured on stage, but behind the scenes he was, according to Ball, less serene. 'Kevin Colson was so nervous he developed a huge mouth abscess!' Moore walked off. The show went on.

Aspects was every bit as operatic as *Phantom*, but with a chamber-music feel to it. The orchestral textures are delicate, the waltzes and duets seductive. Every so often, Lloyd Webber launches into full-blooded

Puccinian arias such as 'Love Changes Everything', which opens and closes the evening. The critics were mixed, everyone was surprised. 'Never expect the expected from Andrew Lloyd Webber,' began the *Daily Mail*'s influential critic Jack Tinker in his review. 'This is uncharted territory on so many fronts. Not least the theme which floats through fast-shifting passions and long-term affections which effectively bind together five people across three generations; a sort of *la ronde en famille*.' Posing the question as to whether the *Phantom* composer had pulled off another multi-million-dollar smash, he concludes: 'The fact is that he has achieved something far more subtle, possibly even more rewarding.' In fact Tinker, like many, criticised Nunn's production for its overextravagance, for being heavy-handed where a light touch was called for.

Riding on the back of *Phantom*, *Aspects Of Love* opened with a £2 million box-office advance. If the show proved not to be a perennial money-spinner like its predecessor, its writers never expected it to be. New York never 'got it' when it went to Broadway in 1990. (In what Michael Ball says is the worst review he has ever read, so-called 'Butcher of Broadway' Frank Rich tore into the show, comparing its emotional impact to a meeting at the bank.) On Broadway it only played 377 performances, but has a great many admirers. Indeed, its reputation seems to have grown over the years. And, although commentators tend to talk of the show as having flopped, it still ran for three years at London's Prince of Wales Theatre. 'I wish all of my shows would run for three years, thank you very much,' grins Don.

The truth is that *Aspects* did not quite work because it was an intimate story in a giant West End theatre. Lloyd Webber admits this. But there are no medium-sized theatres suitable for musicals in London, a fact UK producers are always complaining about.

Another truth is that Lloyd Webber could not resist searching for 'the hit song' in *Aspects*. Well, he got his hit song. But the one or two big moments tend to stand out from the rest. 'You see, he couldn't decide whether to go the Puccini route, or the Offenbach route,' commented Jule Styne jovially to Don on the opening night. 'He went the Puccini route. But he should have gone the Offenbach route.'

Nevertheless, it is an admirable, enjoyable and affecting musical, with lovable numbers like 'Seeing Is Believing' and 'A Memory of A

Happy Moment'. It's just that it could have been a *great* one. Still, they came close, and (however the saying goes) that's worth a cigar.

13 *Sunset*'s Sunrise

After *Aspects*, Lloyd Webber could see the career that was opening up for Michael Ball, and he asked Don to take care of him. But what had worked with Matt, and then for a few years with Marti Webb, never really clicked with Michael, as both men admit.

'It gets in the way,' admits Don. 'Artists are very demanding, even if they're not demanding. They should have attention. And you've got to spend hours discussing billing, the act and details like that. Michael is the most wonderful guy. As a person, as a talent. He's a joy to be with. He was demanding, but not in a nasty way. Whomever you manage expects you to talk to them ten times a day, and so they should. But for me that all became a waste of a day when I'd rather spend my time writing songs.'

Don wrote more songs for Ball. They did the 1992 Rugby World Cup anthem together, 'No More Steps To Climb' (composed by Rod Argent), and Ball recorded 'Tell Me On A Sunday' for his first album. Ball counts the lyricist as one of his great friends, but their manager–client relationship never worked.

'Don is a very calming influence,' says Ball. 'That was invaluable on *Aspects*, with all that enormous passion everywhere. Charles Hart was feeling the pressure after the huge success of *Phantom*, Andrew's barking mad as always, and then you had Don – unbelievably calm. He must have a Dorian Gray-style painting up in his attic somewhere!'

When it came to management, though, sometimes Ball wished that Black were a little *less* calm. 'He always had so much going on, 17 projects at once. And at that point in my career I needed someone to focus just on me. I was recording my first album, we'd had a lot of trouble with it, and finally we were ready to hear it all back. Don couldn't come because, he said, it was the last episode of his favourite TV show, *GBH*! The writing was on the wall.'

So the two parted company and have been better friends ever since. Everyone seems to have their favourite Don Black line and Michael Ball never tires of hearing Don's habitual parting comment, 'All right, love, I'm off into legend.'

Between *Aspects Of Love* and their next full-scale musical, Black and Lloyd Webber kept themselves busy. The next project they worked on together was a song for the 1992 Olympics in Barcelona. They came up with 'Amigos Para Siempre (Friends For Life)' :

(SARAH BRIGHTMAN):
    I don't have to say,
    A word to you.
    You seem to know,
    Whatever mood I'm going through.
    Feels as though,
    I've known you forever.

(JOSÉ CARRERAS):
    You,
    Can look into my eyes and see,
    The way I feel,
    And how,
    The world is treating me.
    Maybe I have known you forever.

(BOTH):
    Amigos para siempre,
    Means you'll always be my friend.
    Amigos para siempre,
    Means a love that cannot end.
    Friends for life,
    Not just a summer or a spring.
    Amigos para siempre.
    I feel you near me,
    Even when we are apart,
    Just knowing you are in this world,
    Can warm my heart.

Friends for life,
Not just a summer or a spring.
Amigos para siempre.

(SARAH BRIGHTMAN):
We share memories,
I won't forget,
And we'll share more.
My friend,
We haven't started yet.
Something happens,
When we're together.

(JOSÉ CARRERAS):
When,
I look at you,
I wonder why,
There has to come,
A time when we must say goodbye.
I'm alive when we are together.

(BOTH):
Amigos para siempre,
Means you'll always be my friend.
Amigos para siempre,
Means a love that cannot end.
Friends for life,
Not just a summer or a spring.
Amigos para siempre.

Sarah Brightman, by this time Lady Lloyd Webber, joined the tenor José Carreras for the vocals. An odd mix? Well, yes and no. Brightman had a proper soprano voice, as she showed in various Lloyd Webber works, not least *Tell Me On A Sunday,* but more famously in *Requiem* and *Phantom Of The Opera.* Carreras was already massively famous as one of the world's great tenors, but not yet the superstar that the 'Three Tenors' phenomenon was to make him (at which point the 'supertenor' label was attributed to him and his high-C-hitting comrades Luciano Pavarotti and Placido Domingo). He was carving out a niche in crossover records, and had by this time made the big-selling but utterly ludicrous recording of Leonard Bernstein's *West Side Story*, in which the Spanish tenor sang the all-American boy Tony, and the Kiwi soprano Kiri Te Kanawa sang the Puerto Rican Maria. Talk about loopy casting! Just as Carreras had failed to sound remotely American when crooning, albeit most beautifully ('De mos' beautiful soun' dat I ever hyurd, Maria'), Black almost pulled his hair out at the way he mangled his English lyrics.

The strangest thing, he found, was that Carreras speaks English beautifully, but that it never translates to his singing. 'I couldn't understand it,' he says. 'He understood the lyrics, and when he spoke them he showed a feel for the lines. But then he starts singing and it all goes out the window. The man speaks English like Prince Charles and sings as if he's never heard the language before!'

Black later worked with José Carreras on another project. Tenors are supposed to already have all the best tunes, but this one wanted more. Not content with the tenorial canon, Carreras wanted to record a selection of the most famous orchestral interludes. This meant that they needed words and, since the biggest market was English, Don was called upon to supply them. The album was called *Passion*. 'He is a lovely man, and so I enjoyed the prospect of doing more with him. But, again, you do wonder why you bother spending all night writing, because English becomes nearly incomprehensible when he sings it.'

The other significant Lloyd Webber commission of that period was a new song for *Starlight Express*. By 1992, the show had proved itself one of Lloyd Webber's long-runners, becoming in that year the second longest-running British musical, after *Cats*. But the thing about children's entertainment is that kids are smart. They are also often far more hip and up-to-the-minute than adults, so if something feels outdated they will be among the first to pick up on it.

Starlight was amongst other things a parody of musical styles, so it was imperative those styles be recognisable to the audience. And, after eight years, its composer felt it was losing touch. So he ordered a major revamp, and drafted in Black to write a central love song. He came up with 'Next Time You Fall In Love'.

(Pearl):

> I guess I'm not too good at keeping love alive for long,
> I think I've found the answers but the answer's always wrong.
> My first love was my true love and it should have been my last.
> The only time I'm happy's when I'm dreaming in the past.
> Next time you fall in love,
> It better be with me,
> The way it used to be.
> Back then was when,
> We touched the starlight
>
> Sometimes you turn away from what your heart tells you is right,
> And so you settle for whatever gets you through the night.
> The flame you thought was dead may suddenly begin to burn,
> And broken hearts can be repaired, that's something that you learn.
>
> Next time you fall in love,
> It better be with me,
> The way it used to be.
> Back then was when,
> We touched the starlight.

(Rusty):

> I've re-lived every moment that I ever shared with you,
> What fools we were to end a dream that looked like coming true.
> Next time you fall in love,
> It better be with me,
> The way it used to be.

(Both):

> Back then was when,
> We touched the starlight.'

'Next Time You Fall In Love' felt fresh and was a lovely song. When I took my 5-year-old cousin Ellen to the show (*Starlight Express* being one of those shows, like *The Lion King* and *Chitty Chitty Bang Bang*, that should only be judged with an attendant child), she declared that her favourite character was Pearl. 'Why?' I asked. 'Because she's really in love,' she insisted, with a knowledgeable pout. 'How do you know?' She looked at me like I was crazy, or possibly dimmer than she had hoped. 'Because she sang that song with Rusty, and it's obvious.'

The number gave the musical's lead locomotives a human dimension, and human feelings that had understandably been lacking in a musical about trains. And it's not me saying that. Never argue with 5-year-old girls. You're on a hiding to nothing.

His next full musical with Lloyd Webber was as big as they come, in terms of cost, size and pressure. Don was about to tackle a legend, one of Hollywood's most famous – *Sunset Boulevard*.

The idea had first come up years earlier, after *Tell Me On A Sunday*. The composer arranged a private screening of the film in Dean Street in London's Soho. Don needed no reminder of the Billy Wilder *noir* classic (starring Gloria Swanson and William Holden) – it was one of his favourites, but any excuse to see it again... After the film, Lloyd Webber gave Don two tunes, and Don went back home and immediately started writing. He came up with two songs: one tune was a swirling melody that he instantly recognised as one of Lloyd Webber's best, called 'One Star'; the other was for the sinister butler, entitled 'Madam Takes A Lot Of Looking After'.

The seeds were sown. And, even though the project was shelved for so long, it never went away. ('One Star', incidentally, did indeed achieve recognition as one of Lloyd Webber's great tunes, but in another musical, with different lyrics. Everyone now knows it as 'Memory'. As a matter of fact, Don and several other lyricists had a bash at supplying the verses for that elusive hit tune when it was put forward for *Cats*. Director Trevor Nunn wrote the version which won out. 'That's the way it goes,' shrugs Don.)

But the wait was worth it. It is doubtful that the pre-*Phantom* Lloyd Webber would have been quite ready for this darkest of stories. And Billy Wilder's 1950 movie shares many similarities with the Gaston Leroux novel on which *Phantom* is based. In the film, a down-on-his-luck Hollywood scriptwriter stumbles into the grand mansion of the faded silent film star Norma Desmond. To pay off his debts, he works on her planned comeback script, *Salomé*. But the unfortunate writer soon runs plain out of luck when Norma becomes infatuated with him.

Through an irresistible mixture of emotional blackmail and proffered riches, she draws him into her web – and, once there, he cannot escape.

Like the Phantom, Norma is one of the silver screen's great monsters. But also like the Phantom, she is to be pitied, finally reaching tragic heights. Leroux's monster is trapped in his home of caves and catacombs; Norma, in her enormous prison of a house. The relationships, too, have similarities – the Phantom uses threats and manipulates emotions to try to win Christine from her young lover, and so does Norma.

Now look at the differences between the Lloyd Webber shows – they're fascinating, because *Sunset* adds new layers of modernity, obviously, but also cynicism. Where *Phantom* is a twisted romance, in *Sunset* romance never has a chance. Christine has her white knight in Raoul. Who does *Sunset*'s Joe Gillis have? Betty, the one girl he truly loves – but she is engaged to his best friend. So their affair, conducted during work while the trusting friend is away, is every bit as squalid as his affair with Norma. He knows it, which is why he reveals the truth to her. But the real truth even he does not know is that she could never have been his salvation in the first place. And walking away will not help either, because this is Norma's show. Like all stars, she demands centre stage, even if she must sacrifice his life and her sanity to win it. She goes off to prison, so who or what is the winner? Hollywood is the ruthless world that breeds both the self-deluding Normas and the failing Joes, and then crushes them when it has had its fun. This is no romance. This is a story of a destructive world. It makes the monsters. And Joe realises that he is well on the way to becoming one himself.

For *Sunset*, Lloyd Webber paired Black with the theatre and film writer Christopher Hampton. Coincidentally, Hampton had long thought the film would make a good musical, and had approached Paramount Studios for the rights. They had replied that somebody else was already negotiating for them. That somebody turned out to be Andrew Lloyd Webber. Hampton discovered this during lunch with his friend at the Carlton Tower one day, when Lloyd Webber was preparing to begin work on *Phantom*. 'He told me that he was planning to do *Phantom Of The Opera*, and asked if I would like to write the book,' says Hampton. 'I told him it was a terrible idea for a musical!' However, he suggested *Sunset Boulevard* instead, and the composer revealed that he was already thinking of the Wilder for later on.

When *Sunset*'s time came, Hampton was disappointed to learn that Don Black had already been promised the lyrics, but Lloyd Webber thought they would work well together.

It was an inspired idea. They both know the way Hollywood works, and are both familiar with its seedy underside. And the *Dangerous Liaisons* writer knows how to propel a story with the speed and tension of a thriller. They hammered out a script over six weeks (spread out over six months to accommodate Hampton's busy movie schedule) at Lloyd Webber's villa in the south of France. 'The combination of Don and Christopher worked so well,' says Lloyd Webber admiringly, 'and Don delivered his best libretto yet for me.'

Stylistically *Sunset* had to inhabit two worlds. There was the snappy, snapping consumer society of Hollywood, where nobody stands still for fear of being tomorrow's nobody, but in Norma's mansion time itself stands still. She had to live from grand moment to grand moment, from aria to aria. Always enacting the grand scene.

'The big songs were mainly down to me,' says Don. '"With One Look", "As If We Never Said Goodbye", that was all very me. The storytelling, and the recitative, that was Christopher.' So Hampton supplied the snap and crackle, the smart cynicism expressed in songs like 'The Lady's Paying' (where a salesman urges Joe to buy his most expensive items with Norma's money), but it was Black's big numbers that went pop. Both 'The Perfect Year', in which Norma tries to seduce Joe on New Year's Eve, and 'As If We Never Said Goodbye', her nervous return to the film studio which made her so famous, hit the charts. Barbra Streisand put 'As If We Never Said Goodbye' in the Top 20, and Dina Carroll took 'The Perfect Year' to No.3 in the UK.

Black grew to admire Hampton enormously – 'His way with language is brilliant, he can find the exact language to fit the piece' – but at times, his inexperience in musicals told, and Don was there to steady the ship. 'He sometimes comes up with words you can use in a play but which wouldn't fit in a song. And I'd say, "This is the big moment, and if you want someone to record this you can't include the word 'anachronism'!"'

Meanwhile, Lloyd Webber came up with a musical structure to echo what Black and Hampton were doing. It's apparent right from the overture. The show begins with great Gothic minor chords, resonant with decaying grandeur, battered resilience and half-remembered dreams.

It's rich and sonorous – this is the sound for the scenes in Norma's mansion. Then, just as the melody begins to resolve, in comes the edgy, nagging patter that characterises the Hollywood scenes, itself interrupted by Joe's sung narration: 'I guess it was five am, a homicide had been reported from one of those crazy mansions up on Sunset'. Then, 'If you want to know the real facts, you've come to right party', and we're into the crazed bustle of 'Let's Have Lunch'.

The contrasts are stark, revealing the incongruities of both worlds. The irony, of course, is that Norma is the great unifying theme – this wrecked woman has seen her own fast Hollywood world transformed into her ruined Gothic mansion of yesterday. The writers knew what they were doing. 'For the first sequence in her house,' explains Hampton, 'we decided to arrest time, building up the claustrophobia by not leaving the house for a long period.'

'As always, I look for the thing people can relate to. Everybody can relate to Norma Desmond,' says Don. 'Forget the insanity and the Hollywood trappings. This is a woman who has been something. Who's been there, who's had everything. And then it's gone. And then there's that desperate glimpse of a second chance, a chance to maybe get it all back. Everybody I know in show business knows that feeling. From my sister-in-law Julie Rogers, who had a big 1960s No.1 in America with "The Wedding", to Val Doonican, who was big ten years ago. I can relate to that. I've had Oscars and then I haven't. Something happens when you think, "I've cracked it!" and then you go through a barren period. The yearning to get back and be safe and secure again, we all know that.'

And that sense of, in Norma's case, clinging onto her powers as a legendary silent screen actress is evident in the dark poetry of 'With One Look', one of Don Black's finest moments.

With one look I can break your heart,
With one look I play every part.
I can make your sad heart sing.
With one look you'll know all you need to know.

With one smile I'm the girl next door,
Or the love that you've hungered for.

When I speak it's with my soul.
I can play any role.

No words can tell the stories my eyes tell,
Watch me when I frown, you can't write that down.
You know I'm right, it's there in black and white.
When I look your way, you'll hear what I say.

Yes, with one look I put words to shame,
Just one look sets the screen aflame.
Silent music starts to play.
One tear in my eye makes the whole world cry.

With one look they'll forgive the past,
They'll rejoice I've returned at last,
To my people in the dark,
Still out there in the dark.

With one look I'll ignite a blaze,
I'll return to my glory days.
They'll say Norma's back at last.

This time I am staying,
I'm staying for good.
I'll be back where I was born to be.
With one look, I'll be me.

If 'With One Look' has Black's signature all over it, the blockbuster title song perhpas has more traces of Hampton, and brilliantly catches the desperation of those who have finally seen Hollywood for what it is.

Sure, I came out here to make my name,
Wanted my pool, my dose of fame,
Wanted my parking-space at Warner's.

But after a year, a one-room hell,
A murphy bed, a rancid smell,

Wallpaper peeling at the corners.

Sunset Boulevard, twisting boulevard,
Secretive and rich, a little scary.
Sunset Boulevard, tempting boulevard,
Waiting there to swallow the unwary.

Dreams are not enough to win the war,
Out here they're always keeping score,
Beneath the tan the battle rages.

Smile a rented smile, fill someone's glass,
Kiss someone's wife, kiss someone's ass,
We do whatever pays the wages.

Sunset Boulevard, headline boulevard,
Getting here is only the beginning.
Sunset Boulevard, jackpot boulevard,
Once you've won you have to go on winning.

You think I've sold out? Dead right, I've sold out.
I've just been waiting, for the right offer.
Comfortable quarters, regular rations,
Twenty-four hour, five-star room service.

And if I'm honest, I like the lady,
I can't help being touched by her folly,
I'm treading water, taking the money,
Watching her sunset.
Well, I'm a writer.

LA's changed a lot over the years,
Since those brave gold-rush pioneers,
Came in their creaky covered wagons.

Far as they could go, end of the line,
Their dreams were yours, their dreams were mine,

But in those dreams were hidden dragons.

Sunset Boulevard, frenzied boulevard,
Swamped with every kind of false emotion.
Sunset Boulevard, brutal boulevard,
Just like you we'll wind up in the ocean.

She was sinking fast, I threw a rope,
Now I have suits and she has hope,
It seemed an elegant solution.

One day this must end, it isn't real,
Still I'll enjoy a hearty meal,
Before tomorrow's execution.

Sunset Boulevard, ruthless boulevard,
Destination for the stony hearted.
Sunset Boulevard, lethal boulevard,
Everyone's forgotten how they started,
Here on Sunset Boulevard.'

Sunset teems with wonderful songs. As well as the two above, there's the jazzy 'Let's Have Lunch', Max's admiring 'The Greatest Star Of All', and a clutch for Norma – 'Surrender', 'New Ways To Dream' (a marvellously evocative hymn to the silent screen, which Black and Hampton wrote overnight), 'The Perfect Year' and 'As If We Never Said Goodbye'. A feast for the cast, especially the leading lady, it was Hampton's great achievement to keep propelling the story forward. There are a lot of big numbers, but they never hold up the action. On the contrary, by taking us deeper and deeper into Norma's twisted character, we can see more and more how this tale must end. It's engrossing stuff.

While some might have thought it a daunting task to musicalise one of Hollywood's most famous films, Black – ever the optimist – was far from cowed. 'I didn't look at the negatives,' he says. 'I was hooked as soon as Andrew played me the tunes. He was at the piano, playing and saying, "And this is where she comes down the staircase." And these incredible melodies were pouring out. I think it's his best score. Heaven.'

In fact, dramatically not much was changed from the film, and Hampton wisely kept in many of the movie's best lines (the most famous of which is Norma's imperious reply to Joe's statement that she used to be big – 'I *am* big. It's the pictures that got small.'). Billy Wilder came to see the show, and afterwards the old man said to its writers, 'You boys are very clever. You didn't change anything.'

It was not the first time that Wilder had been approached about a musical of *Sunset*. Stephen Sondheim had considered the subject back in the 1960s, after finishing his Roman farce *A Funny Thing Happened On The Way To The Forum*. According to Sondheim's biographer Meryle Secrest, 'Wilder told him he was quite wrong to think of the story as a musical. It could only be written as an opera, because "it's about a dethroned queen".' Sondheim agreed, telling Secrest, 'It's such a flamboyant subject you can't do it as a musical. The minute they talk you would scream with laughter because they're such bigger than life figures, and you can't go swarming around that stage the way the lady would have to, and then sit down and have camp dialogue.' He kept that view when the director Hal Prince later asked him to do it as a vehicle for Angela Lansbury in 1981. An opera – albeit in a musical theatre idiom – is exactly what Lloyd Webber delivered.

Whenever and wherever it is done, the show stands and falls by its Norma. It was a great role, and needed a great presence. 'Lots of names were being bandied around,' remembers Don. 'Meryl Streep, Glenn Close.' Close was recommended by Hampton, who had worked with her on his movie *Dangerous Liaisons*. She played the part when the show opened in Los Angeles and was apparently magnificent (she later recorded it), but she did not impress Don on first hearing. 'She came over to audition at Andrew's flat. I thought she was nothing special. It seemed to me a thin voice. She was very pleasant, but the voice seemed reedy, when we needed something ballsy. Afterwards, to my surprise, Andrew enthused, "She could be absolutely fine." I looked at him, astonished. "Could she get those big notes?" He had no doubts at all. And he was right. He could see that she had the capacity, the breath, and with work she could be – and she was – brilliant.' For the world première in London, though, they went with the American singer who had made a stir as the original Fantine in *Les Misérables* – Patti LuPone. Alongside her were Kevin Anderson as Joe and Daniel Benzali as the butler, Max.

Everywhere *Sunset* opened it made headlines (sometimes as much for who did *not* appear as for who did – Faye Dunaway was withdrawn from the show in America because she reportedly was not up to the demands of the role, and rushed into giving an angry press conference). A troop of ultra-distinguished Normas starred in the show in London, Los Angeles and New York. After LuPone came Glenn Close, Elaine Paige, Rita Moreno, Petula Clark and Betty Buckley. Don loved them all.

'They were all terrific. It's a hard part to be bad in. Glenn Close is such an actress that you hang on everything she says. Betty Buckley was mad. Well, the character's supposed to be, but Betty herself has that unhinged feel about her, which was great for the role. People said Petula Clark was a bit domestic, but she toured it successfully for 18 months in America. They were all good. I said in my speech on the last night, "I hate to close this show but it's getting ridiculous. We're considering Boy George."'

That the show closed at all was, say its authors, the fault of cripplingly bad economics. 'It should have run for years longer,' says Don. 'It was overproduced and cost too much money Purely financial nonsense. Someone took their eye off the ball. It just cost so much that we couldn't afford to run it.'

This was at a time when Lloyd Webber's Really Useful Group was in financial trouble. Whereas, in 1994, they had raked in profits of over £46 million, by 1997 they were reportedly facing a £10 million shortfall. There were problems on a corporate level, but a culture of overspending had swept through the company. Lloyd Webber once told me that *Sunset Boulevard* had been budgeted to break even at 85 per cent audience capacity every performance. Instead, he said, 85 per cent is the highest figure a cautious producer should bank on ever making. To calculate it as your break-even point was ridiculous. Had things been properly handled, both composer and lyricist are adamant that the show would have run much longer.

The budget for *Sunset* – £3 million in London – was certainly worthy of Norma Desmond, and more than the show could afford. Trevor Nunn's production was lavish: Norma's palatial home was decked out with all of the trimmings, including the famously lavish staircase. For its transtlantic transfer, Lloyd Webber decided to première the show in Los Angeles rather than in New York, where it cost a jaw-dropping $12 million to mount.

The show was well received in London, where Hollywood satire was the seasonal theme (*Sunset* opened just as the highly praised Cy Coleman show, *City Of Angels*, unexpectedly closed). The general feeling was that *Sunset* was less clever than *City Of Angels*, but sophisticated enough and more of a crowd-pleaser. 'It is often gorgeous to look at, sometimes enchanting to hear and…merits the century-long run it may well achieve,' judged Benedict Nightingale in *The Times*, who also called Black and Hampton's book 'absorbing stuff'. Little was he to know that the exorbitant finances had doomed the show before one audience member had taken his seat.

Expectations were high in LA, where Hollywood turned out in force, with a gala attended by Clint Eastwood, Kirk Douglas, Elizabeth Taylor, Dudley Moore, Jeff Goldblum, Laura Dern, Joan and Jackie Collins, Raquel Welch, James Woods and Darryl Hannah. It's quite an achievement that anybody bothered watching the stage, really! But Glenn Close was on that stage, and giving one of the most admired performances of her illustrious career. So good was she that it was decided that it would be Close, not the London cast's Patti LuPone, who would open on Broadway. LuPone was furious, and the newspapers reported a large undisclosed financial settlement between star and producer. As if the show did not have money troubles enough, there was also the settlement (widely reported as £1 million, and likely to have run at least into the hundreds of thousands) with film star Faye Dunaway when it was decided she was not up to scratch for the role.

Still, *Sunset*'s reputation as one of Lloyd Webber's best is secure (particularly after restructuring put in place for LA was installed in the London show), and there were some thrilling performances. As well as Close, George Hearn was a marvellous, haunted Max, and in New York – the city she had never conquered – Elaine Paige succeeded Close and was a sensation. Don was in the audience for her opening night.

'She got a massive standing ovation, had them in the palm of her hand. I went backstage and she looked at me and just said, "Bloody hell!" She had been in *Cats* and *Evita* there, but this was her big Broadway moment. She seized it, and there was the feeling that she had arrived. I don't know what happened then, because she had rave reviews, and things never quite followed on for her after that in New York the way we all expected them to.'

'Elaine gave a fabulous performance,' says Lloyd Webber. 'I wish we'd gone with her originally in London. We considered her, but Trevor Nunn wanted an American and felt that Patti had more of a patrician edge to her. But Elaine was musically terrific, and Glenn Close was fantastic dramatically.'

Paige remembers *Sunset* as one of her happiest experiences. 'Norma is a gift of a role,' she explains. 'A very good example of the power of Don's lyrics comes from the fact that Andrew asked me to sing the tune which later became "With One Look" at his and Madeleine's wedding. It was then called "Just One Glance" and the lyrics were just OK – not by Don. When Don tackled *Sunset*, and that tune became "With One Look", it was transformed. The character lives in the song. As an actress, it gives you so much to work with. And "As If We Never Said Goodbye" is one of the all-time great songs. Lyric and tune lie perfectly together, and encapsulate Norma's whole life, the sadness of this poor woman whose dreams have gone horribly wrong – and yet she still lives this fantasy life. I think *Sunset* proved Don as one of our great lyricists.'

Sunset ran for over three years at the Adelphi in London and 28 months at New York's Minskoff Theatre. There has since been a UK tour, international productions including Toronto and Australia, and there are persistent rumours of a feature film version, possibly with Close or even Barbra Streisand. For Don, though, the greatest satisfaction was seeing Lloyd Webber's pride in what they had created. For a man for whom, says his friend, nothing is ever finished, everything can be improved upon, there was a rare peace with *Sunset*.

'I have only seen Andrew satisfied once. We were at a performance of *Sunset Boulevard* and it had got to the moment where Norma goes back to Paramount Studios for the first time in years. The studio's spotlight hits her and, moved, she sings "As If We Never Said Goodbye". Andrew glowed, and whispered to me that for a theatrical moment in a show it may be the best thing he has ever written.'

That pride was the composer's only solace at a desperately low time for him. He was fighting to get back control of his company, and could see that all the overspending was crippling the show – yet he could not intervene. 'I was so depressed, I almost sold my shares in the company,' he remembers. 'That show was not a happy time for me. But, looking back at it, it is one of the best things I've done.'

Sunset did not make money. But it was loved. It also won seven Tony Awards, including one for Best Musical. Don jointly bagged two Tonys with Hampton and Lloyd Webber – for Best Score and Best Book. The turnover of famous leading ladies (and their occasional spats) meant that *Sunset* was frequently in the newspapers. With Norma's return to the spotlight, Don Black had his new hit musical.

14 Salaam Bombay – Working With Rahman

It was to be a few years before Don had his next big stage success, but in the interim he stayed as busy as he always does. There was a CD release, *The Don Black Songbook*, in 1993. There were films, including Michael Winner's *Dirty Weekend*, and a TV *Beauty And The Beast*.

He also made the leap to the new era of 007, with Pierce Brosnan now the man fighting terror in his tux. In 1997, he wrote a song for the end credits of *Tomorrow Never Dies*. By this time John Barry had grown bored of Bond and left the series. David Arnold had taken over, and in this movie paid affectionate homage to Barry, his score peppered with musical references to *Goldfinger*, *Thunderball* and *From Russia With Love*. Arnold and Black came up with a song in which, for a change, the woman is in control (funnily enough, this was to be the plot of the next Bond film, *The World Is Not Enough*). kd lang's taking-no-prisoners vocals storm ahead on hard-driving beats and wah-wah horns. It's Bond versus the dominatrix.

Your life is a story,
I've already written
The news is that I,
Am in control.

I have the power,
To make you surrender,
Not only your body,
But your soul.

Tomorrow never dies,
Surrender,

Tomorrow will arrive,
On time.

I'll tease and tantalise,
With every line,
Till you are mine.
Tomorrow never dies,

Whatever you're after
Trust me, I'll deliver.
You'll relish the world,
That I create.

Tomorrow never dies,
Surrender,
Tomorrow will arrive,
On time.

I'll tease and tantalise,
With every line,
Till you are mine.
Tomorrow never dies.

The truth is now,
What I say,
I've taken care,
Of yesterday.

Tomorrow never dies,
Surrender,
Tomorrow will arrive,
On time.

I'll tease and tantalise,
With every line,
Till you are mine.
Tomorrow never dies.

A Sheryl Crow and Mitchell Froom alternative was picked for the opening credits of *Tomorrow Never Dies*, but three years later, for *The World Is Not Enough* (in 2000), Don was back where he likes to be – hitting them between the eyes from the start.

I know how to hurt,
I know how to heal.
I know what to show,
And what to conceal.

I know when to talk,
And I know when to touch,
No-one ever died from wanting too much.

The world is not enough,
But it is such a perfect place to start, my love.
And if you're strong enough,
Together we can take the world apart, my love.

People like us,
Know how to survive.
There's no point of living,
If you can't feel alive.

We know when to kiss,
And we know when to kill,
If we can't have it all,
Then nobody will.

The world is not enough,
But it is such a perfect place to start, my love.
And if you're strong enough,
Together we can take the world apart, my love.

Garbage performed the song, which gets the adventure off to a rousing start – together with an opening sequence that found perhaps the only good use ever for London's Millennium Dome (a thrilling boat chase ends up with a showdown there). Not one of the most distinguished Bond films, it never quite lives up to that early promise, nor does a clever and thoughtful plot quite come off. Still, *Tomorrow Never Dies* (which *is* one of the better Bonds, with a fabulously malign Jonathan Pryce doing villain's duties) and *The World Is Not Enough* grossed an amazing $698 million between them.

Around this time Don started building a broadcasting career, with series such as *How To Write A Musical* and high-profile biography programmes (about fellow songwriters such as Harold Arlen, Dorothy Fields, Jule Styne and Henry Mancini) on BBC Radio. Not to be forgotten either are the many appearances as a guest celebrity on Channel 4's longest-running programme, the quiz show *Countdown*. Restful and genial, *Countdown* is about as far from James Bond as it is possible to get, yet it has a huge fanbase. It's host, Richard Whiteley, is a cult hero amongst those of us who grew up putting off homework with the legitimate excuse that '*Countdown* is educational'. Well, some just watch it for Whiteley's almost-glamorous assistant Carol Vorderman. However, Whiteley's jokes are famously groan-worthy and the celebrity helpers are called to see if they can do any better.

The *Countdown* effect should not be underestimated. 'I still get recognised in the street for that more than for anything else I've done,' says a bemused Don.

A return to the stage coincided with Black's reintroduction to Bond. In 1997, the idea was mooted for a musical version of the hit Neil Simon comedy, *The Goodbye Girl*. The play had been a real charmer, with its plot of a single mother who is not only left by her lover but also finds that he has rented the apartment to an actor (whose home habits include sleeping nude and loudly reciting Shakespeare). Of course, as is the way of these things, they eventually fall in love.

The 1977 movie had been a huge hit for Richard Dreyfuss and Marsha Mason. Dreyfuss's live-wire performance had netted him the Best Actor Oscar that year, and there had been BAFTAs, Golden Globes and a clutch of other accolades as well. As subjects for musicals go, it was perfect. Romance, theatre, comedy, plus killer Neil Simon lines such as 'If you were a Broadway musical, people would be humming your face' – it was all in there. And Marvin Hamlisch, the brilliant composer of *A Chorus Line*, had written the music. It seemed like a sure-fire thing. The only trouble was, in musicals the sure-fire thing simply does not exist.

The show had already opened and failed on Broadway, with Bernadette Peters. Yet it was thought that, with a revamp (Don was called in to replace David Zippel's lyrics), it could be a smash in London. 'Timing is everything with musicals,' says Don ruefully. 'This was a cosy almost two-hander at a time when people wanted their shows to be big.' It also had stars in Gary Wilmot and Ann Crumb, but they were not big enough to set the box-office tills ringing. *The Goodbye Girl* said goodbye before the year was out.

By now, Don was one of the most experienced lyricists in the world. In 1999, to crown his career, the Queen awarded him the OBE, the Order of the British Empire. He may have thought he had seen it all, had done it all. But then along came a project, and a person, quite unlike anything he had come across before.

Andrew Lloyd Webber was no longer just a composer. He had bought the Stoll Moss group of theatres which, including important venues like the Theatre Royal Drury Lane and the London Palladium, made him the most important theatre owner in London. His Really Useful Group needed shows to fill the theatres, so their producing arm – hitherto almost completely involved with the Lloyd Webber canon – began searching for work from other people.

Lloyd Webber felt the opportunity keenly. He cares deeply about musicals and now he had the means, the money and the stages to try and further their cause, because by the turn of the millennium it was beginning to look as though the century that had seen the dawn of musical theatre might also see its sunset. Where, everyone in the business was asking, were the new writers? Look around the West End and Broadway, and who was there? Lloyd Webber, Stephen Sondheim, Kander and Ebb, Marvin Hamlisch, Boublil and Schönberg, Tim Rice, Don, of course, and various established rock stars such as Elton John, Paul Simon and Billy Joel. But most of these people had been writing since the 1960s or 1970s. They were still turning out good shows, but where were the next generation? The fear was that they were putting their talents to use exclusively in the pop charts, or maybe in movies.

Lloyd Webber began trying to think of new directions, somewhere musicals could draw new vitality. There was a disastrous first effort with the Pet Shop Boys' musical, *Closer To Heaven*, a cacophonous confection of (albeit new, which is more than can be said for most pop stars' efforts) pop-style songs strung together by a story of London nightlife and a boy's sexual awakening. Nice idea, but the Pets made the classic mistake of being a pop band making the leap into theatre. In a musical, every song has to advance the action or tell you more about the characters or their context. A pretty tune and a decent drumbeat is not enough. If it's not tightly woven into the story, things soon get boring.

For his next big production Lloyd Webber decided to get much more hands-on, because this was a project he really cared about and had high hopes for. Over the past couple of years he had developed a taste for Hindi pop music, for its rhythmic vitality and imagination. He mentioned this to his friend Shekhar Kapur (director of the film *Elizabeth*), who sent him a tape of Indian composers. Every one that Lloyd Webber liked turned out to be by the same man, a Bollywood composer in his mid-30s called AR Rahman.

To call Rahman a Bollywood composer does not do him justice. He is *the* Bollywood composer, with a mightily impressive CV encompassing films such as the Oscar-nominated *Lagaan*, and the career-making *Roja*. And he is, quite simply, a superstar. Not in the West, except among Asians, but everywhere that the Bollywood movie industry is big – which means India, Pakistan, the Islamic countries, and of course among the Asian diaspora – Rahman is a king. He has sold more CDs than Madonna and Britney Spears. The man is absolutely huge, yet Lloyd Webber and most of his fellow countrymen had never heard of him.

Madras-born Rahman had grown up with the name AS Dileep Kumar, and changed it when he converted to Islam (the initials in his new name stand for "Allah Rakha", though everyone simply refers to him as Rahman). He made his early fortune writing advertising jingles and running a small recording studio, which became one of India's most advanced. But what marks him out from other Indian composers is his gift for melody and for rhythm, and the way he incorporates wide musical influences, from classical to pop (he was awarded a degree in Western Classical Music at Oxford University). The director of *Lagaan*, Ashutosh Gowariker, once confidently told me that Rahman was one of the two or three greatest composers the enormous Indian film industry has ever known.

This, thought Lloyd Webber, could be just the shot in the arm the West End needed. He had for years cherished the hope that new composers from other cultures, with their individual styles, would give musicals new dimensions. The Soviet bloc, he had reasoned, would be the natural source; after all, Russia was the home of Tchaikovsky, of Mussorgsky, of Shostakovich. He had been wrong, and now realised – it was a revelation – that he must look further east. After all, Bollywood already produces dozens of film musicals each year!

He and Kapur contacted Rahman, who was very interested. He called the chance to have a show in the West End 'a dream come true'. Then came the choice of lyricist. Without a doubt it had to be someone who knew musicals inside out, who could point the way should Rahman feel lost in a foreign culture.

So one evening Don received a call from the Lloyd Webber household. Not from Andrew, but from his wife (by this time, he had divorced Sarah Brightman), the energetic and entrepreneurial Madeleine. 'The emphasis was very much from Madeleine to begin with,' he says. 'She suggested, "I think you should meet this boy Rahman, and see how the two of you get on together."'

Don knew that a Bollywood project was in the wind, and was curious to meet the man Lloyd Webber called a 'melodic genius'. 'The Lloyd Webbers had met him a few times and he was extremely quiet. They needed someone who could talk with him and work with him. I suppose they thought that I get on with most people, so I could draw him out. Because he didn't know anything about the theatre. It was to be a much bigger job than just putting words to his music. They needed someone to teach him about musical theatre itself at the same time.'

Don went to the Lloyd Webber's west London house for drinks and to meet Rahman. Small and younger-looking than his years, he is an unassuming character, quick to smile and genuinely friendly, but quiet and with no sense of star charisma about him.

Therefore it came as a shock for Don to see the reaction when he and Rahman, along with Shekhar Kapur, proceeded to the trendy Bombay Brasserie in Gloucester Place for dinner. 'We entered, and the scene was remarkable,' he explains. 'It was like Elvis Presley coming into the room. You could literally hear the whispers sweeping around the place: "It's Rahman! Rahman's here!" People are coming over to ask for his autograph. At least 12 or 15 people came over. And he sat there, smiling and signing.'

It was not, remembers Don, the easiest of meals. 'There were long, long silences at dinner. He was painfully introverted as a person. I was asking, "Have you seen musicals? How do you like to work?" Just to get our feet wet, so I could report to Andrew and Madeleine the next day that we got on well, and so on.'

Rahman had seen no stage musicals. Some film musicals he liked, especially *West Side Story*. He was a great Michael Jackson fan, and was delighted to discover that Don had written 'Ben'. 'But the thing that amazed him', continues Don, 'was that I wrote some of the James Bond songs. He was over the moon. And when he found out I knew John Barry, he went mad! It was like the highlight of his life! One evening I took him to a recording studio where John was working with a 100-piece orchestra, and Rahman had his picture taken with him. He said it was the best night of his life.'

Once Rahman opened up it became clear that the two men could work together, and the project was announced. They would write a musical. It would be about a poor boy from the Bombay slums who becomes a Bollywood film star, runs up against the gangsters who control the industry, falls in love, forgets his roots and rediscovers them just in time to save the slum from destruction. And it would be called *Bombay Dreams*.

Don was the only non-Indian in the writing trio. Meera Syal, writer and star of the TV series *Goodness Gracious Me*, had signed up to write the book. Yet, if India was an alien world to Don, he did not worry. He read books and books about Bombay, watched a dozen Bollywood movies, and took lessons on the culture and foreign concepts such as the Bombay eunuchs (one of the major characters is a eunuch). Besides, as he retorts, 'I don't believe Sheldon Harnick had to go to Russia to write *Fiddler On The Roof*. I don't think it's hard to tune into. And if you're writing a love song, you don't have to know huge detail about Bombay. You need to get a flavour of it. And of what the evening is. I didn't want the lyrics to be too sophisticated. This wasn't the time to start rhyming "Methuselah" with "bamboozler"!'

When his involvement was announced, Don certainly did not seem daunted, saying with characteristic good humour that 'The whole thing is going to be more over-the-top than I normally write – think Technicolor. If I'm stuck, I'll pop down to my Indian restaurant and check out the menu. I'm sure a few Hindi words will creep in. Look out for "chutney" several times – and "chapati". I've already written "It's my chapati and I'll cry if I want to".'

Lloyd Webber installed Rahman in a small room high up in the Palace Theatre. And the younger composer, a great fan of electronic instruments, filled the room to bursting with electric keyboards, computers and synthesisers. 'He's the complete opposite of someone like John Barry,' says Don. 'He just loves his equipment. If he won the Lottery, he'd run to Tottenham Court Road to buy the latest gismo. I spent endless hours watching him fiddling with instruments and gadgets that I knew nothing about.'

This experience was to be new for Don in many other ways, too. For Rahman, an extremely devout Muslim, composing is a deeply religious event. 'Every time I went up to his studio, I had to take my shoes off,' says Black. 'In his tradition, the creative place must be sacred, so you remove your shoes. Then he would light some candles and there would be the smell of incense. It was pleasant for me, but for him it was extremely spiritual.'

Rahman's way of working was, well, different. He comes from a musical culture of improvisation – one thinks of Ravi Shankar's night-long improvisation concerts. What he does *not* do is write structured songs to tight deadlines, as musical theatre demands. It did not take long for his lyricist to find this out, and it came as something of a shock. 'Every other composer I've ever worked with will play you a melody. Rahman will pound with his hands. He'll start with a drumbeat and work something out from there. He has these jamming sessions. I'd say, "What have you got for me?" and he'd say, "I've been jamming," and give me a tape. I'd take that home to play, and there would be just this mishmash, two hours of improvisations and little things tried out, all stopping and starting.'

Mentally donning his deerstalker and cape, Don became what he calls a 'song detective'. Rahman's tapes contained the clues, and somewhere amongst all the red herrings the lyricist had to find where songs, or germs of songs, lay hidden. On the first tape he listened to, in despair at the chaos, suddenly an enchanting, intoxicating few bars sang out – a winding melody that eventually ended up as the opening bars of the show, as the Bombay sun rises over the slums. Don got excited. This was the real thing. Phoning him in delight – 'This bit! This is good. You've got to expand that!' – Don played it back to him down the phone, but he didn't remember having composed it.

When they were together, Don might ask for a ballad, and Rahman would sit at the piano and improvise for 45 minutes. During this the lyricist would have to stay alert, quickly pointing out any snatch of music from which they could build an entire song.

'Getting full-length songs out of him was very difficult,' says Don. 'I don't say it wasn't enjoyable. But it was a long, laborious job to get actual shapes of songs that could be right for the West End and Broadway. And I had to remember the whole time to tread that delicate line, getting the theatricality we needed and yet keeping Rahman's own distinctive voice.'

Much of what Rahman supplied to Black was 'very fast rhythms without any particular melody to them'. Reasoning that the composer's English was too limited for him to be given verses to work to – he was unlikely to get the accents right – Don started throwing titles at him, some of them inspired by the Rumi poetry he was now devouring. One of the titles they got a melody together for, 'The Moon Never Stays Behind The Cloud', did not make it into the show, but a beautiful line from that song (one of Don's favourites) did: 'Precious gifts can come from empty hands'. Rahman's spiritualism was getting to him, and he was being influenced as much by the Indian as the other way around. 'Let's keep the lyrics mystical', the composer kept urging, to which ever-practical Don would reply, 'Fine, but you can only stay mystical for so long. It can't only be about deserts and moons. You do finally have to say something.'

The pair always got on well, but there were frustrations, as Don admits. 'Rahman is very unorthodox in his life patterns. He's up all night, and goes to bed around noon. I'd say, "Rahman, we've got to work tonight." He'd say, "OK, what time? Ten?" We usually compromised at about seven or eight. But then he'd spend an hour and a half getting the computer ready! It would be ten when we started, and I'd come home to Shirley, utterly exhausted, at two or three in the morning.'

When the work was going well, he didn't mind the late nights and early mornings. However, Rahman's sense of urgency, of having an opening night to work towards, was rather less pressing than Don's.

'He has this attitude that everything comes from Allah, which I respect. But because of that, when you're working with him, and trying to figure something out, he'll say, "Don't worry, it'll happen when it will happen." And I'd say, "No, it's got to happen by four o'clock tomorrow because we've got a cast of 30 people waiting to sing it!"'

Rahman would smile and tell his friend not to worry. Lloyd Webber stayed out of the process, not wishing to influence or compromise Rahman's music-making. However, he and Madeleine would often stop by on their way out for dinner to hear what progress had been made. These moments were often acutely embarrassing for the lyricist.

'What could I say? A lot of the time we would have nothing to play them. I'd have been sitting around in the studio for two days but he wouldn't have given me any tunes!' Lloyd Webber, however, understood more of the way Rahman worked. He would listen to two bars and get excited, rubbing his hands and, encouragingly urging Rahman, 'Oh, let's have more of that!'

Rahman, a recording artist to his fingertips, was a great believer in booking recording sessions as a catalyst to creating those elusive moments of magic. And they would be amazing times, says Black.

'He would book a studio for that night. When I'd protest that we didn't have anything to play, he'd reply that we'd have to just play. So we'd book a studio, four or five singers, a few instrumentalists, and there were times when we'd have very little to do. But then I'd see Rahman at his exciting best. He'd turn to a couple of the singers and say "Do this", chanting, "Dang dang de dududu dang", and then he'd get other singers to join in with another rhythm on top, and before you know it he'd have something going, and it'd be great! He loves to work with people. And that's fun and exciting, but it's not the way to find the structured songs you need to further plots.'

The thing which mystified Don the most, at least for the first few times it happened, were Rahman's sudden absences. One moment he was there, the next he was gone. 'He would just get up and leave the room for 20 minutes in the middle of work. It was very disconcerting.

I'd think, "Where the hell is he?" And he'd have gone to another room, no announcement, to privately pray for inspiration.'

One day Don went with Rahman to look at an apartment he had been offered in Brewer Street, in the middle of Soho. To get there they had to walk past the multitude of Soho sex shops and strip joints, and when he got back to his studio Rahman immediately disappeared to pray, feeling the need to cleanse his spirit.

Don would give Rahman lessons in writing musicals – about the purpose of lyrics, about the way they can, they must, elucidate or progress the story, and about rhyming. 'Rhymes focus, enforce, enlighten, clarify,' he would explain. 'You couldn't sing, "Fly me to the moon/And let me play among the stars/Let me see what spring is like/On Jupiter and Saturn." It's wonky.'

Rahman, for his part, found the experience fascinating, describing working with Don as 'a privilege'. And Don came to have tremendous admiration for this quiet, gentle man.

He went to see Rahman give a concert to 20,000 fans in a New York stadium. It sold out, despite the tickets costing $120 each. And, as with everything involving Rahman, it was a unique experience.

'We sat down at 7:30pm, the time it was meant to begin. At 9:30 it still hasn't started. And nobody is moaning. Nobody! The all-Asian audience is just sitting there, patiently waiting. No banging, no whistling. I was there with *Bombay Dreams'* music director Chris Nightingale and, observing all this, he remarked, "They're a noble yet chaotic race." A nice way of putting it.'

The show finally started. Rahman, boyishly handsome in a white Oriental jacket, came out and shyly stood behind his keyboard. As he played, the crowd went mad. At one point, he stopped the show. 'I'd like to present an award to a dear friend,' he announced to the cheering throng. 'Would Don Black come up to accept an award?' Up Don went, in front of the 20,000, for the completely unexpected award. It was inscribed (deep breath), 'Presented To The Outstanding And World-Renowned Lyricist Don Black For His Glorious Contributions To The Sounds Of Music And Expression Of Soulful Feelings Through Poetry On The Occasion Of The Musical Extravaganza AR Rahman Live In Concert – presented by Bharatiya Vidya Bhavan, USA'. Rahman had not said a word about it. He was probably saving his voice for the concert.

They did get a song-list together in the end. And that sensuous, twisting melody from the first tape Rahman gave to Don became not only the Bombay sunrise, but also the basis for one of the show's best numbers, 'Only Love'. My favourite lyrics, though, are to be found in the duet 'How Many Stars', as the lovers admit their feelings for each other. It's deceptively simple and deeply poetic – but poetic in the sense of something almost sacred. It has the subtly varied repetitions of a prayer. And we all pray for love.

How many stars have to shine before your eyes meet mine?
How many stars must I see before you dream like me?

How many tides have to turn before you turn to me?
How many stars have to shine before my heart is free?

How many stars have to shine before your hands hold mine?
How many stars must I see before you come to me?

How many times have to turn before you turn my way?
How many stars have to shine before you say you'll stay?

Everyone needs a sense of belonging,
Someone there who always understands.
That precious gifts can come from empty hands.
Precious gifts can come from empty hands.

How many stars have to shine before we find our way?
How many stars have to shine before we love each day?
How many stars have to shine before we find our way?
How many stars have to shine before we love?
How many stars?

Don's favourite *Bombay Dreams* song – another of his universal thoughts – is that sung by the suddenly homesick Akash as he discovers the seedy underside of Bollywood. 'The Journey Home' was picked up by several critics:

The journey home is never too long,
Your heart arrives before the train.
The journey home is never too long,
Some yesterdays always remain.

I'm going back to when my heart was light,
When my pillow was a ship I sailed through the night.
The journey home is never too long,
When open arms are waiting there.

The journey home is never too long,
There's room to love and room to spare.
I want to feel the way that I did then,
I'll think my wishes through before I wish again.

Not every road you come across is one you have to take.
No, sometimes standing still can be the best move you ever make.'

The journey home is never too long,
Home helps to heal the deepest pain.
The journey home is never too long,
Your heart arrives before the train.

If Andrew Lloyd Webber was hoping to attract new audiences and new writers with *Bombay Dreams*, then finding a cast proved tricky. Despite the proliferation of Indian-centric English films, from *East Is East* to *Bend It Like Beckham*, the pool of sufficiently trained musical performers is small, if growing. Even for the demo, it was important to have Indian voices, because the show needed absolutely the right atmosphere and flavour. Besides which, you cannot very well have an English-sounding Fantine (from *Les Mis*) type of voice belting out a song called 'Shakalaka Baby'.

Don sat in on the final auditions for the show. 'Some were good, but some were terrible. And not many could have done eight shows a week. The training isn't there.'

Many of the participants at the auditions, he discovered, were ashamed to tell their parents where they had gone. That, says Don proudly, is one cultural change the show has made. 'They all want to get into it now. It has become respectable.'

The lead female role of Priya was taken by the similarly named Preeya Kalidas. An experienced actress with movie (*Bend It Like Beckham, East Is East, Sari And Trainers*) and television (*My Family, Doctors*) credits to her name, she had no problem projecting in a large theatre. She had the looks, and a soulful, marvellously controlled voice with the technique to withstand the pressures of show after show. The handsome, capable Raza Jaffrey was the slum-boy-made-good, Akash.

Once rehearsals began, Lloyd Webber became far more involved, keeping a paternal eye on the show's structure, and channelling the Really Useful Group's considerable marketing forces into promoting it. He threw a lavish launch party at the Cinnamon Club in Westminster, and it was then that I got my own taste of Rahman's celebrity. In the minicab home, the Indian driver was enquiring where I had been, in a friendly but faintly disinterested way. I mentioned that I had been at a launch party for a new Andrew Lloyd Webber musical. A raised eyebrow was the only response. 'Well, he's not actually writing this one,' I added. For some reason, I felt obliged to explain. 'He's brought across this chap from India called AR Rahman. Nice man.'

The driver – no exaggeration – pulled over to the side of the road and stared at me, wide-eyed. 'You *met Rahman?*' he asked, voice shaking with excitement. My own eyes widening somewhat now (one hand checking for the door handle, just in case), I replied that, yes, I had. The driver thrust out a hand to grasp and shake mine, as he said, 'Sir, it is an honour to have a man of your status in my car.' Still, I didn't get a discount.

If the creation of the show was a serious endeavour in which its authors were, as Don puts it, 'trying to break barriers', the musical puts the accent squarely on having a great time (despite, in my opinion, the weaknesses of Syal's cartoonish book). It succeeds in at once capturing and having fun with the macho spirit of Bollywood. And musically the clash of cultures meshes to fabulous, thrilling effect. The opening montage of the Bombay slums – in which the chaotic city life is caught in one refrain after another, the crowd singing about 'Contradictions, city of extremes/Anything is possible in Bombay dreams' or just chanting, 'Ding dang, ding-ading dang' – has the feeling of a Rahman jamming session, with bits of Black tossed among the riffs. In numbers like the eunuch's lament, 'Love's Never Easy', you can feel Rahman's cavalier tendencies harnessed to a strong musical theatre structure. In still more songs, especially the joyful dance number 'Shakalaka Baby' (one of those tunes you cannot get out of your head – 'Come and shakalaka with me'), the joins are all but impossible to spot.

It was not until they saw *Bombay Dreams* in front of an audience at the Victoria Apollo Theatre that the writers and producer knew they had something that worked. Don could feel the excitement among the audience: 'It was a fantastic electricity, especially when they started doing the "shakalakas" and all the big bits. The audience was there, in the spirit of the evening, and they were touched. Although there were still things to put right, we could tell that there was a show there and in a few weeks' time it could be great.'

Rahman, Lloyd Webber and Black were all disappointed with the opening night. Don walked around, tension etched into his face, uncharacteristically nervous. Whereas the crowds at the previews had cheered and clapped, the opening-night audience – perhaps overawed by the ultra-hyped occasion, or unsure how to react to parody numbers like 'Shakalaka Baby' – stayed quiet. On the other hand, the reason may have been the below-par performance on the stage. Opening nights are funny times (Michael Ball admits to having spent years trying to work out a way to get over his opening night nerves and never succeeding). The cast knows that the audience is unusual, filled as it is with friends and interested parties all desperate for the show to succeed on the one hand, and critics quietly judging on the other. And sometimes the show is affected. It was so at the *Bombay Dreams* opening. The performances seemed artificial, and leading man Raza Jaffrey was clearly shaken to the pit of his stomach by nerves.

The reviews were mixed, few were dire but then few were adulatory either. And everyone respected what the show was trying to do. Good enough to let the marketing and word-of-mouth take effect. The show stayed busy, becoming one of the hottest tickets in town. And as hoped, it attracted more than your usual white middle-class theatregoers. To begin with, ninety per cent of the audiences were Asian and, according to Don, it still hovers at around the 20 per cent mark.

Within six weeks the show hit its stride. The performers relaxed, started enjoying themselves, and found the party Bollywood atmosphere they needed. 'It became so finely drilled, now it runs like a dream,' says Don. 'Runs' is the operative word, since it is still going strong over a year later, and in a depressed West End it has been one of the few success stories. However, Don's Indian summer was about to be interrupted by a savage storm of criticism.

15 The Making Of A Lyricist

It would be cruel to dwell for too long on the reaction to Black's next project. But the stark contrast between the success of *Bombay Dreams* and the failure of *Romeo And Juliet – The Musical* was hard to escape.

There is an unwritten rule in musical theatre: what works in France will not play in England. Evidence? Well, *Notre-Dame De Paris*, a rock musical of the Victor Hugo novel, was a smash hit in La France, playing to stadiums and making records with its record sales. It came to England, where it was greeted with derision. There have been others to drown on that rocky Channel crossing. The only French musical to succeed in London was *Les Misérables*, which had already flopped in Paris!

Romeo And Juliet, by Gérard Presgurvic, echoed *Notre-Dame*'s fate. It had played to stadiums in France. French friends of mine were telling me how wonderful it was, hyping it to high heaven. But the English like their Shakespeare to have, well, at least something Shakespearean about it. The musical, which had some good talents attached – as well as Black, the innovative David Freeman directed and the resourceful Adam Kenwright produced – tried to be cartoony enough for young people. It was panned. The music, the production and the lyrics. The knives were out, with headlines like 'Never was there a tale of more woe'.

Don was hurt. 'I'm old enough and wise enough to know that sometimes I get it wrong, but I don't think it deserved the lacerating reception it got. It would have been nice if more critics had noted that I'd had an illustrious career and this was a blip, instead of it being an out-and-out roasting.' He read one review, which included the line, 'Don Black should hang his head in shame', and read no more.

'As Dad has got older,' says Clive Black, 'he's felt the pain of failure more, just as he now feels the highs of success more. It's not to do with money now, it's to do with respect from his peers. I think the failure of *Romeo And Juliet* hurt him more than he'd like to admit. He was first in line for criticism, because his was the name everyone knows on the show. When it's an Andrew Lloyd Webber, he's a bit less visible.'

But Don's career has had more than its share of success, so the odd bad judgement call ought to be forgivable. Besides, he could not be miserable for long, as there were new projects to attend to.

Bombay Dreams was still going strong, and now there were plans for it to go to New York (with Tom Meehan, of *The Producers* and *Hairspray*, drafted in to improve the book). He was working on a musical of *Dracula* with Christopher Hampton and Frank Wildhorn, which is at the time of writing headed towards Broadway. Rahman had got back in touch for a song, 'Taj Mahal', for his new movie.

It also looks increasingly as though Black and Wildhorn will join forces again for a new musical based on *Bonnie And Clyde* for Broadway. Kevin McCallum, who worked on *Rent* and Baz Luhrmann's *La Bohème*, is set to produce, with *Rent*'s Michael Grief to direct. And once again the light of enthusiasm shines in Don's eyes, the *Romeo* débâcle perhaps not forgotten, but buried. '*Bonnie And Clyde* could be great. The setting is so evocative, the dust bowl, the Depression.'

Perhaps most exciting of all, Black and John Barry have reunited for a long-overdue follow-up to *Billy*. Barry has long cherished the hope of writing a musical of Graham Greene's tale of gangsters and spiritual corruption, *Brighton Rock*.

Barry approached Greene with the idea 40 years ago, but two things went wrong. First, Greene wanted to write the lyrics himself, and was no lyricist. Then, as Barry amusingly relates, producer Wolf Mankowitz and director Roy Boulting had a fight. 'We had set up a meeting, and there was Wolf Mankowitz, Roy Boulting, myself and Graham Greene sitting round a table. What we did not realise was that Boulting and Mankowitz loathed each other. Evidently they'd fallen out on some film and never got over it. They started in at each other right away, arguing. Graham Greene and I just looked at each other open-mouthed, while they screamed at each other at the tops of their voices. That was the end of *Brighton Rock*, or so I thought.'

The idea was revived when the producer Bill Kenwright – looking for a hit musical to replace *Blood Brothers* when it eventually closes (as it surely must, and probably quite soon, in the wake of the closures of other long-runners *Cats*, *Miss Saigon* and *Starlight Express*) – phoned

Barry. He remembered the *Brighton Rock* dream, and asked the composer if he would like to write it. Barry leaped at the chance. It will be dark, he promises. Having heard some of the early tracks, it also sounds as though it could be great.

In the meantime, lyrics Don wrote in 2001 for Barry's famous themes from *Out Of Africa* (the song is called 'Places') and *Dances With Wolves* ('Here's To The Heroes') have been successful in Europe (going gold in Germany, sung by the tenor Erkan Aki), and there are plans for American and British releases as well.

Black is as busy as ever: a show here, a film there. Everyone comments on how calm he stays ('grounded' is the word many use). And although Don wins the awards and the plaudits (and occasionally dodges the brickbats), it is the quietly formidable Mrs Black who gives him the strength to keep his head. Even more than Don, Shirley judges people as people, and their fame or celebrity pretensions are swept aside.

'Our lives never seemed glamorous to me,' she says with a shrug. 'People do say how lucky I am to meet all these stars and so on. I never think of it like that, and I never did. I can never remember feeling star-struck or in awe of anybody, however important they were. They were just people. We're very peculiar, I think. Family and friends get excited about what we do, but we've never been bothered. If we go somewhere glamorous, it's nice; if not, it's also good.'

There is a wonderful story, which shows Shirley at her no-nonsense best. She and Don had become quite friendly with the writer of *The Godfather*, Mario Puzo. They went to his house in Santa Monica, where Puzo proposed to Don that they write a musical about Napoleon together. In vain, Don tried to persuade him to stick to the area for which he was known – a musical about the Mafia could be *really* fascinating. Neither show ever happened, but they became friendly.

'We played poker with him at his house,' remembers Shirley, 'and he was lovely. He had all his family there, the place was full of his children and grandchildren. It was a real Italian atmosphere, with lots of cooking and the children running around with no shoes on.' Puzo was a great gambler, and fancied himself as a master poker player. So when that night they played poker and Shirley won, he was not a little surprised.

Shirley won real respect from him on a later visit to London. As she explains, Puzo was not a man to trifle with. 'He cultivated the image of a Mafia don from one of his books. There was definitely that about him. He was like a big, cuddly teddy bear, but you also had the feeling of danger. It was better to be on the right side of him.' On this visit, Puzo took the Blacks to the casino at the Ritz, and there he stayed for hours, playing poker. He started to win, was winning big, and Puzo would always play until he lost or was too tired to play any more. Utterly absorbed in the poker, he did not notice the ever-practical Shirley getting more and more worried that he would lose all his money – at one point she made her decision for him. 'Right, that's it. We're leaving. Time to go, Mario,' she declared and, much to the *Godfather* scribe's surprise, she picked up all his chips and took them to be cashed. 'He was so shocked. No one had ever done that to him before!' she laughs. But he got up and meekly followed her out.

Don's love for Shirley is always evident, not least in his affectionate jokes. When she says something to make him proud, he will often crack, 'Isn't she wonderful? I don't why I bother with all the others.'

There is no doubt what is first and foremost in Don's life. Family. 'They are everything to me, in terms of stability and of what's important,' says Don. 'Shirley, my two boys, my sisters, my brothers, we all speak every day. All that can wash away a bad review very quickly.'

Grant and Clive both followed their father into the music business. Clive made some abortive attempts to break into the world of movies (he once wrote to Michael Caine's manager and asked to manage Caine, receiving the succinct reply, 'I do. Fuck off.') before he became, at 27, the youngest ever managing director of EMI Records in the UK. He now runs one of Europe's biggest independent record labels, Edel. Grant has dipped into publishing, management and now seems to have found his calling as a songwriter – a major songwriter, writing both words and music for artists of the calibre of Holly Valance, Liberty X and Dido. (At his first important song meeting, there was a problem about some of the lyrics. Grant excused himself, ran around the corner and hurriedly phoned Don for some advice!) Don could not be more proud – of both of them.

'They're both down-to-earth. I never begrudge anything to my kids because I know they realise the value of it. They know what it's like to be poor because they know where I come from, so they appreciate what we have. I am pleased because they've been brought up with good music, with Stephen Sondheim, Rodgers and Hart. And they've been surrounded by the music of Henry Mancini and John Barry. So Grant, as a writer, knows Cole Porter and Jerome Kern songs, and is writing today with that knowledge. The flame is in good hands.'

And they both dote on him. 'Dad is one of the funniest men I know,' says Grant. 'One of his favourite tricks was on the way to school in the mornings. We would see lots of other kids also going to our school, and he'd call one of them over and ask what time Pele was due to arrive. He'd insist that Pele was giving a talk, and would wonder if the boy knew *when* because he didn't want to miss it. By the time we got to school, all our friends would run up and say, "Pele's coming in today!"'

Clive remembers his father trying to prove his macho credentials to his boys. 'He'd take us to football matches, which he didn't like and had no idea really how to play. And he'd sit there reading a book. If the other team would score, though, he jump up and indignantly shout, "He was offside!"' Another time, Don took them to what Clive calls a 'dude ranch' in Arizona. 'It was a real men's place, all horse rides and baked beans. He *hated* it. But he didn't want to show that to us. So he stuck it out for two days, and then suddenly announced, "Sod this, we're going to Miami." Hours later, we were feasting on chicken and chips in a plush Miami hotel, and he was much happier.'

Don and Shirley now live in an elegant apartment next to London's Holland Park, near Kensington High Street. One of their neighbours and friends is the film director and restaurant critic Michael Winner. 'I had worked with Don and we had become friends,' says Winner. 'So when Shirley told me they were looking to move, I recommended my road. There was a flat going with a nice garden, I told them. Shirley protested that she didn't like Holland Park and anyway she didn't want a garden. But they moved in, and I got a call from Shirley saying, "You must come round, it's beautiful, and you should see my garden."'

Although family is the most vital part of Don's life, writing is also very important to him. 'He doesn't like to go for long stretches without writing something. He can't do it,' says Shirley. 'The other day he said, "I haven't written for three weeks. I've got to write something." He doesn't question where it comes from, he just sits there and it comes. And he can write anywhere – in the kitchen, on a plane, even with noise, so long as it isn't music. But he has to write.'

And that is why, at the age of 64, Don's diary is fuller than ever. Retirement? He dismisses the suggestion. 'I'll never retire. There's no reason to, because I love writing lyrics. It's just me and a pen and a piece of paper, so I can go to the park and scribble a few lines and call a composer. It's not hard work, is it?'

Hard work? Not when you thoroughly know your craft. But, as fellow lyricist Tim Rice points out, lyric-writing is trickier than many people think. 'Composers hog the limelight. There's a mystique about them. People think they can do something no one else can do. That is manifestly untrue. If every child was taught music from an early age as they are taught English, then there would be a great many more composers. Writing lyrics is not a case of sauntering to your desk and jotting down a few lines at a time. It is hard work, although you may enjoy it, and Don is one of the cleverest lyricists around.'

As Don admits, although every writer has their own style, there are invaluable points of technique which he has picked up over the years. So, to help budding songwriters, I asked him to list them. Who knows? Perhaps it will inspire the next Don Black.

Don Black's Ten Golden Rules
Of Lyric-Writing

1: HUG THE TUNE

'Each word has to sit comfortably on each note of the melody. They have to hug the contours of the tune and they have to sing. When this happens, the simplest thoughts become beautiful. Also, a good lyric should sound spontaneous.'

2: THE UNIVERSAL THOUGHT

'Always look for an original thought about the human condition; a universal thought that people can respond to will add to its emotional impact. Think of Cole Porter. "Whenever skies look grey to me and troubles begin to brew/Whenever the icy winds begin to blow I concentrate on you." It's true: whenever you're feeling down you think of someone you love. "Love changes everything" – that's very true.'

It is also, says Don, important to make your mark right from the beginning. Let them know what the song is about as soon as it begins.

'If you take a song like "By The Time I Get To Phoenix" by Jim Webb, there's a marvellous opening line – "By the time I get to Phoenix, she'll be rising". You're there, you get the picture so early on. I try and do that with every song. There's another Jim Webb song, which begins, "This time we almost made it, didn't we girl?" The whole dramatic situation is set up right at the beginning. It's the same with all great songs.'

3: NOTE-TAKING

'Always keep a notebook and jot down snatches of ideas. These will come in handy. I had the title "Tell Me On A Sunday" on a scrap of paper for a long while before I did the show. I thought, "There is an idea in there somewhere." And when Andrew played me his melody, those words seemed to sit beautifully.'

4: A LYRICIST OF ALL WORLDS

'Don't be a lyrical snob. It is just as difficult to write a song for Britney Spears as it is for a Broadway show. It's a very different craft, but equally challenging. Listen to as much contemporary music as you can, also jazz, folk music, country song and, of course, show music. Soak it all. This should be a labour of love.'

5: KEEP THE FAITH

'The world is full of lyrical critics. Most people think they can do it. They can't. As most people aren't musicians, they can't spurt out phrases like "I hate that B flat in bar 16", but it is easy for them to rubbish the words. Either they rubbish them or they dismiss them with clichés like "banal". Tim Rice also gets very annoyed about this. He once wrote to *Variety* magazine because they reviewed *Phantom Of The Opera*, a very long review, without mentioning the lyrics. Tim's letter asked, "Did they la la the whole libretto?" But if you believe you have written something special, don't be deterred by the detractors.'

6: LOOK AGAIN

'Don't fall in love with everything you write just because it's finished. Take another look – hone and refine.'

7: YOU AND YOUR SONGS

'Always try and write for yourself. Don't copy and don't follow. You are unique. There's only one of you. Try and put your own individual signature on each song.'

8: A TIME FOR RHYME

'I have always been a stickler about rhymes. Mark Steyn, the great expert on the songwriter's craft, said, "rhyme reinforces, clarifies and focuses". That's so true. An example: if the lyric to "Come Fly With Me" went "Come fly with me, let's fly, let's fly away,/If you could use some exotic booze/There's a bar in far Calcutta"... Ouch! It's like nails on a blackboard or somebody singing off-key. A rhyme is also an aid to the ear. Of course, rhyme doesn't seem to be that important when listening to the songs of Bob Dylan or Tom Waits. They are fine poetic storytellers and their imagery is remarkable. But not many people sing their songs apart from them – those are specific songs particular to them, their own stories and their individual styles.'

9: VERSES FOR EVERY OCCASION

'Theatre writing, as I said, is different to pop writing. A theatre lyricist's job is to illuminate character and dramatise situations. Pop music lyrics are all about sounds and they rarely strive for clarity. It is fun to write pop songs. You are not restricted by any story-line. But in a way that makes it harder.

'Alan Jay Lerner once told me that he never wrote a song that wasn't for a film or a show. He found it impossible to create a self-induced scenario. For that matter, he also found it difficult to write the lyrics first. He preferred the rigid framework of a melody. The confinement helped him. I agree with that, but I've also known where to have more fun writing songs, more freedom. Writing for Robbie Williams would be just as enjoyable as writing for Marvin Hamlisch, but you have to tailor your style to the product. And remember – do have fun. We're only trying to write songs, not change the world.'

10: SUCCESS IS WHERE THE HEART IS

'I think it's possible to teach people how to write songs, but you can't teach them to love what they do, and you can't teach them taste. To be a professional songwriter, you have to relish great songs. What is a great song? A song that reaches a level of emotion that leaves the listener drained, moved, changed. So – and this is the most important rule of all – if you can listen to Oscar Hammerstein and not admire his folksy genius, if you can listen to Stephen Sondheim and not marvel at his graceful solutions, if you can listen to Lerner, Mercer, Hart and not be bowled over by their concise eloquence, and if you can listen to the score of Gershwin's *Porgy And Bess* without getting goosebumps, then you're in the wrong game. Forget it.'

To illustrate some of these rules, and just for the fascinating fun of it, I asked him to take me through one of his most famous songs. As we went through parts of it, he pointed out why he did what he did.

Let's take 'Tell Me On A Sunday'.

Don't write a letter when you want to leave,
– *That says a hell of a lot in a few words. You've got the situation and you compound it with*

Don't call me at three a.m. from a friend's apartment.
– *You've got a bit more, and now the thing is to gradually unfold, illuminate the character.*

I'd like to choose how I hear the news.
– *She's vulnerable, she knows it's not going to work out. There's a truth there, people start affairs and almost never look far ahead. You don't think how it's going to be in ten years' time.*

Take me to a park that's covered with trees.

Tell me on a Sunday please.
– *In other words, let me down very, very gently if you can.*

Don't want to know who's to blame,

It won't help, knowing.

Don't want to fight day and night,

Bad enough you're going.
– *I like songs that have a conversational shrug in them. This is a spoken thought, a soliloquy, so conversational mannerisms are appropriate if you can get it right. It's important to have a good ear for real conversations, hard to put into songs but worth it if you can, because it helps get at the truth of a situation. What I try to bring is an intensity to ordinary, everyday feelings. Without sounding too lofty, that's my aim.*

At the end of the song, we later added the coda, which I like very much:

Don't run off in the pouring rain,

Don't call me as they call your plane,

Take the hurt out of all the pain.

Take me to a park that's covered with trees,

Tell me on a Sunday please.
– *Don't dramatically run off in the pouring rain, don't glibly call me as they call your plane – it's the various, true, ways of saying goodbye. So we know at the end of that song that this girl is vulnerable, she's used to affairs ending abruptly and has no doubt experienced some of these other ways of parting before and she has a poetic, romantic side to her.*

And all the way through, these intense feelings are being given force by the rhymes, until they almost burst through them.'

It is a cause of sadness to Black that, these days, talent is not enough on its own to guarantee success. There has always been an element of perspiration required to promote inspiration, but the music industry is a harder place. 'The industry wasn't ruthless when I started, the way it is today,' he laments. 'These days the record industry revolves around marketing, around the singers as products. The songs themselves barely register much of the time.'

In the golden days of Tin Pan Alley, publishers cared about the songs. 'My first publisher, Dick James, loved a song. When you'd written a song for him, he'd welcome you into his office and tell his secretary to turn the phones off so he could listen to it. He'd play it, and if he liked it, he'd say, "Put that middle bit on again, it's unbelievable!" You've got more chance of winning the Lottery than having a publisher act like that today. Now, they just ask for the titles so they can register them. Very rarely do you hear the sentence, "Can I hear it?"'

Clive Black, who as a record-company boss, knows all about today's industry, agrees. 'The business has got harder. And it has changed. It's now the *business* of music, rather than making music and then trying to make some money out of it.'

Yet it can still be done. The success of Grant and Clive, weaned and raised on Don's golden rules and sense of values, proves it. And, as for their dad, he's still wrestling with those elephants. As he looks back at his life so far, there was one clear point which defined what he had made of himself. Grant's bar mitzvah in 1974 – in contrast to Don's own, modest do at home in Hackney – was a lavish, showbiz affair at the Grosvenor Rooms in Willesden. There were books of matches with Grant's name on, guests in evening dress and a band. And, everywhere, Don's showbiz friends.

As he sat next to his son after dinner while Grant made his speech about becoming a man, Don looked around the room. There were plenty of witnesses to his success: John Barry, Elmer Bernstein, Johnny Mercer, even two members of Grant's beloved Chelsea Football Club (John Hollis and Dave Webb – Don had called in a favour). And, closest to him, more important than all the celebrities who had turned up, were seated Don's family members. It was a good metaphor for his life.

At the very end of Grant's boyhood, it was clear to all – clear to him – that Betsy's quiet son from the East End was a confident, talented, loved man. Never mind the elephants, he had taken on life and won.

Appendix 1: Don Black Musicals

Maybe That's Your Problem – (Walter Scharf, Lionel Chetwynd) – 1971
Billy – (John Barry, Dick Clement and Ian La Frenais) – 1974
Barmitzvah Boy – (Jule Styne, Jack Rosenthal) – 1978
Tell Me On A Sunday – (Andrew Lloyd Webber) – 1979
Song And Dance – (Andrew Lloyd Webber) – 1982
Abbacadabra – (Benny Andersson, Bjorn Ulvaeus) – 1983
Dear Anyone – (Geoff Stephens, Jack Rosenthal) – 1983
Merlin – (Elmer Bernstein, Richard Levinson and William Link) – 1983
The Little Prince And The Aviator – (John Barry, Hugh Wheeler) – 1983
Budgie – (Mort Shuman, Keith Waterhouse and Willis Hall) – 1988
Aspects Of Love – (Andrew Lloyd Webber, lyrics with Charles Hart) – 1989
Starlight Express (additional lyrics) – (Andrew Lloyd Webber, Richard Stilgoe) – 1992
Radio Times (additional lyrics with Chris Walker) – (Noel Gay, Abi Grant) – 1992
Sunset Boulevard – (Andrew Lloyd Webber, lyrics with Christopher Hampton) – 1993
The Goodbye Girl – (Marvin Hamlisch, Neil Simon) – 1997
Dracula – (Frank Wildhorn, lyrics with Christopher Hampton) – 2001
Bombay Dreams – (AR Rahman, Meera Syal) – 2002
Dance Of The Vampires (one song) – (Jim Steinman, David Ives and Michael Kunze) – 2002
Whistle Down The Wind (tour, one additional song called 'The Gang') – (Andrew Lloyd Webber, Jim Steinman, Patrcia Knop) – 2002
Romeo And Juliet – The Musical – 2002
Tell Me On A Sunday (new version) – (Andrew Lloyd Webber) – 2003

Future plans include *Brighton Rock* with John Barry and *Bonnie And Clyde* with Frank Wildhorn.

Appendix 2: Don Black Filmography

Very Important Person – (Reg Owen) – 1961
Thunderball – (John Barry) – 1965
Born Free – (John Barry) – 1966
The Chase – (John Barry) – 1966
Pretty Polly (also known as *A Matter Of Innocence*) – (Michel Legrand)
– 1967
I'll Never Forget What's' Is Name – (Francis Lai) – 1967
Stranger In The House – (John Scott) – 1967
To Sir With Love – (Mark London) – 1967
The Long Duel – (John Scott) – 1967
The Vengeance Of Fu Manchu – (Malcolm Lockyer) – 1967
Isadora – (Maurice Jarre) – 1968
Mayerling – (Francis Lai) – 1968
First Love – (Mark London) – 1968
House Of A Thousand Dolls – (Mark London) – 1968
Boom! – (Johnny Dankworth) – 1968
The Southern Star – (Georges Garvarentz) – 1968
Sinful Davey – (Ken Thorne) – 1968
The Party – (Henry Mancini) – 1968
Hot Millions – (Laurie Johnson) – 1968
Work Is A Four-Letter Word – (Guy Wolfenden) – 1968
La Leçon Particulière (also known as *Change Of Heart*) – (Francis Lai)
– 1969
Where's Jack? – (Elmer Bernstein) – 1969
Mr Jericho – (George Martin) – 1969
A Walk In The Spring Rain – (Elmer Bernstein) – 1969
In Search Of Gregory – (Ron Grainer) – 1969
The Midas Run – (Elmer Bernstein) – 1969
Some Girls Do – (Charles Blackwell) – 1969

Run Wild, Run Free – (David Whitaker) – 1969
The Guru – (Mark London) – 1969
The Kremlin Letter – (Mark London) – 1969
The Italian Job – (Quincy Jones) – 1969
True Grit – (Elmer Bernstein) – 1969
Goodbye Gemini – (Denis King) – 1970
Hoffman – (Ron Granier) – 1970
The Last Valley – (John Barry) – 1970
Walkabout – (John Barry) – 1970
Diamonds Are Forever – (John Barry) – 1971
Mary, Queen Of Scots – (John Barry) – 1971
Pancho Villa – (John Cacavas) – 1971
She'll Follow You Anywhere – (Gordon Rose) – 1971
Public Eye (also known as *Follow Follow*) – (John Barry) – 1971
Alice's Adventures In Wonderland – (John Barry) – 1972
Ben – (Walter Scharf) – 1972
Gasp – (Walter Scharf) – 1972
Antony And Cleopatra – (John Scott) – 1973
Cahill – US Marshal – (Elmer Bernstein) – 1973
Walking Tall – (Walter Scharf) – 1973
The Belstone Fox – (Laurie Johnson) – 1973
A Doll's House – (John Barry) – 1973
Paul And Michelle – (Michel Colombier) – 1974
Gold – (Elmer Bernstein) – 1974
Golden Needles – (Lalo Schifrin) – 1974
The Man With The Golden Gun – (John Barry) – 1974
Tamarind Seed – (John Barry) – 1974
The Dove – (John Barry) – 1974
Love Among The Ruins – (John Barry) – 1975
The Wilby Conspiracy – (Stanley Myers) – 1975
Doc Savage: The Man Of Bronze – (John Philip Sousa) – 1975
Satan's Harvest – (Denis King) – 1975
Won Ton Ton, The Dog Who Saved Hollywood – (Elmer Bernstein) – 1976
Buttercup Chain – (Richard Rodney Bennett) – 1976
Gulliver's Travels (screenplay and lyrics) – (Michel Legrand) – 1976
The Pink Panther Strikes Again – (Henry Mancini) – 1976

The Bitch – (Biddu) – 1979
Ashanti – (Michael Melvoin) – 1979
The Nude Bomb (also known as *The Return Of Maxwell Smart*) – (Lalo
Schifrin) – 1980
Honky Tonk Freeway – (Elmer Bernstein, George Martin) – 1981
The Golden Seal – (Dana Kaproff, John Barry) – 1983
Svengali – (John Barry) – 1983
Scandalous! – (Dave Grusin) – 1984
The Worst Witch (TV film) – (Charles Strouse) – 1985
Out Of Africa – (John Barry) – 1985
Dances With Wolves – (John Barry) – 1990
Freddie As F.R.o.7 – (David Dundas) – 1992
Dirty Weekend – (David Fanshawe) – 1993
Beauty And The Beast (TV and video) – (Rachel Portman) – 1997
Tomorrow Never Dies – (David Arnold) – 1997
The World Is Not Enough – (David Arnold) – 2000
Thomas And The Magic Railroad – (Hummie Mann) – 2000
Tom's Midnight Garden – (Debbie Wiseman) – 2000
Christmas Carol – (Steve Mac/Wayne Hector) – 2001
The Little Robots (TV series) – (Debbie Wiseman) – 2003

Index

———————— PUBLIC LIBRARY————————

Presented to the
Library

**In honor of the dedicated
volunteer service of**

Irene Romero

A Passion for
COLLECTING

Original title "Esprit Collection," by Jean Demachy and François Baudot
published by Editions Filipacchi in 2004
Copyright © 2004 Editions Filipacchi
Copyright © 2004 Filipacchi Publishing, Inc. for the U.S. edition

ISBN: 2-85018-840-9

Translated from French by Simon Pleasance and Fronza Woods
Edited by Jennifer Ladonne
Art Direction by Lili Neyman

Printed in France by Imprimerie Clerc

FRANÇOIS BAUDOT
JEAN DEMACHY

A Passion for
COLLECTING

DECORATING WITH ART AND ANTIQUES

filipacchi
publishing

Contents

"Tell me what you collect, and I'll tell you who you are."

Behind every collection there is an idea; an idea arising from a personality; a personality formed by a way of life. The act of collecting cannot be separated from the collector, and the collector assumes a thousand and one faces. But whether the collector is naturally cultivated, initiated to the calling by experts keen to pass on their know-how, or, as is perhaps most often the case, an inspired autodidact, those who accumulate things, trade, barter and chase down objects to the four corners of the earth all have one thing in common: an unquenchable passion. That tremendous appetite for an ideal, for just the right object that will bring that unparalleled moment of complete satisfaction. To the collector, art galleries, auction houses, secondhand shops, flea markets and yard sales all represent one thing—the fantasy of limitless possibility. The collector's profile—extravagant or modest, limited by resources or completely unbounded by time or personal means—is truly eclectic, from financiers to adventurers, clergymen, couturiers, laborers, business people, the wise and the frivolous. Yet deeply etched in the character of each and every one of them is the will to discover, the lure of possession, the thrill of amassing quantities of objects. And, like desire, collecting never satisfies the appetite it creates. Rather, each object acts as fuel for an ever-increasing flame. For collecting represents an urge as old as the world itself: the desire to own. "He who collects, also discards," goes the saying, but it takes a strong character to obey this principle. At the end of the day, even when a collection is reduced to one single object— the quintessence of a life of quests and eliminations—this

quests and eliminations—this object occupies such a place in the mind and life of its owner that it becomes indistinguishable from the collector himself. In this book, we bring together collections assembled by many different personalities, each one of them portrayed exclusively by the collection that bears his or her signature. Just as the ornate pattern of an oriental carpet contains its meaning hidden within, each choice the collector makes sends a message to the world at large. It is up to the viewer perusing these pages to reach her own conclusion of those who have agreed to open their doors to reveal the objects of their passion. No matter how large or grand the container, it will invariably be smaller than the dreams it holds. As is abundantly clear on these pages, these are not the fruits of a passing whim, they are the spoils of a quest that could easily span a lifetime.

Just as there are countless types of collectors, so are there countless reasons to collect. Some collect to be noticed, others to become sole possessor of the object of their passion. Some seek only their own pleasure, others the pleasure of sharing. Likewise, there are many types of collections; too many to count. From the horizontal collection, which calculates sets and series of things, categorizes and counts them: stamps, moths and butterflies, watches, coins, etc., to the vertical collection, which has much more room for personalization and individuality as it jumps from one branch to the next in the genealogical tree of objects. When such collections have advanced to the stage where every aspect of the collector's environment is infected with his mania, we witness some of collecting's finest hours. These are the

collectors we've chosen to feature here: those whose collections have infiltrated their lives to the extent that home itself is subservient to the collection's purpose. Steering clear of categorization, allowing all epochs, ages and eras equal status on equal terrain, the seeker, the flâneur and friend of chance encounters does not shy from eclecticism. This is the collector who perhaps more than anyone reflects our age, rich as it is in contrasts and contradictions. Be the collector imperious or attentive, compulsive or calculating, he or she must be ready to transcend categorization and listen to the objects themselves. Like the great sculptor Rodin bent over a sculpture ear to its chest like a physician listening to his patient's heartbeat, the collector must feel the rhythms and whisperings of their possessions and divine a meaning relevant to our times. This is what Maurice Rheims called "the strange life of objects." And this is precisely what this book aims to capture. There are those who believe in an object's soul, the indelible essence that pervades all things of beauty and the life breathed into objects that are loved.

But where there is love, there is also jealousy. Collectors tend to be a possessive bunch and to penetrate their world and gain access to their secret chambers, much resistance must be overcome. Even while surrounded by advisers, dealers and accomplices, the collector is basically a loner. The splendor of collections that herald their owners as prophets of our time also serves to cocoon them among their acquisitions. But their singular existence does not prevent them from being forces in the world. Kings and monarchs, Rothschilds and Rockefellers have all in their day found a way of expanding their power by means of their collections. These days, modern diviners and tastemakers may not stake their name and reputation on the collections they assemble but their influence can often be measured in terms of the conquests they make by way of the recognition of their vision.

There remains the least predictable aspect of collecting, or the aspect that collectors most choose to ignore—the decorative value of their collections. No one who has created cabinets of curiosities, libraries of rare books, galleries or lofts filled with antiques or stuffed with paintings claims to use decoration as his guide. It is rejected. It is scorned. It is dodged. In the collector's view, it is a matter of exhorting destiny, not exalting decor. And yet the most successful of collections have an undeniable visual appeal, as is evident in each one of the photographs included here.

Since being photographed, many of the installations featured in this book have known other fortunes. When a collector dies, evolves or simply moves on, there may be no more left of the fruit of her lifetime quest and compulsive accumulation, than an inventory or sale catalogue. But the greatest collections give rise to new collections; when a piece from a legendary grouping arrives at auction it becomes the seed that germinates a whole new collection or a new jewel in the crown of an already existing one. And there are those collections, long since disbanded, that are still discussed, still dreamed of, and in their mythic proportions, still possess the immense power to inspire.

9

Versace loved to collect houses—in Milan, Como, Miami—if only to hold the artworks and furniture he adored. Each home had its own signature style, matching the spirit of the place. In his Manhattan mansion he opted for avant-garde style. Tragically, his New York pied-à-terre would turn out to be the Milanese couturier's final creation.

In his personal rooms on the top floor of his Fifth Avenue home, Gianni Versace gave a prominent place to his portrait in broken plates by New York artist Julian Schnabel. On either side of the central door, behind a crimson-upholstered sofa and an Empire armchair, hang two large canvases painted in the 1980s by the late Jean-Michel Basquiat.

Gianni VERSACE

Shortly before his tragic death, Gianni Versace was working on his town house just off of Manhattan's Central Park. With four floors equipped with every up-to-the-moment technological innovation, the fashion maestro was keen to redefine themes in keeping with the spirit of the U.S. So he left behind the decorative ruins he loved—as exemplified by his palace in southern Italy—and struck up a fertile dialogue with high-profile American artists, such as Julian Schnabel, the visual artist, filmmaker and musician. In Schnabel, Versace found something better than an artistic adviser or decorator, he found a soul mate. The many-faceted, protean artist not only made Versace's portrait in his signature broken plates, but also designed his steel bed, wall frescoes and marble floors, resulting in a coherent—if eclectic—whole to which the house's proprietor added an impressive collection of modern and contemporary drawings paintings, sculptures and antique furniture. The couturier's love of everything Empire might have clashed with the bolder, more violent strokes of his chosen artworks, but not here, where an often baffling yet totally symbiotic style emerges between opulent fabrics of Versace's own design and monumental artworks; from the virile lines of Pablo Picasso to the large graffiti works of Jean-Michel Basquiat.

11

Preceding spread: The large ground-floor sitting room is decorated with a collection of colorful Venetian glass vases from the Seguso, Venini, Barovier and Toso glassworks of Murano. The walls in marble trompe-l'oeil are lined with a collection of Picasso drawings produced between the 1920s and the 1960s. In the center *La Maternité à l'orange*, a portrait of Françoise Gilot with Paloma and Claude (1952). The furniture is a mix of 1940s Art Deco and Empire. The armchairs and ottoman are in a quilted black velvet.

Opposite:
The 18th-century inspired hallway is a perfect example of his characteristic mix of over-the-top opulence and contemporary art. Two neoclassical Russian sconces flank Roy Lichtenstein's famous painting *Blue Nude* over a gilded French baroque table.

Right:
On the first-floor landing, beneath a Jean-Michel Basquiat painting, a 1940s console table displays a series of hand-blown Venetian glass vases from the 1950s.

For the great couturier's bedroom, Julian Schnabel designed a massive bed in brushed steel. The motif of the inlaid marble floor was inspired by a print from Versace's Winter 1996 collection. The pedestal table and chairs are Empire, the quilted silk bedspread is a house of Versace design. On the wall, *Amoco*, a magnificent and ambitious fresco jointly painted by Andy Warhol and Jean-Michel Basquiat in the 1980s.

16

The mammoth of international publishing finds his best inspiration in his 19th-century workspace and residence in Cologne, Germany. It is here that he ponders new ideas and entertains friends—here, too, that his passion for the arts is exhibited to best advantage.

Benedikt TASCHEN

Taschen, who was a millionaire by 40, is passionate but not effusive, an odd mixture of anarchist and introvert. In Cologne, where he lives and works, his publishing house became an instant success. Today, on the city's loveliest avenue, the publisher occupies one of the rare 19th-century homes spared by allied bombs. In the impressive hallway, the conservative-chic of this large Baroque mansion still finds room for the very latest in contemporary art. Taschen collects the avant-garde with great enthusiasm. In his home there is not a single working space left unembellished by a roving group of artworks that change location according to the master of the house's whim. "Changing the place of a painting or sculpture is like giving it a new identity. Living with art makes life more pleasant. You feel you're in a real home," says one of Taschen's associates, himself afflicted by the collecting bug like many others working for the publisher. In the basement of his private residence, Taschen has installed sliding panels for easy access to his large canvases, like so many slides in their sleeves. Behind the director's desk, a work by Jeff Koons depicts the artist with his ex-girlfriend, La Cicciolina, both nude in an unambiguous posture. No doubt a clever means to put Benedikt Taschen's visitors at ease!

In the basement of Taschen's private home in Cologne, an "inflatable" dinghy made in bronze by the American artist Jeff Koons. On the wall, a chromatic series by Gunther Förg.

Behind the
"Elephant Chair"
by sculptor
Bernard Rancillac,
works by Albert
Oehlen, Mike
Kelley and Martin
Kippenberger.

Benedikt Taschen began by publishing books about the contemporary artists he admired.
Now he collects the real thing.

In his patrician two-bedroom Manhattan apartment, the doyen of New York couturiers created a contemporary dwelling steeped in European neoclassicism. Blass, who died in 2002, bequeathed all of his possessions to cultural and charitable organizations.

Bill BLASS

The exquisitely courteous Bill Blass brought a whole new definition to American style, combining the very best of "old Europe" with a new-world aesthetic. He was just as comfortable designing clothes for Manhattan's most fashionable women as he was perfecting a classic style of interior design often described as "Philadelphian." Born in Indiana in 1922, this self-taught man developed an early appreciation for the refinement of late 18th-century European style, as strictly applied by the architects of American independence. With his passion for that neo-Palladianism that flourished everywhere where culture flourished—from St. Petersburg to Philadelphia—Bill Blass became a passionate collector of furniture and artworks that harkened back to that exceedingly structured and vaguely militaristic style where the relics of ancient Rome mingle with reminiscences of the Napoleonic era. Lustrous parquet floors, spare lines and masculine touches prevailed. Mahogany, marble and bronze, stark whites and shades of stone culminated in an aristocratic atmosphere, where the loft vied with the chateau. For Blass, however, the reference was less Josephine at Malmaison than Jefferson at Monticello. All that, tinged with a certain nostalgia for the Republic of Athens.

In his Manhattan apartment, a corner of Blass's bedroom and study. On a 19th-century table, the couturier juxtaposed different periods and different civilizations: ancient China, Hellenistic Greece, 19th-century American. In the foreground, a pair of Italian stools. Articulated clamp lights in copper-coated brass illuminate a collection of antique helmets.

Preceding spread:
In this large living room overlooking the East River, a mix of Empire furniture and antique busts and torsos.
The deep sofa covered in sumptuous white silk was designed by Blass himself. Above the mantelpiece, a large Picasso drawing depicts Picasso's lover Marie-Thérèse Walter sleeping (1930s).

Left:
In the bedroom the bed is raised just high enough to allow unobstructed views of the river.
A large equestrian bronze of General Bonaparte.
In the center of the room, on the gueridon, a period reproduction of the Vendôme column and a Regency globe. Leather-covered armchair from the art deco period.

Tina Chow, the gifted jewelry designer who left a legacy of stunningly original works, also accumulated an outstanding collection of Parisian art deco furniture and objects with her husband Michael, a well-known New York City restaurateur.

Tina CHOW

Tina Chow was fragile and sensitive and lived halfway between East and West. For a few brief years she reigned over New York high society in the heady Warhol milieu. As they ushered in new trends and a distinctive urban style all their own, Tina and Michael Chow furnished their uptown loft with rare pieces from the 1920s and 1930s, then relatively unknown. Today, all that remains of their exquisite creation is a few photographs. But those photographs capture a rare beauty—and though ephemeral we must be grateful for this small glimpse into their rarified world. In this light-filled former artist's studio, black lacquered forms stand out against beige silk walls. Most of the furniture was designed by that master of art deco furniture, Emile-Jacques Ruhlmann. Streamlined Jean Dunand vases and one or two Eileen Gray pieces—also important pioneers of that period—punctuate the deliberately spare decor, which has served as a model for many lovers of the period. This reprise constitutes a kind of tribute to the 1920s as well as to the '80s. Many of the pieces pictured here fetched considerable sums at auction and are now scattered throughout the world enriching a few museums and the very best collections.

In Tina Chow's lofty apartment, a grand piano made of Macassar ebony designed by Emile-Jacques Ruhlmann holds some of the bangle bracelets and rock-crystal jewelry that made her famous in the early 1980s. An outstanding two-tone bronze vase, sculpted and etched by Jean Dunand, and a lacquer wardrobe from a set of furniture designed by Jean Dunand in 1924 for a gentleman's bedroom.

The spiral
staircase was
designed by
Michael Chow
inspired by a
Le Corbusier
drawing. A
lacquered metal
Ruhlmann chair
with a leather
seat. On the
easel, also
designed by
Ruhlmann,
a Jean-Michel
Basquiat drawing.

A sweeping view of the stunning high-ceilinged living room. Neutral walls covered in ivory-colored raw silk offsets precious wood and the sheen of lacquered chairs by Emile-Jacques Ruhlmann. A rosewood lectern displays a sketchbook of portraits of Michael by artist Larry Rivers. On the right of the fireplace, balanced on a lacquer column by Eileen Gray, a rare 1920s finned metal vase by Jean Dunand. On the marble mantelpiece, designed by Ruhlmann in the neoclassical style, an unusual cachepot and a plaster frame designed by Diego and Alberto Giacometti in the 1930s for decorator Jean-Michel Frank.

Rhapsody in black
and white...in the 1980s
the vertical city of
New York returned to
the opulent lines of
art deco style.

In front of a large black-lacquer wardrobe by Jean Dunand, etched with a rendition of "The Ass and the Hedgehog" based on a drawing by Jean Lambert-Rucki (1920s), sits a famous gaming table in Chinese lacquer with eggshell inlay. Matching chairs were cleverly made to fit just under the table to form a perfect cube. This one-of-a-kind piece was commissioned by the couturière Madeleine Vionnet from Jean Dunand.

37

On a low Ruhlmann table in metal and frosted glass, Tina Chow arranged her jewelry next to a 1930s cubist yellow plaster vase by Alberto Giacometti. In the foreground, a stool from the same period designed by Eileen Gray.

Opposite: A view from the loggia: early 20th-century alabaster hanging lights.

Born in Brittany, Roger Prigent emigrated to New York City at the age of 20, eventually to become one of the star photographers of American fashion. But a passion for collecting would prove to be his strongest. Now in his 60s, he has redefined himself as one of Manhattan's top antiques dealers.

Roger PRIGENT

Prigent, an energetic Frenchman who attained eminence in the fashion magazines of the golden '60s, found that having photographed all the most beautiful women of his day, he could now move on to beautiful objects. A bachelor, an indefatigable traveler with insatiable curiosity and a virtuoso photographer—who is a close friend of Richard Avedon—in his youth he nurtured a secret passion for all things classic. On his travels he was forever accumulating curiosities, in due course forming an outstanding collection that in the 1970s would finally settle him on antiques dealing. He called his first store Malmaison, a veritable Aladdin's cave for decorators and upper-east-side ladies alike. "Malmaison" means "bad house," but he showed this etymology to be paradoxical indeed. Prigent's house and antique store have over the decades become a delicious mix of the classical, Napoleonic and simply eclectic. All this blends perfectly with 1930s paintings, art deco furniture and Cartier bibelots. Roger Prigent is an eternally young man who, when he realized that his eyesight was slowly fading, decided to organize a sale of his collection so his finds could enrich other people's lives. But his sense of beauty is still unmatched, and the curiosity of this hunter of life's beautiful objects and images is unabated.

On top of a rare Empire-style bookcase, terra-cotta Greek vases copied from antiquity (early 19th-century Italian). On the floor, two framed ink drawings by Eugene Berman and a seascape in oils by his brother Leonid (late 1930s).

On an Empire
desk by the
furniture maker
Jacob-Desmalter,
a selection of
Greek urns, a
porphyry gorgon
mask and silver-
plated bronze
casts taken from
antiquity (early
19th-century).
Behind, a drawing
in colored pencil
by Jean Cocteau.

Following spread:
In Prigent's
bedroom,
a remarkable
mahogany
Empire bed
by Jacob-
Desmalter
borrows the
model of
Bonaparte's bed
at Malmaison.
The 1930s mural
comes from the
smoking room
of an American
steamship.
Table and bronze
bowls in the early
19th-century
Pompeian
style, like the
mahogany chairs
also by Jacob-
Desmalter.

43

On the banks
of the Seine
a completely
restored 17th-
century building
houses a top-
notch collection of
modern and
primitive art—
bright colors,
irrepressible forms
and powerful
ideas.

Patricia LAIGNEAU

In the ample living
room, oversize
yellow sofas
blend with the
primary colors of
contemporary
artworks.
Between the
sofas, a coffee
table by Jean-
Michel Wilmotte
with a sculpture
by Vincent Debré
and a Murano
glass ashtray.
Top, a gouache by
Fernand Léger
and on the
background wall
a painting by
Gaston Chaissac.
On the left,
18th-century
Provençal oil jars.

This sunny triplex at the top of a Paris mansion houses a superb collection, where primal sculpture, vintage furniture and works of art from the latter half of the 20th century all intermingle. From Alexander Calder to Jean-Charles Blais, Arman to Oceanic sculptures—a mix of bold tastes and colors were assembled by a collector couple determined to create an environment completely of the moment. Designed to resemble a ship's prow, these former top-floor apartments and maid's rooms were transformed to become three open floors exhibiting museum-quality works illuminated by many windows and skylights. But the artwork is not confined to within, from these windows some of the world's most cherished monuments are visible—Paris's Notre Dame cathedral, for one. And when night falls, the spotlights of pleasure boats traversing the Seine sweep across the works of art: a drum from New Hebrides, Mumuye tribal sculptures from Nigeria, Jean Dubuffet canvases, Niki de Saint-Phalle's *Nanas*, a screen by David Tremlett. Every object, every placement and every relationship has been carefully considered to achieve maximum effect. Two decades of patient acquisition, five years of renovation, three floors of pure magnificence, where the ancient and the modern mix to greatest advantage.

The main living
room and dining
room are on the
apartment's
second level.
Above, views of a
skylit balcony
where the
gallery and study
reside. In the
foreground, to the
right, a New
Hebridean drum.
On the low table a
Nana by Niki de
Saint-Phalle.
The carpet was
designed by Jean-
Michel Wilmotte
and the sofas by
the mistress of
the house. On the
wall, to the right, a
large painting by
Pierre Le Clerc,
and at the very
rear a painting by
Jean Dubuffet.

49

Like a ship's prow, whose end forms a cozy room "below-deck," one can recline on natural-colored canvas sofas brightened by large cashmere shawls (Hermès). On the left, under the stairs, Arman's *Le violoncelle en colère* (The Angry Cello); on the pillar in the foreground, a Calder, and above center a Jean-Charles Blais.

On the top floor, beneath the roof, is the master of the house's study, library and gym. The chair and recliner were designed by René Herbst and the desk by Franco Albini (Knoll) with a Tizio lamp. In the left foreground a collection of Mumuye sculptures from Nigeria. The center sculpture is by Philippe Migno and the rug by Jean-Michel Wilmotte.

From the New Hebrides to Dubuffet, all cohabit just fine in their waterside gallery.

Left:
One of the apartment's more utilitarian ideas: David Tremlett's striking four-leaf screen hides the television, video and stereo systems. To the right, an eye-catching head sculpted by Rennerz and to the left a Jean Dubuffet transfer.

Opposite:
On the lower level, left, a sculpture titled *Head* by Richard di Rosa next to a drawing by Robert Combas. The banister is based on a 17th-century design. On the upper landing, above a Mazarin desk, a canvas by Gérard Schneider; to the right, an acrylic by François Boisrond.

This austere yet supremely elegant collection of Ming furniture acquired by master-collector Philippe de Baker is one of the world's finest and most comprehensive, with Ming furniture spanning the 16th and 17th centuries.

Philippe DE BAKER

In the large living room, a remarkable early 17th-century folding armchair designed for a Ming dignitary (Yuanhubei Jiaoyi) in the shape of a horseshoe complete with its own footrest. A stunning collection of Tsong-period porcelain lining the shelves along the back wall (10th and 11th centuries). On the zitan-wood table, two pieces of imperial tableware.

The door of this comfortable Brabant cottage opens to reveal the unexpected—the Ming empire re-created in objects and furniture patiently assembled by an ardent traveler who adores 17th-century China. Contemporaneous with the reign of France's Sun King, Louis XIV, the high style of the Middle Empire was quite different from the sumptuous rooms of Versailles, even if these two powers were mutually intrigued with each other. With the accession of the emperor Long Qing, a golden age of furniture-making began in China. Crafted from unusually hard species of tropical wood, these objects— whose repertory of forms aimed at a spare simplicity—were nothing less than masterpieces. With a minimalist aesthetic that far predated any such aesthetic in the West, these pieces were designed for the elite of the imperial court. In the latter part of the 20th century, political upheavals in China led to the destruction of much of this furniture. All that remains today are a few thousand pieces scattered throughout the world. The collection formed by Mr. de Baker, accounts for an estimated ten percent of these surviving pieces, making it a profoundly important collection. And he's gone to great lengths to create an atmosphere that allows this magnificent collection to be seen at its best.

A long journey for the princely furniture of the Middle Empire to the heart of the Brabant.

Left:
This small drawing room, whose silvery gray hue was inspired by noble Peking homes, reproduces the furnishings of a 16th- or 17th-century Chinese man of letters. In that period there was a preference for simplicity, exemplified by this daybed (Luohan Chuang), only two examples of which are known to exist today.

Opposite:
A folding chair (Jiaoyishi Tangyi) for outdoor use. Ming craftsmen excelled in the use of the most precious hardwoods, such as this piece in huali, a variety of rosewood.

This consumate image-maker has a hand in influencing the art of his time on a daily basis. As a champion of popular films, the producer of "Asterix" reveals in his own home a flair far removed from the simple tastes of the Gallic village.

Claude BERRI

O n Rue de Lille in Paris's Faubourg Saint-Germain, the attic of an 18th-century mansion was partly raised to create the feel of an artist's atelier. France's most famous filmmaker and producer helped to redefine a new French style—the "bourgeois bohemian," or "Bobo" style. The series of immaculate rooms where he houses his collections—designed in collaboration with architect Yannis Tsiomis and decorator France Loeb—represent nothing less than a manifesto for contemporary art. The spare, abstract monochromes of Yves Klein, Robert Ryman and Piero Manzoni interact with Lucio Fontana's slashed canvases and Cy Twombly's palimpsests. Alongside these works, Berri has arranged singular pieces of furniture by Jean-Michel Frank, Pierre Chareau and Eugène Printz—the very best of the early 20th-century moderns. Yet Claude Berri is not a mere hoarder of valuable objects, the man of action in him constantly vies with the purist, and the possession of beautiful objects is not enough to satisfy him. No matter how luxurious his Parisian home may be, he could reappraise and rethink it from one moment to the next; it is not so much a hedonistic satisfaction that drives him as a ceaseless quest to understand the true spirit of modern art, and, in his discrete way, help others to appreciate its genius.

In the small sitting room, a 1960s coffee table and bronze stool sculpted by Diego Giacometti share the space with a series of works by the Italian artist Lucio Fontana (circa 1958).

Berri's home brings together great works of the 20th century—from decorative pieces from the 1920s and '30s to the great abstract artists of the '90s.

In the study, in the midst of Jean-Michel Frank furniture, tables by Pierre Chareau and Diego Giacometti; light sculptures by Dan Flavin (*Untitled* and *Monument for V.Tatlin,* 1964) flank the windows. On the left, three works by Jean Dubuffet, and in the corner, *Untitled Black Board,* 1968, by Cy Twombly.

A strong sense of composition, crucial to the art of directing,

Behind a pair of
Pierre Chareau
chairs, the
bookcase is given
the crowning
touch with Jean
Dubuffet's *Mire*.
To the left, two
Joseph Cornell
boxes next to a
monochrome
by Ad Reinhardt.
To the right,
a sculpture by
Lucio Fontana.

extends in the most felicitous way to his home.

A glimpse of the sizable living room (right); furniture by Sue and Mare, on the wall, *Untitled*, a large canvas by Cy Twombly. Another view of the living room, on the left, shows a Ryman monochrome behind a hammered bronze table by Diego Giacometti.

In spite of his marked eclecticism, this enterprising dealer has become a period specialist in what is commonly known as "1940s style." This apartment, designed in the late 19th century, offers a fine synthesis of this style, which actually spanned the 1930s to the immediate postwar years.

Yves GASTOU

In front of a large canvas by James Brown (1989), an iron console table by Diego Giacometti and two stoneware vases. The plaster and terra-cotta pieces are maquettes made by the sculptor Léon-Ernest Drivier (a student of Rodin) for the nymphs in the Trocadéro pond (1937).

Beneath the lofty Third Republic ceilings of his classy Right Bank apartment in Paris, Yves Gastou has assembled an astonishing collection. Furniture that until recently was all but ignored, before a few discerning connoisseurs helped collectors on both sides of the Atlantic rediscover its merits. This is especially the case with variations on the mirror theme as defined by Serge Roche and Gilbert Poillerat's ironworks. Carpets, rugs and tapestries, and neoclassical-inspired seats by André Arbus along with the baroque scrollwork of gilded wrought iron gates. A whole new generation has now fallen head over heels for this neglected period that their parents turned their backs on. And not without good reason; those years were full of memories of the hard times endured just before, during and immediately after World War II. Where collecting is concerned it has often been the trying times that smile on people of limited means. Today, prices for the 1940s and early '50s pieces are on a par with those of more widely appreciated 18th-century furniture. No longer considered kitsch, these florid lines and voluptuous forms represent a style more in keeping with the relaxed attitudes of today.

In the living room,
on a wool carpet
by Garouste and
Bonetti, a coffee
table, armchair
and wrought-iron
gate by Gilbert
Poillerat (circa
1940). The seats
are by André
Arbus and the pair
of 1940s oak and
bronze buffets
highlight pieces
by Ettore Sottsass
and a pair of
beaten silver
vases by
James Brown.
On the wall,
an Aubusson
tapestry based
on an André
Arbus drawing.

In the dining room a beautiful diversity in the works of wrought-iron craftsman Gilbert Poillerat: a monumental chandelier, console and large dining table, all in wrought iron. The mirror-clad obelisks are by Gilbert Poillerat and Etienne Kohlmann (circa 1940), the gold leaf-covered wrought iron chairs by René Drouet. On the mantelpiece, a Sèvres porcelain centerpiece by Couturier and on the right a large sculpture by Axel Cassel.

True to
the spirit of the
United States and
meticulously
designed down to
the tiniest detail,
the home of a
great man of
American fashion
forms the
backdrop for a
rare collection of
modern art.

Doug TOMPKINS

On the heights of San Francisco, in the midst of a luminous garden, a vast contemporary house serves as the showcase for a collection of important modern paintings. Spare almost to the point of austerity, everything in this white-clad space is designed to highlight the work of the artists represented. It's easy to forget that you're actually in the midst of a large American city, for the aura of a country getaway prevails here. Architect Willis Polk helped create this airy dwelling with its many windows and views that temp the eye almost as much as the large canvases by such greats as Balthus, Bacon and Botero. Even the furniture is pared down to the essentials with white the ongoing theme. The owner's preference is for the clean lines of art deco-style—with some pieces made to measure—in a constant search for harmony. Like the simple backdrop of a stage set giving pride of place to each and every work, there are rarely more than one or two artworks per room, so the canvases never vie with one another. Nothing like the sterility of a gallery space here, yet each room keeps an ongoing dialogue with the environment outside, with an appreciative nod to the sapphire blue of California skies.

In the guest
bungalow,
black furniture
contrasts with
white walls.
Tripolina folding
armchairs
in leather. The
carpet is from the
art deco period.

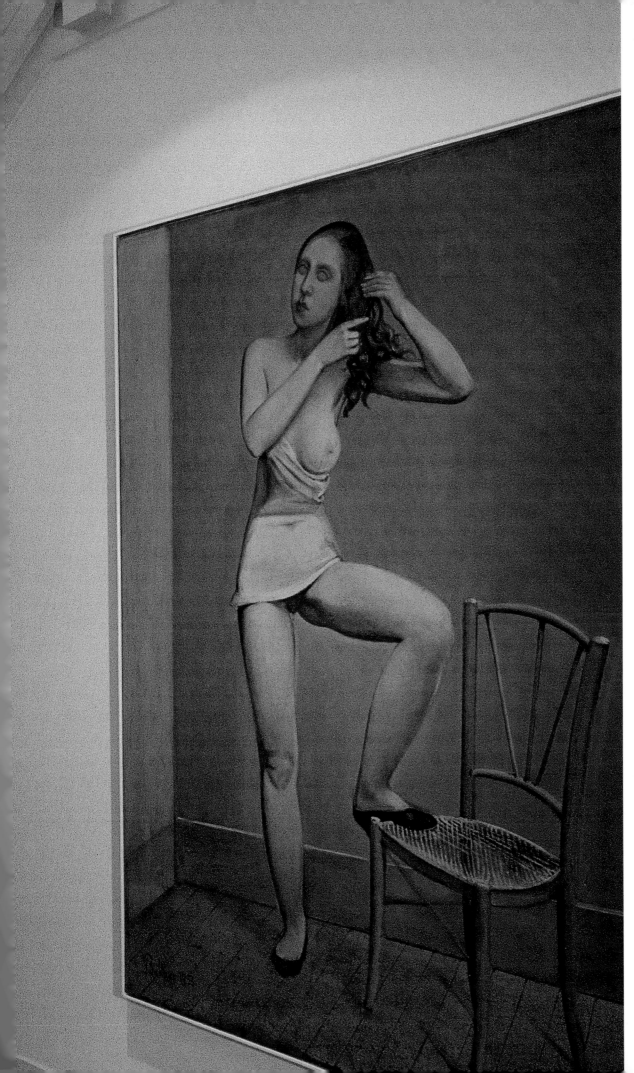

Alice, one of the paintings that brought the painter Balthus to the fore in 1933. To the left, at the foot of the stairs, stands a Jaraï funeral post (Vietnam, 19th century).

Following spread: On the wall, *George Dyer,* a triptych by Francis Bacon (1970s) where inlays depict the artist's self-portrait and the profile of Lucian Freud.

Left:
Jyriama
sculpture
(Kenya,
19th century).

Opposite:
Three American
Folk Art puppets.

Enigmatic variations against immaculate
backgrounds; works that couldn't be more different
come face to face and
bring out the best in each other.

80

Hellenic pediments, Pompeian bronzes, custom-made trompe-l'oeil drapery wallpaper. In this rarified and antiquated setting, time has suspended its flight.

Paloma PICASSO

The first portraits of her show her in a house in Vallauris with her father in what may be the most beautiful and rare paintings of the collection. Paloma Picasso has since become an artist in her own right. When the demands of her work led her to set up a home in New York City, she opted for a large apartment in Yorkville, a Manhattan neighborhood that has more in common with the palatial old buildings of Europe than with the surrounding vertical lines. Paloma's private home contains an outstanding collection of works by her father. But she has been keen to preserve her independence from the great master, and has distributed them carefully throughout the different rooms interspersed with the 19th-century neoclassical objects and art deco furniture she loves, in contrast with the modern art and emphasizing its raw power. This residence is more in keeping with the homes of early 20th-century pioneer collectors. The ones who didn't hesitate to mix canvases, whose innovative proportions would soon change the face of painting with the more refined pieces of classical collecting. The hallway bronze of a young girl skipping rope depicts the owner of the house as a girl. Now a woman, she has forged her own formidable place in the world of beautiful artworks and in her own personal environment.

In the hallway, trompe-l'oeil wallpaper and an inlaid marble floor. The bronze sculpture *La Petite à la corde* (Girl with Skipping Rope) by Pablo Picasso (1950). Cherry-colored solid mahogany door. In the living room, glimpses of 19th-century bronzes.

A daughter's singular and personal homage to the

Paloma Picasso has imbued the living room with a powerful and unique style. Here, restoration bronzes rub shoulders with furniture by Emile-Jacques Ruhlmann and works by her father.

greatest Catalan painter of all.

ARMAN

Born in 1928, the young Armand Fernandez—now known simply as Arman—thought he'd become a teacher. Yet he ended up at the School of Fine Arts, in Nice, and there had his first exhibition in 1956. Four years later, he cofounded the New Realists group, and the rest is history. Today he divides his time between his studio houses in Paris and New York City. Interested from the very beginning in new ways of seeing things, his early work focused more and more on accumulations of objects regarded as incongruous. He still creates compulsively "to the top of the walls" in his words, and collects both outstanding artworks as well as the most prosaic of objects. In his Manhattan building, where he lives with his wife and team of assistants, the heir to Duchamp and dadaism quenches his need to amass things. Noteworthy 18th-century Japanese suits of armor are offset by an eloquent series of bakelite radios. African masks present a striking contrast to a series of identical desk lamps, neatly arrayed in metal pigeonholes. Arman himself mischievously throws people off his track—it's not always so easy to tell an actual Arman work from these unexpected encounters. Is it from the gallery walls or the flea market? Just the question he hopes to inspire—with no ready answers.

An exceptional Japanese helmet in the shape of a hare was worn by Yamabushi warrior monks.

A collection of collections: from the extremely valuable to the truly prosaic...the lines between found objects and works of art become blurred.

Left:
In Arman's study, American bakelite radios from the 1930s to the '50s.

Opposite:
In the hallway, *Persistence des impressions* (1991), a work by Arman made from a group of copper desk lamps with opaline green shades, a ubiquitous American model. On the left, a Dogon statue (Mali) and in the foreground a Japanese suit of armor in steel and black lacquer.

Preceding spread, left:
In the dining room, the tables and chairs are by Arman. On the far wall, above a collection of Japanese helmets and *Eight Guitars,* a sculpture painting by Arman. On the shelf to the left, a collection of Gabonese sculptures.

Preceding spread, right:
On the bookshelves to the right, a collection of fetishes from Zaire and African masks. On the floor Warhol's famous *Brillo Boxes* and two unmistakable Warhol paintings.

Left:
In the living room, in front of a Frank Stella painting (1960s), the sofas and armchairs were designed by Arman.

95

Nicolas Berggruen asked Peter Marino to decorate his apartment on the top floor of Manhattan's Pierre Hotel where he lives year-round. In the most discreet fashion, major works of the late 20th century are shown to full effect in these handsomely appointed rooms.

Nicolas BERGGRUEN

Several luxury hotels in the United States have private apartments rented on a yearly basis and decorated to suit the personal tastes of a tiny handful of the world's elite. In this ultra-sophisticated apartment in the Pierre Hotel tower (with stunning views over Central Park), decorator Peter Marino has designed a warmly refined setting for the collections of a young Swiss art lover and collector. The many works of Andy Warhol go nicely with the Parisian furniture and objects designed between the wars—a thriving period for the decorative arts. Pieces by Dupré-Lafon and Jean-Michel Frank blend with the white-oak bookshelves and the distinctive neutrality of an abode designed more to persuade than to dazzle. Berggruen has thoroughly succeeded in reconciling his taste for a discreet classicism with his love of daring contemporary art. A financial manager specializing in capital investments, he is expert in backing up the prescience of his choices. From Warhol's Factory period to the short yet brilliant career of Jean-Michel Basquiat, many of the works on view here illustrate some of the highlights of the art-world heyday of late 1970s and early '80s. Here, these works reclaim their stature as masterpieces and blend seamlessly with the very European brand of refinement that sets these rooms apart.

Above a Dupré-Lafon writing desk, a painting by Francesco Clemente. A period Empire chair in black horsehair.

Limed white-oak
bookshelves
designed by
Peter Marino
frame *Tuxedo*
by Jean-Michel
Basquiat (1982).
Sanded
Hungarian oak
furniture designed
by Jean-Michel
Frank from the
late 1930s.
Bronze lamps
by Alberto
Giacometti. The
sofa and chairs
are based on a
design by the
Marino agency.

99

Yesterday, Andy Warhol was collecting Jean-Michel Frank; today, they are found side by side in the Pierre Hotel.

Opposite:
In the guest room, a large painted screen by Andy Warhol (1957) frames a black lacquer desk with a tortoiseshell veneer on brushed steel legs (Jansen Company, 1960s). A leather-clad mock bamboo lamp created by Jacques Adnet (1940s), chair by Jean Royère and straw frame by Jean-Michel Frank.

Right:
In the living room, above a steel console, an Andy Warhol ink drawing from the *Rorschach* series (1984) exhibited on a mirror of woven steel.

Left:
To the left in the hall, a bronze standard lamp by Alberto Giacometti. Beneath a large canvas by Anselm Kiefer (1980s), a pair of oak stools designed by André Arbus in 1950.

Opposite:
In the master bedroom, next to a colonial bed (19th century), an Anglo-Indian table with a crystal and silver-plate pitcher by Christopher Dresser, circa 1860. A 19th-century armchair in mahogany (Jacob). At the head of the bed, a round mirror by Line Vautrin. On the left wall, a monumental canvas in the *Rorschach* series (1984) and a silkscreened portrait from the famous *Jackie* series (1970), both by Andy Warhol.

Pierre HEBEY

On a chest of
drawers by
the furniture-
maker Jean
Pascaud,
decorated with
panels designed
by Jean Boullet,
two plaster
masks carved by
Giacometti rub
shoulders with
Justice, an original
piece by Niki de
Saint-Phalle.
Above, a painting
by Alechinsky.

Pierre Hebey has taken refuge in west Paris on the edge of the Bois de Boulogne, where he opens his doors only with reluctance. Once he had allowed our photographer across the threshold, he permitted himself these observations about this "collectomania": "I make different collections... at the same time. There's no furniture section and no painting section. Collecting is a mystery. You never get to the bottom of it. Why am I a collector? I don't know the answer. The oddest thing is this wish to own things, this need to possess. No one in my family has been a collector. You're born a collector; you don't become one out of conviction or belief. In 1946, when I got my law degree, my father asked me what I wanted. I asked him for a Magritte. He didn't want to give me the painting, he gave me a car instead—it cost the same. I became interested in paintings because of the editor and publisher Maurice Nadeau, champion of the surrealists. So I started out from literature and ended up with painting. But intuition isn't enough. You need it to begin with but lots of people have intuition....When I started collecting art deco at the flea markets there were just five or six of us collecting, that's all! Collecting calls for a lot of effort and time, but that is precisely the fun of it! A collector never stops."

In the living room, two Ruhlmann
armchairs; to the left, on the floor
a sculpture by François-Raoul Larche
depicting the American dancer Loie Fuller.
On the table, *My Friend Pierrot* by Max
Ernst and a Jean Lambert-Rucki sculpture.
On the Printz library table in front of the
bookcases, *Roger and Angelica on the
Hippogriff* by Antoine-Louis Barye
(circa 1850). To the far left, a Printz desk
holds a sculpture by Gustave Doré titled
Ratapoil. On the back wall, center, a large
Alechinsky canvas, to the left, Fernand
Léger's *The Keys* above an ink drawing
by Henri Michaux. On the right, a
Marc Chagall canvas above a smaller
Chagall drawing. On the Printz bookcases,
a bird's head by Max Ernst and a bird
by Gustave Miklos.

In the bedroom, on an African-style table by Sue and Mare, a lamp by Dupré-Lafont and sculptures by Emmanuel Frémiet, Jules Dalou, Auguste Rodin and Jean-Baptiste Carpeaux; lions by Barye. On the left, a small painting by Henri Michaux. To the right, a large Alechinsky ink drawing.

108

The collector does not indulge in decoration. It is decoration that is at the beck and call of the collector.

A standing lamp by Ruhlmann and the edge of a Dupray table. Behind the chair designed by Pierre-Emile Legrain, an Alechinsky drawing titled *The Binche Carnival*. To the right, on the wall next to a Max Ernst sculpture, a series of original gouaches from a book signed Bram van Velde.

Following spread: At the edge of the garden, a set of three Max Ernst sculptures; behind the Reinhoud fountain, a sculpture by Japanese artist Techi Gahara, and a *Nana* by Niki de Saint-Phalle.

In Biarritz, the house owned by Pierre Hebey
and his wife, Geneviève, elegantly expresses
their taste for rare things with simplicity and a
discreet sense of balance.

Right:
A gouache of an owl by Paul Jouve in the 1920s-style bedroom. Desk by Charlotte Alix and Louis Sognot. The standing lamp on the left is by André Arbus.

Opposite:
A tribute to Japan: a bamboo and lacquer chair.

Left:
An interplay of
verticals and
horizontals:
a rare German
armchair by Johan
Rhode beneath a
painting by
Robert Crippa.

Opposite:
Against the
background
of a Thonet
wardrobe, an
armchair and
desk by Carlo
Bugatti, a vase
by Alexandre
Bigot and a
Murano glass
bowl.

Following spread:
Frames sold at
the Guggenheim
Museum in New
York City. In the
photo right of
center, Catherine
Deneuve with
Geneviève and
Pierre Hebey in
Biarritz.

All great creations shock at their inception;
some collectors learn how to understand them and
live with them sooner than others.

she got 3 wishes

These two women designed a space in New York City that serves as both home and office: a place to bring up their children and the site for a contemporary collection still in its infancy, but no less ambitious.

Dorothy BERWIN
Dominique LEVY

Dorothy Berwin is an English film producer; Dominique Levy a modern art consultant of Belgian and Egyptian extraction who runs her company Dominique Fine Art from home. They have settled in lower Manhattan's Tribeca, where semi-industrial brick buildings offer superb spaces lit by lofty skylights. Starting out with next to nothing—apart from the classic proportions of the Greek-style molded cast-iron 19th-century pillars—the two artists consulted American architect Steven Lerner to help show their contemporary acquisitions to best effect. Avant-garde artworks, especially photographs, hang side by side with industrial furniture of the 1950s and other artworks often collected with the help of the London gallery owner David Gill. Furniture by Marc Newson and Jean Prouvé, separated by 75 years, go hand-in-hand with photographs by Nan Goldin and Gregory Crewdson, Dan Flavin neons and Richard Serra drawings. In the main room, the color scheme is inspired by a large canvas by German artist Franz Ackermann. This interaction recurs in the outstanding chandeliers that draw the eye up toward the soaring ceilings. With collecting, the important thing is to maintain a balance between offsetting the acquisitions while insuring that the house doesn't end up looking like a gallery.

In the library, photographs by Anna Gaskell and Nan Goldin, bookshelves by Jean Prouvé. On the right, a bridge chair designed by Robin Day.

119

In the main room, a color scheme drawn around a large canvas by German artist Franz Ackermann. The chandelier, designed by Jeff Zimmerman, is nothing less than a sculpture in gray and aubergine-colored molten glass. The dining room table is by Stephanie Bergman.

Collectors without borders, the avant-garde
is not limited to paintings but extends well beyond.

Left:
The desk,
designed by
Martin Szekely
at Berwin's
request, is at
once a sculpture
and a functional
object. In the
background,
a Franz
Ackermann
canvas.

Opposite:
A chair by Marc
Newson, on
the wall, a
photograph by
Rineke Dijkstra.
The 1940s
bookshelves are
by Jean Prouvé
and Charlotte
Perriand.

Maroun SALLOUM

I n another life, he could well have been his own best customer. Maroun Salloum buys the things he loves then squirrels them away in storerooms. Such and such a "thing" will always come out at just the right moment. For as much as he makes purchases on a love-at-first-sight basis, the antiques dealer devotes himself equally to patient searches for things he dreams of—objects that may be modest or pedigreed but never commonplace. This man has the taste, the eye, and above all a true sense of the hunt. Despite the graciousness of the welcome one receives at his shop on the far end of a courtyard on Quai Voltaire, Maroun Salloum is a reserved man. At the School of Fine Arts in Paris he studied architecture and set his sights on industrial design. It was then that he started hunting for his first antiques, to fund his firm. He was so good at it that just one year after taking his degree his mind was made up: he would be a dealer. From then on he would spend most of his time roaming the world, tracking down rare objects, from Prague to Paris, Moscow to Manhattan. After concentrating on Greco-Roman, neoclassicism and Ming China, Salloum nowadays focuses mainly on the roots of the 20th century and the innovative forms of the European avant-garde. This solitary knight still asserts that the important thing is to love.

The serene mysteries
of Asia mix
seamlessly with
central European
treasures.

In the living room,
a pair of
armchairs
designed by
Josef Hoffmann
(1905). On a table
in front of the
bookshelves a
Cambodian
Buddha from the
late 17th century.
To the right,
a Fontana Arte
lamp (1938).

127

Left:
Another view of
the living room,
on the
bookshelves,
a pair of 18th-
century Chinese
porcelain vases
mix with an Italian
folk art vase.
Between the
books,
a collection of
New World
objects.

Opposite:
On the wall,
a Henri Bellery-
Desfontaines
mirror (France,
circa 1910). On a
Russian chest
(Talaskino school,
1900), a Sainte-
Barbe bronze by
Arno Breker (circa
1950) and a
"Ferro Battuto"
set by Duilio
Cambellotti.

Living in a luxury hotel all year round suits Pierre Bergé's sense of gracious living. Although he owns several residences, for many years now he has kept rooms at the Lutétia Hotel, on Boulevard Raspail in Paris. His modest suite overflows with beautiful things, which just goes to show that for certain art lovers, too much barely suffices.

In the bedroom, over the night-stand, a drawing by Victor Hugo and a Georges Braque painting. On the table, a lamp by Jean-Michel Frank.

Pierre BERGE

An entire world re-created in a hotel. In his Jacques Grange-decorated suite, the former managing director of the House of Yves Saint Laurent recalled a time when as an ambitious youngster he walked Coco Chanel to the Ritz, where she lived until her death. Now it seems he's following in the great couturier's footsteps in creating a permanent home in a place that is for most a temporary luxury afforded for only a few blissful days. The 650 square feet that Bergé has fashioned with singular flair and an expert's sense of proportion, seem to have expanded to three times their size, so well chosen are the masterpieces that flesh out the true volume of these rooms. Nothing was included without serious reflection; even the merest door handle could not escape the connoisseur's eye. Starting with the leopard-patterned carpet, ideal for Ficelle's siesta (Bergé's wily Jack Russell who is the favorite treasure of this precious interior). The atmosphere is essentially 18th century with one or two objects from the 16th or 17th centuries. But in this sumptuous cocktail of exquisite pieces, one is also treated to works by the likes of Jean Cocteau and Jean-Michel Frank, and outstanding pieces by Picasso, Braque, Toulouse-Lautrec, Degas and Derain.

131

In front of
the bedroom
bookshelves,
a striking terra-
cotta sculpture
of Louis XIV.

In the hotel suite where he resides year-round,
an art lover gathers together his many different passions.

Opposite:
On the early 19th-century console table, two bronzes depicting Henri IV and Maria de Medici (Moatti), onyx and horn bowls and a collection of "vanitas" skulls.

Right:
In the living room, an extraordinary Renaissance Italian chest with marble-veneer drawers. Beneath a portrait by Géricault, two antique profiles, a marble Apollo and a collection of 17th-century Italian vases.

From the Renaissance to the 1930s, a cabinet of curiosities and a cozy place to live.

Playful design, crazy colors, eclectic mixes of plastic, wood and steel, find themselves together on display on the first floor of an old Nice mansion just a stone's throw from the Italian coast.

Christophe NOIREL

Life is an endless cycle: one discards what one once loved and ends up with bitter regrets about what was mercilessly tossed out 20 years before. Take, for instance, the furniture of the 1970s, spurned in the '80s and '90s and because they were often fabricated of materials too delicate to last, they have now mostly vanished. But the tide has turned; now, the colorful lamps of Verner Panton, furniture by Joe Colombo and Eero Aarnio and other greats of the era are being zealously tracked down by a new generation of collectors bewitched by these space-age confections, just as their parents were smitten by the furniture of the 1930s and '40s. Gallery owner Christophe Noirel adopts a maniacal approach to reclaiming that lost era: apart from wall-to-wall shag carpeting, he has tracked down and exhibited some of the finest examples of the futurism that was in vogue 30 years back. His treasure trove looks fantastical and represents less cynical times when titling a film *2001, A Space Odyssey* was enough to ensure an enthusiastic following eager to penetrate the depths of the future. Although the decors of the third millennium never fulfilled their Jetson-inspired promise, it is still possible to put together such collections. Henceforth, it is a good idea to think before you empty your attic....

In a corner of the living room, a Ball chair by Finnish designer Eero Aarnio (mid-1960s). The orange- and red-plastic furniture is the work of Raymond Levy, and the two lamps are by Giancarlo Mattioli.

139

Requiem for a decade in plastic: a vision never fully realized but happily (and profitably) resurrected.

Preceding spread: Furnished to resemble an actual living room, Christophe Noirel's gallery houses the greatest of the Italian designers. Lamps and lanterns by Guzzini and a "Safari" couch by Poltronova, the designer portion of the Italian Archizoom group.

<u>Above:</u>
The gallery owner is also the creator of these wall paintings, reinforcing the 1970s spirit exemplified by the furniture. Blue walls match the Verner Panton carpet. The green and orange "Pastil" armchairs are Aarnio creations; the "Tongue" chair is by Pierre Paulin, and the red chaise longue is an Italian piece made of resin.

<u>Opposite:</u> Two "Pastil" chairs by Aarnio and two lamps by Guzzini.

A specialist in objects that were unsellable for almost 20 years, this collector rummages through old estates to find treasures overlooked by less inquisitive colleagues. His tastes, which are not confined to any particular period, steer him toward those things relegated to the sidelines of history.

Antoine BROCCARDO

Because he's always had the passion of a collector, Antoine Broccardo was a natural for antiques dealing—his way of reconciling the functional with the decorative. This unearther of things invisible to most, first plied his trade in a tiny five-by-twenty-foot booth. Russian folk art from the late 19th century, objects with surrealist leanings, old architectural photographs, particularly of Italy, neo-Roman, Second Empire-era cast-iron pieces fashioned after excavated objects—like the famous treasure of Boscoreale (today in the Louvre)—theatre props and furniture originating from Central Europe between the wars. Nothing interesting leaves this curious collector indifferent, and his collection is enriched day in and day out by new items he records in detail. For some 20 years—he is barely 40—Broccardo has been an outstanding specialist of the period from the 1930s to the '50s with an in-depth knowledge of its treasures. This sense of secondhand goods combined with a fondness for unexpected encounters lend his lair a sense of theatricality, calling to mind the charades that André Breton and his friends were so fond of. As the collector might say to himself about his finds of the day: "My first is a giant chess piece, my second a plaster house, my third a paper sparrow-hawk...."

Against a backdrop of the Parthenon (carbon print by Alinari, 1860), a rare set of neo-Roman goblets in gilded and silvered bronze made from the antique model for the goldsmith Constant Sevin in 1868. The mask of Greek tragedy by Sartori dates from the 1950s.

In the game of chance, the inquisitive person
finds the biggest thrills in the most unexpected places.

Opposite:
Multiplying the
space with five
chrome-mounted
mirrors in
this screen by
Jacques Adnet.

Right:
On the
bookshelves,
a still life in
the Surrealist
style: black glass
globe vase
(Ernest
Boisceau); die-
shaped cup-and-
ball game
(1940s); a giant
pawn from
a mahogany
chess set by Man
Ray; a plaster
head from the
1930s; a set of
abstract forms
(1920s,
Netherlands),
dominated by
an écorché
anatomical figure
(late 18th
century).

Left:
On a whimsical cherry-wood console (German, 1910) a pair of Swedish polished brass candlesticks from the 1920s. Above, a Serge Roche mirror (1930s).

Opposite:
In the foreground, on a chrome-plated table, an Egyptian-style gilded bronze statue titled *Joseph* by Just Becquet (1903). next to the head of Actaeon in patinated bronze, a work by Janine Janet (circa 1950) from the Balenciaga collection. On the left wall, a work in red chalk by Yakovlev.

Restricted
Growth
(small version)

Peter Hutchinson
1968

As a creator of perfumes, Frédéric Malle has a soft spot for subtle harmonies. But where his collections are concerned, his keen sense of style more befits a dandy than a thoroughly modern guy.

Frédéric MALLE

This maverick perfumer loves nothing more than to find harmony in unexpected combinations. And just like his craft, his apartment seeks out that perfect balance between furnishings and artworks from many periods and persuasions. Housed in an arc-shaped apartment on the top floor of a building overlooking Paris's Place de l'Odéon, Malle has found a perfect refuge for his particular pairing of tasteful neoclassicism with such far-flung items as Andy Warhol's *Electric Chairs*, assorted teak pieces from Borneo, furniture by Ruhlmann and Knoll (borrowed from his mother), Swedish modern pieces found at flea markets and plenty of photos of family and friends. Malle has an inquisitive mind, yet maintains strict rules for buying: never just any old thing, and never with any speculative intent. Even with a limited tolerance for searching, in his view, collecting is the best way of giving an order to things. An avowed amateur, he is nonetheless the product of generations of collectors. "After dreaming about my grandfather's collection, then my father's, I'm now only interested in the works produced by people of my age, and I hope this will be mutual," declares Malle, whose perfume lines have already launched some 20 fabulously creative fragrances under his aegis.

In Malle's bedroom, a photograph by John Coplans, a Paul Hutchinson collage and a bronze head by Delamarre.

151

In the living room, an Arco standing lamp designed by Achille Castiglioni (1962). The daybed (left foreground) is by Jacques Adnet (1950). The wardrobe is by Emile-Jacques Ruhlmann and the desk and chair by Jules Leleu (1940s).
The low wicker chair is the work of Poul Kjaerholm (1960). The photo seen just through the arch is by Suzanne Lafont (1986).

Following spread, left page:
A plasma screen with a Jean-Charles Blais animation. The armchair is by Jacobsen and the stool by Sori Yanagi (Japan, 1954).

Following spread, right page:
In the dining room, on madder-colored walls, five prints from a series of ten entitled *Electric Chair* by Andy Warhol (1963). A ceiling lamp by Louis Poulsen (1957). The chairs, redone in black leather, date from the 19th century (England).
On the right, a teak fertility statue from Borneo (early 19th century).

153

This denizen of Brussels, a great connoisseur of art from the 1950s and '60s, satisfies his passion for Danish modern while thoroughly upgrading the look.

Jean-Claude JACQUEMART

Owner of the Atmospheres boutique, Jean-Claude Jacquemart has just set up home in Brussels' Grande-Place, all the better to express his passion for the 1950s-style furnishings he eagerly collects. Jacquemart was completely smitten by this once-underappreciated period in international design and grew particularly fond of the exquisite glass and earthenware it produced. The pottery of Arne Bang, Axel Salto and the Saxbo works—all souvenirs of prestigious Milan Triennials past—take center stage. To highlight their rich and surprising colors, he has chosen the abundant light of a top floor apartment in a contemporary building and furnished it with pieces by Charles Eames, Florence Knoll and Finn Juhl, as well as lesser-known artists like the Danes Kofod Larsen and Peter Hvidt. His collection reveals a practiced eye daring in its scope: Vasarely silkscreened works, pieces by Eero Saarinen and Isamu Noguchi and primal Nepalese and African sculptures all come together to form a brilliant whole. In many ways, the now retro furniture and objects that Jacquemart loves presaged today's more interesting designers but with softer lines and more human forms. So it is not surprising that mixing modern pieces from the post-war era with much more contemporary works would make a great success.

A reference to 1950s design: three Danish nesting tables, table lamp by Arik Levy and a display of Italian glassware by Gio Ponti, with vases made by the Rosenthal company (Germany).

Great design of the 1950s fills this penthouse apartment in an unabashedly modern building.

Opposite:
In the dining room, lit by a Noguchi lamp, stoneware pots by Arne Bang rest on a Saarinen table surrounded by Hvidt chairs. Two framed Saverys drawings on the back wall with Dogon statues and headrest on the window sill.

Right:
In the living room, a wide window sill holds a statue by Hatié, a small Scarpa bronze, a primal Nepalese piece, and a 1920s painting from the Belgian school alongside pieces of Scandinavian pottery. A leather settee (Knoll International) and American lamps from the 1950s.

Left:
On the right
side of the
hallway, a painting
by Michel Mouffe
and a Thai "aka"
statue.
On the left,
a bookcase by
Sylvie Baucher-
Feron holds a fine
collection of Elfi
Plashus Swedish
vases. Behind
the bookshelves,
two Tanzanian
statues.

Opposite:
In the bathroom,
a David Mellor
stool and shelves
holding a series
of Danish,
Italian and
Dutch glassware
from the 1950s
and '60s.

This dauntless London antiques dealer shamelessly mixes periods and styles with gleeful abandon. His offhanded pairings, while sometimes outrageous, mostly add up to an unparalleled panache.

Gordon WATSON

This apartment might well be labeled banal were it not for the constant distraction of unexpected encounters and surprising juxtapositions. The London art dealer Gordon Watson systematically creates shock waves and that's how he likes it. Arts and crafts furniture commingles with Andy Warhol paintings and one or two plaster pieces with the surreal theatricality that Jean Cocteau would have adored, a Christian Boltanski installation and a piece of art deco furniture thrown in for good measure. "I hate museums because you can't buy anything in them," declares this compulsive collector and expert organizer of empty spaces. He has come to realize that when his treasures are brought out sparingly, they assume greater proportions. A specialist of the 1930s and '40s who learned his trade at Sotheby's, Watson opened a gallery some 20 years ago where, along with his associate Lewis Kaplan, he displays willy-nilly objects as diverse as jewelry, silver flatware, glass and furniture all bearing signatures of some of the great designers and craftsmen of the 20th century. Hardly confined to the era of his expertise, this art lover is constantly juxtaposing the most subversive of contemporary works with the merely highly collectable and getting away with it.

In the main room, in front of a "reliquary" sculpture by Christian Boltanski, two armchairs inspired by a Jean-Michel Frank piece and a 1940s wrought-iron table.

163

Pale maple-wood parquet and white walls for a penthouse living room in a 19th-century building in central London. On the table in the foreground, ceramics by Jean Cocteau stand side by side with a candlestick by Marina Terzieff and a Carpeaux bronze. The 1920s chairs in patinated oak were designed by Robert Thomson. On the wall, plaster sconces by Serge Roche.

In the living room, a carpet by John Harwood based on a drawing by Jean Cocteau. Above a Robert Thomson library table, a triptych by Christian Boltanski and vases by Magdalena Odundo.

The truism that one needn't be a tycoon to build a distinctive collection is brilliantly evident here. With a limited budget, this young Londoner filled his tiny apartment with curiosities that combine the haphazard with the bizarre.

Hubert ZANDBERG

Hubert Zandberg alighted in London as a law student five years ago. Soon after, he met the decorator David Champion and in no time at all became his associate. In due course, Zandberg moved into a 500-square-foot Portobello apartment where he did away with doors and painted the whole place black. Against such a backdrop, he was soon showing off his secondhand and flea-market finds from neighborhood haunts. Far from emphasizing the diminutive proportions of the room, its dimensions seem to increase by the very fact that it is filled to overflowing. Here, the eye is courted by a hundred details from countless perspectives created by seemingly limitless objects—no doubt strangers until now—all thrown together as if in some surrealist charade. On the low ceiling, Hubert created a frieze made up of 40 herbarium plates, all framed himself. The apartment is a cabinet of curiosities—a collection of Dogon ladders, stuffed hunting trophies, butterflies from around the world, even the toilet rolls arrayed on metal shelves resemble an art object. One day, however, he'll have to sell or, better still, make his way to roomier quarters; for when a collector can no longer distinguish his bed from the rest of the room, it's clearly time to make a move.

In the living room, on a black-lacquer table, an oil painting by David Champion, a collection of miniature Dogon ladders, a clock lamp (1930) and on a French chair from the 1920s, four African earrings.

In the living room, above a neoclassical-style love seat covered in two shades of linen, two boxes of butterflies, a mirror by Line Vautrin and Asian fish traps around a photo by David Gamble showing the hallway of Andy Warhol's house, an inspiration for Zandberg. A pair of woven string armchairs, designed by the master of the house himself. In the foreground, on the table, a set of objects in horn and bone, and a series of skulls. On the right of the window, on a Chinese lacquer chest, a bundle of miniature ladders of Dogon origin.

Right:
In the bedroom, a photograph by Georges Dureau, on a black lacquer table, an antique bowling ball and a contemporary lyre-shaped lamp.

Opposite:
An eclectic mix around the four-poster bed in this less than 100-square-foot bedroom: architect's lamp from the 1950s, stuffed head of an English bulldog, a stuffed pink flamingo, a series of Victorian glass eyes, tortoise shells and iron herbalist's boxes commonly used in the late 19th century to keep botanical specimens. The console and stool were designed by David Champion and Hubert Zandberg.

Combinations never seen before; fresh perspectives, explosive effects.

The former president of Canal+, a popular French TV station, is an admirer of post-war Americana. His collection is a lot like him—made up of objects with a great sense of fun. Many of these lively (and sometimes kitsch) pieces have become sought-after rarities.

In Pierre Lescure's office, a saucy lamp from the 1940s fitted with a system of vanes that spin when the lamp warms up, revealing the scant attire of its pinups.

Pierre LESCURE

Lurking behind the serious face of a big boss, Pierre Lescure cleverly disguises what he's really up to. Why does he vanish several times a month between Paris and New York? Where does he go with that conspiratorial air? Why, to haggle over objects steeped in the lore of the American dream. Flea markets, obscure shops known only to the initiated few, rambles from the London suburbs to the New York docks—for this child of jazz and comics, nurtured on Cinemascope and technicolor, treasures can only ever be "made in the USA." The Lescure collection is fascinating for many reasons, not least of which that it takes things just over the top. The obsessive effort exercised by its author to analyze, appraise and exhibit this nostalgia belies its studied disorder. Not one item in this grown-man's toy store evades his grasp: such and such an issue of *Popular Mechanics*, the silver Zeppelin-shaped shaker or the Speed Graphic camera (just like the ones used by the Untouchables in 1940s Chicago), a pinup girl for truckers, or a collectible lunchbox, jukeboxes and the first Mickey Mouse wind-up robot, an amazing rocket-ship radio complete with countdown—a fantasy world re-created with all the abandon of the eternally young.

After thirty years of hoarding objects found in American flea markets during his travels, in May 2004 Pierre Lescure decided to break up his collection of now rare objects which was sold off at Sotheby's.
In the foreground, on an armchair inspired by Salvador Dali, a plaster dummy used in the 1950s to advertise corsets and brassieres.
On the walls, various hyperrealist canvases (USA, 1960s and 70s).

Following spread, left page:
A rare radio set made of blue reflecting glass, Sparton model (1935-1940).

Following spread, right page:
A mixture of comics, books and kitsch: nostalgia from a more carefree time.

177

David HOLDER

The first thing I bought was a set of Perriand and Prouvé bookshelves," explains the young collector. The desk would be the start of a great collection. The novice read every conceivable book about the period from 1950 to the '70s, grilled the specialists and scoured the showrooms. Then he set up house in a three-floor 1920s mansion. In his bright and spacious living room, light plays on different clusters of objects: one or two beautiful tribal pieces, paintings by Robert Combas, Peter Klasen and Tom Wesselmann, sculptures by Arman and Nathalie Decoster, a rug designed by Garouste and Bonetti. The walls, painted an eggshell white, seem to fade away behind these significant pieces, where Marilyn looms like the classic she is. Between photos by Peter Beard and Helmut Newton, the furnishings are more in the spirit of Le Corbusier; spare resting places and backdrops for his favorite items from the rue de Seine galleries, and more significant pieces from the Basel Art Fair and the Venice Biennale. But there is no lack of inventiveness in this nascent collection, "In ten years' time, I'll probably sell everything so I can move forward and buy in a better way," declared Holder a few years ago. History will soon bear witness to this wise resolution.

Schlosser's 1966 huge oil painting, *Naufrage* (Shipwreck), above the buffet.

In the studio, a simple and comfortable pure white sofa (The Conran Shop). On the Garouste and Bonetti carpet, a coffee table by Charles and Ray Eames. On the window sill, an ink drawing by Arman lit by a Noguchi lamp (1960). On the fireplace, flanked by two Jacobsen armchairs, a sculpture by Francesca Guerrier, plaster bear by Georges Guyot, bronze bear by Raymond Delamarre and a chicken by Arman.

Design purgatory lasts for thirty years. After that, it either finds its place in the pantheon of greats or is forgotten.

London gallerist and collector David Gill is a talent-spotter who enjoys mixing high and low as dictated by his latest finds. In addition to his loft gallery, he owns a snug pied-à-terre where he can give free rein to his deeply individualistic sense of interior design.

On the wall, *Hydra*, a decorative linen, velvet and PVC patchwork tapestry with gilded scallop motifs, hemmed with beaten-iron rings and a black ceramic bead fringe. *Samson and Delilah*, a bronze, black patinated console with a scagliola top and varnished clay cubist vases, all by Garouste and Bonetti. Wicker poodle (1940s), with a red collar (Hermès).

David GILL

No nugget of 20th-century gold is left unmined in his home near London's Fulham Road and in his London gallery, where David Gill has brought together examples of some of the last century's more inspired, if sometimes underappreciated, moments. Spiced with a typically London eclecticism, his gallery is also a shrine to the eccentric, eschewing the more prosaic examples of the great 20th-century movements for more interesting one-of-a-kind pieces. Not necessarily to everyone's taste, for those seeking something outside the mainstream, it is most certainly a vital stop on their search. Mirrors by Serge Roche, the great ornamenter of the 1940s, clay vases designed by Constance Spry, the maverick floral designer of the 1930s and '40s. Gill's home is no exception. Here, furniture designed by Syrie Maugham, Somerset's wife, works by Emilio Terry, T.H. Robsjohn-Gibbings, Marc du Plantier and Line Vautrin elegantly defer to the younger generations: textiles by Ulrika, furniture by Garouste and Bonetti, silverware by Richard Vallis and ceramics by Grayson Perry. Together these different generations of often surprising yet always inspired pieces add up to something unique and extraordinary.

In the
background,
a baroque-style
armchair from the
Hardy Amies
fashion house.
Center, a metal
sculpture by Tom
Dixon. A half-
round, half-square
polyurethane and
faux-leather
chair. A pair of
low divans by
Printz (1935).
In the foreground
a pale-green silk-
covered wing
chair from an
apartment
designed by Le
Corbusier for the
art patron Charles
de Beistegui, on
the Champs-
Elysées.
Framed photo
by Wolfgang
Tillmans (of
model Kate
Moss).

Wood and white molded plastic table (Garouste and Bonetti). Porcelain vase (Grillo Demo), architectural maquette and terra-cotta catchall.

Whether outrageous or discreet, no European city encourages all-out eccentricity quite like London.

of the 20th century.

In Gill's living room, two neo-Grecian mahogany chairs with bakelite imitation Wedgwood medallions are creations of T.H. Robsjohn-Gibbings (USA, 1940s). The pair of low turquoise-lacquered bookcases were designed by Syrie Maugham (1935). On the bookcases ceramic pieces by Jean Cocteau, beside a "Pineapple" lamp by Line Vautrin. A wicker poodle wearing a Hermès collar. For the fireplace, bronze andirons by Garouste and Bonetti (1989), and on the mantelpiece a pair of Serge Roche candlesticks (1930) on either side of a Richard Vallis silver bowl (1933). Above the fireplace, an oil by Eugene Berman, in between two Larry Bell gouaches (1990).

Left:
On a marble-topped console table, a still-life arrangement including a large sculpted silver candleholder by Richard Vallis (1994), a Beardsley-esque ceramic "light bowl" and a neoclassical-style black basalt cup, both by Oriel Harwood (1993). To the right, an urn with inscriptions by Grayson Perry (1993), all original works made on commission for David Gill.

Opposite:
View of the dining room from the hallway through a mirror-and-chrome screen from the 1930s. Bronze table custom-made for the room by Garouste and Bonetti (1990), set of chairs by André Arbus (1938), terra-cotta vases by Constance Spry (1935), crystal door knob and gold thread trimming by Ulrika (1992).

196

In the living room, a collection of enamel, bronze and silver boxes by Line Vautrin (1940-1960) on two nesting tables by Printz. Gold-striped velvet pillows by Ulrika.

<u>Opposite:</u>
Beneath a draft for a painted scarf by Jean Cocteau, two low high-backed Shaker-style chairs made in the 1950s by the Chiavari works from a design by Gio Ponti.

When three heads are better than one: a designer, a decorator and an antiques dealer, all from different parts of the world, live together in this former London pub. Three distinct sensibilities with one thing in common: a well-developed flair for the dramatic.

Hassan ABDULLAH
Michel LASSERRE
Stefan KARLSON

W hen a Malaysian, a Frenchman and a Swede decide to live together in Notting Hill—one of London's trendiest neighborhoods—the mixture could not fail to be interesting. Especially if housed in a late 19th-century one-time tavern, where several floors of fabulous finds from places as far-flung as India, South America, Italy, Sweden and France; from periods spanning several centuries find a welcome home. With 6,500 square feet to work with, their particular brand of tongue-in-cheek chic, including a veritable zoo of exotic stuffed animals (some sporting tiaras, intended, one supposes, to lend a touch of glamour), has plenty of room to flourish. The many young artists living in this part of London are pleased to make a visit to the "pub" to find inspiration and delight in whatever might be new that week. London is still fertile terrain for the kinds of eccentricities these three collectors love to cultivate. Without vast funds at their disposal, Abdullah, Lasserre and Karlson, a trio clearly driven by the same sense of adventure, discover new ways to indulge their collectomania. Dreams of Marie-Antoinette do not preclude rock 'n' roll, it's the mix that keeps everything fresh and everyone on their toes.

Original 19th-century pub windows extol the virtues of British beverages. On a pine refectory bench, books and binders holding selected issues of the old *London Gazette*. A souvenir from Bengal, a stuffed tiger sizes up a polar-bear rug on the wide-plank floor.

These three hip Londoners have at least one thing in common: an inordinate love for the spoils of the decorative arts.

Preceding spread:
Flanking the Regency fireplace, two trompe-l'oeil marble pedestals display the bust of a Roman emperor and a plaster of Adonis. Among this collection of 19th- and early 20th-century furniture, paintings and objects, a low, armless chair in purple felt, a 21st-century piece, has landed in the middle of the room as if from another planet.

Left:
On this friendly stuffed and winged bulldog sparkles a theatrical tiara made of pearls, and paste.

Opposite:
Behind a wooden dummy, a series of oil portraits from many different European cities.

For Charles de Beistegui, the Château de Groussay was a theater set meticulously and sumptuously fabricated to bring his extravagant fantasies to life. Now Groussay is in the hands of a television producer who is gradually opening to the public this still magical chateau.

Jean-Louis REMILLEUX

In the chateau's library, the Dutch-inspired grisaille-caisson trompe-l'oeil ceiling was painted in the late 1930s, the romantic chandelier, designed by Charles de Beistegui and made by the bronze-smith Thoulouze, illuminates two floors of bookshelves and a mahogany balustrade.

Time seems suspended here through an endless succession of reception rooms, galleries and vestibules, whose footmen, long since departed, seem to have joined Cinderella and de Beistegui himself in an eternally blissful paradise. Jean-Louis Remilleux, the current owner of the Groussay estate, also traffics in dreams. He has worked to re-create Beistegui's English-style grounds with Chinese and Palladian follies, the estate's own private theater inspired by the Residenztheater in Munich, an English-style library on two floors, and the chateau's great reception hall, hung with the same peacock-feather silk brocade that once embellished Marie-Antoinette's bedroom at Versailles. Despite Groussay's noble proportions, it was completely reimagined by de Beistegui in the 1930s as a residence...for one! But with the dual purpose of throwing those legendary parties people still talk about—the owner took great pleasure in impressing others with his lavish entertainments. Now it seems the same wish is at work in this bewitching chateau less than an hour outside of Paris. It is Remilleux's purpose to make visitors believe for a few brief moments that the duchess of Charest might rustle down those famous corkscrew stairs in all her pearls and silk for no other purpose than to invite them to afternoon tea.

The art of bringing a historical estate back to life without disturbing the enchantment of years past.

Opposite:
To the left of the mahogany corkscrew staircase, a rare velvet-clad reading chair with an adjustable lectern.

Right:
On the 19th-century desk, Empire candelabras and Sèvres biscuit ware sit politely among stuffed parrots.

The walls of the immense arc-shaped gallery are covered with an 18th-century print wallpaper. The inside of the hearth is covered in classic blue and white Delft tiles. A set of Dutch chandeliers and a collection of exotic stuffed animals. The made-to-measure benches are Empire-style, while the door and fireplace were inspired by a 17th-century design.

210

Index

Credits

Photographs by Gilles de Chabaneix: **pp. 60-67.** Pierre-Olivier Deschamps: **pp. 104-111, 112-117, 144-149, 186-199.** Jacques Dirand: **front cover, pp. 24-29, 46-55, 68-73, 162-167.** Andrea Ferrari: **pp. 138-143.** Marianne Haas: **pp. 6 (top), 8 (top and bottom), 30-39, 40-45, 74-81, 82-87, 130-137.** John Hall: **pp. 5, 88-95.** Jean-François Jaussaud: **pp. 118-123.** Guillaume de Laubier: **back cover, pp. 7 (top and bottom), 8 (center), 9 (top and bottom), 10-17, 18-23, 56-59, 124-129, 150-155, 156-161, 168-173, 174-179, 180-185, 206-211.** Gilles Trillard: **pp. 200-205.** William Waldron: **pp. 96-103.**

Stories produced by Alexandra d'Arnoux: **pp. 74-81.** François Baudot: **pp. 6, 7, 8, 9, 10-17, 18-23, 24-29, 30-39, 40-45, 56-59, 60-67, 88-95, 96-103, 104-111, 118-123, 124-129, 144-149, 150-155, 174-179, 186-199, 206-211.** Marie-Claire Blanckaert: **pp. 130-137, 156-161, 168-173, 180-185, 200-205.** Marie Kalt: **pp. 68-73, 162-167.** Françoise Labro: **pp. 46-55.** Fabienne Rousso: **pp. 82-87.** Laure Verchère: **pp. 112-117.**